UTSA
Memorial Fund
in memory of

Nicholas J. Weber

From a Gift
to UTSA by

the donors to the
UTSA Memorial Fund

HARPSICHORD
IN
AMERICA

HARPSICHORD
IN
AMERICA
A Twentieth-Century Revival

LARRY PALMER

INDIANA
UNIVERSITY
PRESS

Bloomington and Indianapolis

Manufactured in the United States of America

Library of Congress Cataloging-in-Publication Data

Palmer, Larry.
Harpsichord in America.

Bibliography: p.
Includes index.
1. Harpsichord. 2. Harpsichordists—United States.
3. Harpsichord makers—United States. I. Title.
ML651.P3   1989   786.2'21'0973   88-45446
ISBN 0-253-32710-5

1 2 3 4 5 93 92 91 90 89

For Momo Aldrich

The dead are really sometimes too diffident and are willing to wait too long for the sad meed of posthumous fame.

. . . I merely want to suggest that perhaps it is wrong always to play the same things, which might make quite decent people think that music was only born yesterday; whereas it has a past whose ashes are worth stirring, for within them lingers that unquenchable flame to which the present will always owe something of its radiance.

Claude Debussy, "Neglect"
from *Monsieur Croche, the Dilettante Hater*

CONTENTS

Illustrations

Preface

This book tells the story of an improbable occurrence. It is a quixotic tale of the return to prominence of an instrument discarded by time, forgotten by the general public, and replaced in common usage by a larger, louder instrument. It is the story of an intrepid band of dreamers—men and women, some academic, some temperamental, some frankly quite mad—all determined that their chosen instrument should live again to make music.

The tale is populated by craftsmen, artists, and amateurs. Working independently in many cases, together in some, they accomplished their "impossible" mission: the sleeping beauty known as the harpsichord was awakened. Music of the past came to be performed in a style perhaps close to that known by its composers. And in this improbable happening, now a century in the making, there lies a fascinating story.

I have chosen, whenever possible, to let the protagonists and the reporters of the events tell their own stories in order to capture more closely the flavor of the time. Except for obvious typographical errors in the originals, spellings have not been modernized and terminology has not been updated.

The first six decades of the twentieth century are the years in which most of the rediscovery happened. When a principal character lived beyond 1960 it seemed logical to take the story a few years further; but, for the most part, the first seventy-five years of the harpsichord revival are the focus of this chronicle.

Acknowledgments

My debts to many people must be acknowledged, now that the story has been written: To Madeleine Aldrich (Momo), who shared her memories and her photographs as well as the good life during my annual trips to Honolulu; to the late Sue Stidham, my closest friend and sometime student, who believed in this project so passionately that she provided the word-processing equipment on which it could be written; to Shannon Steel, who made the equipment work; to Richard Barnes, who read the complete manuscript with a critical eye and helped to ferret out information about recordings and the use of the harpsichord in jazz; to Howard Schott, Richard Pearce-Moses, and Charles M. Gatlin, Jr., who corrected factual and stylistic errors in the manuscript; and to Isolde Ahlgrimm, my first harpsichord teacher and abiding friend, especially for sharing her notes about Mrs. Thomas's lesson with Landowska, as well as for the inspiring musicianship and teaching that made me love the harpsichord and its music in the first place.

To my students, over the years, in the biennially offered course at Southern Methodist University, "The Harpsichord in the 20th Century"; especially to Lewis Baratz, Dean Billmeyer, Henry McDowell, Jonathan Maedche, Robert Poovey, Marilyn Roark, Marilyn Saker, Jane Schmidt, Jan Van Otterloo, and Thomas Whiteside for research projects that provided information used directly in the writing of this book. Their questions and interest often led me to examine the depths of my own lack of knowledge about the subject and eventually convinced me that this book was needed.

To librarians (may their tribe increase), especially the invaluable Joan Schuitema (also a harpsichord major) for her countless hours of research help; to Robert Skinner, Fine Arts Librarian at SMU, for encouragement and tangible support; to Harold E. Samuel of Yale University's Music Library, for his help in locating photographs; and to William Parsons, of the Library of Congress, for his abiding interest in this project.

To friends and colleagues on two continents who provided information, pictures, transportation, and lodging: John Ardoin, Roban Bieber, Margaret Power Biggs, Kenneth Cooper, William Dowd, Catherine Dower, Miriam Clapp Duncan, Stan Freeman, Mano Hardies, James Holloway, Ben Hyams, Fred Hyde, Jane Johnson, Roy Kehl, Igor Kipnis, Richard Kurth, Dorothy Lane, Arthur Lawrence, Willard Martin, Helen Merrill, Daniel Pinkham, Virginia Pleasants, Clyde Putman, D. Samuel Quigley, Denise Restout, Elsa Richards, John Chappell Stowe, Temple S. Timberlake, Richard Torrence, Ephraim Truesdell, Gavin Williamson, H. Ross Wood, and Brett Zumsteg.

To Eugene Bonelli, Dean of the Meadows School of the Arts, Southern Methodist University, for sabbatical support in 1979; and to Robin Robertson, Associate Dean for General Education, Dedman College, SMU, for a generous CORE research grant that enabled me to spend a summer writing.

And, finally, a very large debt of gratitude to Hal Haney, who made *The Harpsichord* a viable journal during his eight years as editor and publisher. In so doing he preserved a considerable segment of the revival's story for succeeding generations.

I also gratefully acknowledge permissions to quote extensively from
the following sources:

Mabel Dolmetsch, *Personal Recollections of Arnold Dometsch* (London: Routledge & Kegan Paul, 1957). By permission of the Mabel Dolmetsch Estate.

Robert Evett, "The Romantic Bach," *New Republic,* 28 July 1952.

Hal Haney, interview with Claude Jean Chiasson, *The Harpsichord* V:3 (1972).

Eta Harich-Schneider, *Charaktere und Katastrophen,* copyright 1978. By permission of Verlag Ullstein.

Ralph Kirkpatrick, *Early Years,* copyright © 1985. By permission of Peter Lang Publishing, Inc.

Musical America: John Caffrey, "John Challis and Julius Wahl: Harpsichords for Americans," February 1950; review of Wanda Landowska's Town Hall recital (signed R.S.), March 1949; review of Ralph Kirkpatrick's Town Hall recital (signed R.K.), 1 February 1954.

Newsweek, article about Wanda Landowska, 23 February 1948.

Alice Pentlange, script for the radio program "So You Haven't the Time," Van Buren Papers, Harold B. Lee Library, Brigham Young University.

Josephine Robertson, "Harpsichord Popularity Is Seen Growing," *Cleveland Plain Dealer,* 15 December 1960.

Halina Rodzinski, *Our Two Lives,* copyright © 1976 Halina Rodzinski. Reprinted with the permission of Charles Scribner's Sons, an imprint of Macmillan Publishing Company.

Virgil Thomson, "Rhythmic Grandeurs," reprinted in *The Musical Scene* (New York: Alfred A. Knopf, 1945).

Time: "Harpsichordist," 12 October 1936; "Musical Antiques," 30 October 1939; "Man from Ypsilanti," 24 January 1944; "Harpsichordists Out of Tune," 3 February 1947; "Grandma Bachante," 20 June 1949; personality story about Wanda Landowska, 1 December 1952; "Midnights in Manhattan," 24 May 1954; "The Plectra Pluckers," 15 August 1960; "Romantic Revival," 30 May 1969. Copyright © Time, Inc. All rights reserved. Reprinted by permission from TIME.

Fernando Valenti, "Scarlatti Forever," *High Fidelity,* November 1954. All rights reserved.

Yale Alumni Publications: Eva J. O'Meara, "Historic Instruments in the Steinert Collection," *The Yale Alumni Weekly,* 29 March 1928; Willie Ruff, "A Musician's Legacy: Ralph Kirkpatrick Remembered," *Yale Alumni Magazine,* April 1985.

HARPSICHORD
IN
AMERICA

PROLOG

THE HARPSICHORD IN DECLINE

EUROPE IN THE NINETEENTH CENTURY

"Make what you want; this upstart [the piano] will *never* replace the majestic clavecin!" In any listing of erroneous predictions these vehement words from French composer Claude-Bénigne Balbastre (1727–1799) to instrument maker Pascal Taskin (1723–1793) would resound with irony, for the production of harpsichords in France ceased in 1789 at the outbreak of the French Revolution. Indeed this political upheaval resulted not only in the cessation of harpsichord production but also in the destruction of countless noble instruments (as well as countless noble persons).[1] Although the charter of the Paris Conservatoire (1795) allowed for six professors of harpsichord, they were soon vastly underemployed; and the last prize in harpsichord playing was awarded in 1798.[2]

Production of harpsichords in England slowed to a trickle as the eighteenth century waned; Jacob Kirckman produced his last harpsichord in 1809, but the instrument had been outmoded for several years. A Mrs. Piozzi wrote that in 1803 one could buy the finest of Kirckman's harpsichords for a guinea, whereas in earlier times people had so prized these instruments that nameboards from them were placed on less-desirable examples from other makers.[3] When the dramatist Charles Dibdin auctioned off his theatre in Leicester Place, London, in 1805 there was not a single bid for the Shudi harpsichord, but a Hancock grand piano sold for seventy pounds.[4] In little more than a decade the upstart had triumphed!

Here and there, of course, quilled instruments were still being used: Giuseppe Verdi, a child in the 1820s, learned his notes on a polygonal spinet now housed in the Museo Teatrale alla Scala, Milan.[5] A spinet by Alessandro Riva of Bergamo was made as late as 1839.[6] Clavichord production also held on far into the nineteenth century: Johann Michael Voit and Son of Schweinfurth produced instrument number 399 in 1811.[7] Donald Boalch lists Swedish instruments by Carl Nordquist and Eric Wessberg from the years 1818 and 1821; and there is even a clavichord dated 1852 in the Skara Museum.[8] In Stuttgart a maker named Hofmann built two clavichords for Mr. Joseph Street, an English amateur, about the year 1857.[9] Several clavichords were produced in the Finsbury Park section of London after 1880, and a Mr. Dove, another late nineteenth-century Londoner, made harpsichords and spinets in the tradition of the English builder Baker Harris.[10]

So, in a technical sense, harpsichords and clavichords did not "die out." Beethoven's *Moonlight Sonata* was published in 1802 for "harpsichord or pianoforte," a designation that would continue through the publication of Franz Liszt's very pianistic *Tre Sonneti del Petrarca* in 1846.[11] Conservative musicians of the early nineteenth century kept using the instrument to which they had become accustomed in youth: Carl Zelter, Mendelssohn's teacher, was discovered at "his old two-manual harpsichord" when Eduard Devrient and Mendelssohn visited him in 1829 to propose the first modern performance of Bach's *Saint Matthew Passion*.[12] Rossini learned music at a "poor old instrument" and used a harpsichord for the recitatives in his operas at least as late as 1816.[13] The harpsichord remained on the Polish musical scene beyond the turn of the nineteenth century, as well; thus Chopin might have played on a quilled instrument as a young student. Boalch lists a Polish maker, Mazlowski, active in Poznan as late as 1805.[14]

The poem "A Toccata of Galuppi's" by Robert Browning (1812–1889), in his two-volume opus *Men and Women* (1855), ensured the immortality of the rarely performed Italian composer Baldassare Galuppi (1706–1785) and called to mind another age with the line "While you sat and played Toccatas, stately at the clavichord. . . ."[15]

Throughout the nineteenth century the harpsichord remained a household instrument in some out-of-the-way communities. An English curate, the Rev. Francis Kilvert (1840–1879), recorded daily events in an unaffected, buoyant account of life near the Welsh border. For Wednesday, 26 October 1870, he wrote,

> Carrie Gore let me in to the Mill kitchen through the meal room and loft over the machinery; and there was Mrs. Gore making up the bread into loaves and putting them into the oven. Good-natured nice Carrie, with her brown hair arranged in a bush around her jolly broad open frank face, and her fine lusty arms bare, entertained me by playing on the jingling old harpsichord, sitting very stiff and straight and upright to the work with her chair drawn in as near as possible to the key-board so that she was obliged to lean a little back quite stiff. She played some hymn tunes correctly, but what I admired most was her good nature, good breeding and perfect manners in sitting down to play directly she was asked. . . .[16]

Of course, a few pianists continued to have an interest in "old music" and would, on occasion, try their hands at the old instruments. Ignaz Moscheles (1794–1870) appeared in historical concerts in the Hanover Square Concert Rooms and in the Italian Opera House, London. In 1837 on three successive occasions he played the music of Scarlatti and his contemporaries on a Shudi harpsichord built in 1771, still (at that time) in the possession of Broadwood's, the piano manufacturers. In her memoir, *Life of Moscheles, with Selections from his Diaries and Correspondence* (1873), his wife wrote

> When the cover was lifted, one saw a contrivance somewhat in the shape of a Venetian blind, which, like the shutter covering the swell part of the organ, was acted upon by the pedals—by using this, greater sonority was given to the tone,

which otherwise, was rather thin, and less agreeable. Moscheles gave much attention to the invention, and turned it to good account. The upper and lower keyboards of the instrument were evidently intended for the rendering of such passages of Scarlatti and other masters as on modern pianos require constant crossing of the hands; and one row of keys being connected with two, and the other with three strings, certain shades are produced in the quality of the sound.[17]

Moscheles also programmed Bach's *Concerto* in D minor with string quartet accompaniment. The critics were of the opinion that the size of the crowds at these concerts should be enough to induce the pianist to repeat them the next season, with even more of the interesting old repertoire.

There is no record that Moscheles continued to be involved with the harpsichord after 1846, when he emigrated to Leipzig to assist Mendelssohn in the founding of the Leipzig Conservatory. Moscheles, a serious scholar, wrote toward the end of his life, "The influx of pianists is as great as ever. . . . They do not see that music is still to me as my own life blood, and while they are burying me, I am quietly feeding on the toccatas and fugues of old Bach. . . ."[18] This sentiment leads one to believe that his interest in early music, if not early instruments, remained undiminished after his departure from England.

After Moscheles left London several other artists took up his idea of historic concerts: Charles Salaman (1814–1901) began his series in 1855, using a Kirckman harpsichord; Ernst Pauer (1826–1905) gave concerts in Willis's Rooms between 1861 and 1867, playing the same Shudi harpsichord used by Moscheles; and Carl Engel (1818–1882), from Hanover, arrived in England about 1845 and achieved a certain fame for the collection of early instruments he assembled at his house in Kensington. These instruments, acquired by the Victoria and Albert Museum in 1875, formed the basis of the outstanding collection there. Engel played his instruments regularly in public and lectured extensively on the subject of early keyboard music.[19]

By far the most remarkable of this group was Alfred James Hipkins (1826–1903), who joined the piano firm of John Broadwood and Sons in 1840 to learn tuning. He remained there for the rest of his life, becoming a superb (if self-taught) executant on all keyboard instruments and a world authority on tuning, musical pitch, and the history of musical instruments. At the request of Ernst Pauer, Hipkins contributed program notes for Pauer's historic concerts in the 1860s. Subsequently Hipkins gave historic concerts and lecture recitals of his own. In 1885 he presented a lecture on spinets, harpsichords, and clavichords in the Music Room of the International Inventions Exhibition. He concluded his remarks on the history of the harpsichord by introducing the musical examples he would play:

> I will now play upon two harpsichords (one by Shudi, dated 1771, and one by Shudi and Broadwood, dated 1781) a Prelude, Saraband and Cebell (or Gavotte), composed by Henry Purcell; a Menuetto and the air, with variations, known as the "Harmonious Blacksmith," by Handel, and a Sonata by Domenico Scarlatti. This selection will show the special characteristics of the harpsichord and its limitations.

But it must be remembered that the adornment of shakes, turns, and other graces were more cultivated in the best days of the harpsichord than emphasis, accent, and those ever-varying changes of power that help to make our modern music what it is. I must not omit to say that the belief once prevalent among musicians, and that I find still exists, that Scarlatti's handcrossings were due to the use of two keyboards, is not justified. Technically the hand-crossings are intentional, and, moreover, double keyboard harpsichords have found little favour in his, or at any time, in Italy.[20]

In 1886, in another notable performance for the Royal Musical Association, Hipkins played on five different instruments (his page turner was none other than the pianist Anton Rubinstein).[21] Hipkins was the first artist since the eighteenth century to perform segments of Bach's *Goldberg Variations* at the harpsichord. In his book, *A Description and History of the Pianoforte and of the Older Keyboard Stringed Instruments* (1896), Hipkins's statement that the two-keyboard variations should "be played on unisons only" showed sound scholarship, a discriminating ear, and an intuitive sense of the way in which a double-manual harpsichord should be used.[22]

Hipkins, a contributor to the first *Grove Dictionary of Music,* reported that "in 1879 Mr. G. J. Chatterton of London, incited by my article upon the clavichord, which had then appeared in Sir George Grove's Dictionary, successfully transformed an old square piano into one—the reverse process to that which obtained . . . about the middle of the last century."[23]

PARIS: A PIANIST, A PRINCE, AND THREE COMPOSERS

The Harpsichord Comes into Fashion Again

Musical performances with the harpsichord, the forerunner of the piano, seem to have become fashionable in Paris. On the 11th of the past month [February 1888], according to the "Guide Musicale," such an event took place there. . . . The tone of the harpsichord joined with the flute and viola da gamba [in sonatas of J. S. Bach] in a charming manner, most especially, however, with the flute! And what spirited and attractive playing in the amusing pieces by Rameau: La Vézinet, L'Indiscrète, La Timide, and Tambourin for harpsichord, viola da gamba and flute. Truly, if the performers MM. Diémer, Delsart and Taffanel had appeared in white wigs and knee britches, the listeners could have believed themselves transported back in time. The solo playing of M. Diémer at the harpsichord showed with elegance and skilled use of the registers which of the varied tonal shadings could be brought out [at this instrument]. . . .[24]

In the late 1860s, Louis Diémer (1843–1919), professor of pianoforte at the Paris Conservatoire, had organized a small group of musicians interested in performing music of the past. He had won a first prize in piano at the Conservatoire in 1856, and the Viennese critic Eduard Hanslick called him "a delicate and graceful artist." But, as such things are wont to be, his fellow pianist Mark Hambourg described Diémer's playing as "dry-as-dust . . . with a hard, rattling tone."[25] George Bernard Shaw, writing of a London recital, described Diémer as "a remarkably clever, self-reliant, and brilliant pianist, artistically rather stale, and quite breath-bereavingly unscrupulous in using the works of the great composers as stalking horses for his own powers. The mere recollection of his version of the Zauberflöte overture causes the pen to drop from my hand."[26]

For his pioneering early-music concerts in Paris, Diémer was fortunate in being able to borrow a harpsichord made by Pascal Taskin in 1769 that was still in the possession of Taskin's descendents.[27] In 1882 this magnificent instrument had been restored by Louis Tomasini. Shortly thereafter it was loaned to the Paris firm of Érard, which wished to study the instrument with the thought of making a modern copy of it. Soon after Érard's had the idea of such an antiquarian venture, the firm of Pleyel decided to open a harpsichord department. Its "re-creation" of a harpsichord, shown in 1889, had three sets of strings with six pedals for the operation of these registers.[28] Harpsichords by Érard and by Tomasini were also exhibited at the Paris Exposition—a veritable explosion of new-antique keyboards!

Both Érard and Pleyel built instruments of five octaves. Their harpsichords were graceful, elegant, and beautifully decorated, but with open framing at the bottom, as in the modern piano. The bracing was much heavier than that used by Taskin (a typical example of the doctrine of progress: bigger was naturally better!). No metal was used in the framing at this time, although stringing and bridges were heavier than in the eighteenth-century instrument. For its first harpsichords Érard remained more faithful to Taskin's original design; already an English-style lute had been added to the Pleyel. Érard used quill plectra for one 8-foot register; Pleyel used leather plectra for all the registers. Both builders employed wooden jacks and traditional felt dampers. Keyboards were built to the dimensions of the contemporary piano rather than to the slightly smaller octave of the eighteenth-century keyboard instruments.[29]

A typical program given by Diémer and the Société des Instrumens Anciens included both ensemble pieces by Bach and Rameau and harpsichord solos—always small, light, antique—in the vein of Daquin's *Le Coucou* and Rameau's *La Poule*.[30] Even in these small-scale works one might imagine that Lazare Lévy's description of Diémer's pianism would apply to his harpsichord playing as well: "astonishing precision . . . his legendary trills, the sobriety of his style. . . ."[31]

The first "modern" composition for harpsichord was written for Diémer by Francis Thomé (1850–1909), a popular composer of salon music and sentimental piano pieces. Thomé's greatest hit, *Simple Aveu,* graced the music rack of nearly every parlor piano at the turn of the century. His *Rigodon* [sic], "Pièce de Clavecin," opus 97, written about 1892, was dedicated "à son ami Diémer." This work was intended to suggest the frivolous, decadent mood of many late eighteenth-century French composers, and it gave Diémer a further opportunity to demonstrate

RIGODON

PIÈCE DE CLAVECIN

Francis THOMÉ Op. 97

À son ami DIÉMER

The first harpsichord composition of the twentieth-century revival: Francis Thomé's *Rigodon*, pièce de clavecin, published by Lemoine, c. 1893.

his trills. The work remained relatively unknown in the twentieth century until Igor Kipnis discovered a copy in an antiquarian shop in London and recorded it as part of a selection of favorite harpsichord encores.[32]

Charles-Marie Widor (1844–1937), organist of the Church of St. Sulpice in Paris, was another sometime devotee of the harpsichord.

> Widor, who looked upon St. Sulpice as his home—for sixty years he mounted, with sprightly step, the difficult stairway leading to the great organ—had two habits: before leaving the church he would pause with his friends before the magnificent murals painted by Delacroix in the Chapel of the Angels, making his guests admire them. "Isn't it beautiful, isn't it splendid," he would cry. "Isn't it worthy of Rubens?" And he would go to the *clavecin* of Marie Antoinette, which he had placed in one of the small chapels, and would play a few measures of the Mozart Sonata in A, saying over and over: "Yes, yes, he was the god of music."[33]

Elsewhere in Paris, the harpsichord could be heard at the salon of Prince Edmond de Polignac (1834–1901), an amateur composer of some ability. Through his marriage to the American heiress Winnaretta Singer, Prince Edmond obtained the financial resources necessary to indulge his passion for music. Both the Prince and Princesse de Polignac were devoted to music of the Baroque era, and at their salon this music could be presented on an eighteenth-century harpsichord. Rameau's opera *Dardanus* was given its only nineteenth-century performance in the Polignac music room. The production made an extraordinary impression on both musicians and literary figures who heard the work.[34]

Through association with the Polignacs Maurice Ravel (1875–1937) became familiar enough with the harpsichord to specify the accompaniment of his early song *D'Anne jouant de l'Espinette* (1896) as "clavecin ou piano (en sourdine)."[35] While nothing could be more pianistic than this accompaniment, the idea, drawn from the poetry, of using a harpsichord, could have been an apt one. It is unfortunate that Ravel never used the harpsichord again, for some of his musical thoughts are well suited to the instrument. Ravel performed the song, with M. Hardy-Thé, to whom it is dedicated, in a concert at the Salle Érard on 27 January 1900. At the harpsichord? Probably not, although private hearings for the Polignac circle might well have featured the old instrument.[36]

The first use of the harpsichord in a twentieth-century orchestral score came surprisingly early: in the opera *Thérèse* by Jules Massenet (1842–1912),[37] which is set at the time of the French Revolution. It was composed during the winter of 1905 and the spring of 1906. Its first performance took place at the Monte Carlo Opera on 7 February 1907, with the offstage harpsichord played by Louis Diémer.[38] The opera was popular with the public; it was given during the following three seasons in Monte Carlo and was staged in Paris in 1911.[39] The harpsichord was heard, with string accompaniment, in a *Menuet lent mélancolique*. With great charm it suggested an eighteenth-century past. Even more laudable was Massenet's scoring— muted strings playing pizzicato allowed the harpsichord to be heard. Many later attempts to use the harpsichord have been far less successful.

CHAPTER

1

A PASSION FOR COLLECTING

MORRIS STEINERT

A boyhood impression rather than the general American interest in shipping segments of Europe back home led Morris Steinert to begin his collecting of keyboard instruments. Born in Scheinfeld, Bavaria, Steinert (1831–1912) showed an early love for music. His elder brother Louis engaged the aged local cantor-organist, Dazian, to teach the boy the rudiments of music. At that time there was no piano in Scheinfeld, but the cantor had a clavichord on which Morris had his first lessons. Many years later, after emigration to the United States and the establishment of a successful piano business in New Haven, Steinert returned to Scheinfeld, determined to find this clavichord.

After a few days in my native town, I began the search for my clavichord, which, according to information received from my brother Louis, then residing in Coblenz, had been left in Scheinfeld, as it was so old and dilapidated that he considered it a useless piece of furniture; he also stated that he had no record of it. I was not daunted, however, and after a day's search I succeeded in tracing it to the tower abode of old Dazian, who must have taken it after my brother left. I was told that Dazian had died many years before, that his successor, his brother Joseph, had also passed beyond, and that Herr Bayer now held the position of Stadt Musikus.

Going to the tower, I mounted the steep, winding stairs to the living rooms, in search of Herr Bayer. Very much out of breath, I knocked at the door and inquired of the pleasant-faced elderly woman who opened it for the Herr Stadt Musikus, and was told by her that he was in the field hoeing potatoes. Descending, I hastened to him, and recognized him as the flute-player of old Dazian's band. He was now a man of seventy-five years, aged and bent. We exchanged greetings, for he well remembered me as the boy taught by his uncle, and he also knew that I now lived in America. Herr Bayer had before him a large basket which was full of potatoes, and which, by my help, he strapped upon his back, and together we started for his tower home.

Upon asking him about my old clavichord, he told me that his uncle had an old clavichord which must have belonged to the Steinert family, that he had kept it for many years, using it to compose and arrange music, and that it was in the old tower.

The American instrument collector Morris Steinert.

Again, I mounted the steep stairs, the old musician in advance with his potatoes on his back, and entering the principal living-room saw the old clavichord standing in one corner. With my heart full of joy I purchased the instrument, and, what is more, the violoncello upon which I took my first lesson, half a dozen violins and several violas, all instruments which belonged to and were loved by my old instructor, Dazian.[1]

Steinert had a remarkably antiquarian (and therefore, progressive) viewpoint for his time:

I was deeply interested in collecting old instruments that were used in the past, and that must have served the great composers of the seventeenth, eighteenth, and early part of the nineteenth century, and I based my work upon a closer investigation than the accepted view of our modern musicians, who think that the compositions of these classical tone poets sound better when played upon the present pianoforte. With this opinion I could not agree, and I ascribed their wrong views on the subject to their ignorance and unacquaintance with the instruments I speak of. . . .[2]

Steinert was even more ahead of his time in that he wished to have the instruments restored to playing condition. After assembling his "quite respectable collection" not only from the area around Scheinfeld but also from other sections of Germany, he had the instruments shipped to the United States, where he studied their construction, repaired them, and learned how to play them. "This was a great undertaking on my part, and it took me several years to put them into proper order and play them intelligently."[3] The first nineteenth-century concerts of historic keyboard instruments heard in the United States may have been these events described by Steinert:

Finally, having them in good condition, I engaged the services of Mr. [Henry] Krehbiel, the eminent musical critic of the *New York Tribune,* a gentleman who is profoundly interested in the study of the evolution of the pianoforte, and with him I began a lecture tour. While I played the old keyed instruments, playing Bach and the school which is in keeping with their mechanical construction, also improvising upon them, Mr. Krehbiel lectured, and my two sons, Henry and Albert, assisted me in rendering chamber music upon the violin and viola. These lectures were given gratuitously at Yale, Harvard, Brown, Smith, Vassar, Andover, Professor Lambert's School of Music in New York City, Springfield, and the Music Hall, Boston, I also secured Mr. Arthur Friedheim, the pianist, who played upon the modern pianoforte, in contrast to the old school and old instruments of my collection.[4]

Steinert and his band of early music explorers were quite successful in their musical ventures. Word spread, and the reputation of this unique playable collection grew.[5] Steinert was requested to exhibit part of his collection at the Smithsonian Institution in Washington, which he "most cheerfully did." Another invitation, from Princess Pauline von Metternich, led to the exhibition of some of the choicest instruments at the Exhibition of Music and Drama in Vienna (1892); this in turn led to a similar exhibit at the Chicago World's Fair of 1893:

While in Vienna the Commissioner from America to Great Britain, Mr. McCormick of Chicago, came to visit the exhibition and to solicit musical loan collections for the "World's Fair." . . . He called on Geheimrath (Doctor) von Ausspitzer, and told him his object in coming to Vienna, and Doctor von Ausspitzer informed him that the man who had the most interesting collection was an American, Mr. Steinert, of New Haven, Connecticut, and he advised him to see me. Mr. McCormick, who lived in the same hotel, paid me a visit and solicited my co-operation. While I did not promise to send my collection, for I felt that I had been a showman quite long enough, I left the question open, and as he was not finally successful he left. Upon my return to the United States, I entered into correspondence with Doctor Peabody, and we arranged upon satisfactory terms for my loan collection to be shown in Chicago. I received two thousand dollars for my services, which amount did not cover one half of the expense of taking my collection there.[6]

(During the trip to Europe, Steinert made excellent purchases to augment his collection, adding a double-manual Hass harpsichord of 1710 and, from the British Exhibit in Vienna, a Hans Ruckers mother-and-child virginal of 1579, both instruments highly decorated and both rare examples.[7])

The Chicago Columbian Exposition was the largest showing of Steinert's collection thus far; one particular harpsichord—Napoleon's—was singled out for an article in *Musical Courier*. It was an instrument built by Jacob Kirckman of London in 1755 and given by the sometimes impetuous emperor to a sergeant who served in the palace. After Napoleon's banishment, the sergeant emigrated to the United States, settled in Scituate, Massachusetts, and eventually sold the instrument to Simon Bates in 1833. Steinert purchased the instrument from the Bates family.[8]

Steinert continued his lecture career for several more years, largely at schools and universities in the eastern part of the United States. In 1900 he donated about forty instruments to Yale University's School of Music, creating the foundation of the great collection now housed there.[9]

MORE HISTORIC HARPSICHORDS, MORE COLLECTORS

The public's interest in an old keyboard instrument was often connected with the details of its former ownership. In 1889 a short article that appeared in the Milwaukee *Yenowines News* was reprinted in *The American Musician* for 30 November and again in *Musical Courier* for 18 December under the title "A Harpsichord Romance." The article recounted the story of the Shudi and Broadwood double-manual harpsichord of 1789 that was discovered by William Rohlfing, the owner of a Milwaukee music store. While on a trip to Annapolis, Maryland, he found the instrument in the loft of an old college building and learned that it had once belonged to Charles Carroll of Carrollton, a signer of the Declaration of Independence. Rohlfing was able to purchase the historic instrument and present it to the firm of Knabe and Company, the piano manufacturers, in Annapolis. The article stated, however, that Milwaukee was the present home of the instrument.[10]

Yet another instrument with a historic connection was a Longman and Broderip double-manual harpsichord of 1793 in Washington's home, Mount Vernon. It belonged to Nelly Custis, "beloved granddaughter and adopted daughter" of the nation's first president. She took it to Woodlawn Plantation, not far from Mount Vernon, where she lived with her husband, Washington's nephew Lawrence Lewis. In 1860, long after harpsichords were out of style, this keyboard instrument was the first piece of furniture returned to Mount Vernon when the furnishings of the vacant mansion were reassembled.[11]

The St. Louis World's Fair in 1904 featured an instrument associated with a famous composer rather than with a political figure: the harpsichord on which Gioacchino Rossini took lessons from Giuseppe Malerbi in 1802. In a letter to Cav. Luigi Ferrucci, librarian of the Mediceo-Laurenziana Library in Florence, dated Passy, October 18, 1868, Rossini wrote,

> My Dear Luigi: Nothing could give me more delight than you telling me about the harpsichord or cembalo, still existing at your cousin Malerbi's. You undoubtedly know that in my childhood and during my sojourn in Lugo I used to play on that poor instrument! I call it a poor instrument now that I have become a pianist of some value, but I have always recommended it as a good deal preferable to the noisy pianofortes for the instruction of the true singing. If you will go to the theatre you will certainly notice how my advices have been taken and put into practice.[12]

Most private collectors after Morris Steinert did not have an interest in playing their acquisitions. They were attracted by the artistic and antiquarian features of the instruments. Mrs. John Crosby Brown discovered an ivory lute in Florence in the 1870s, fell in love with it, and purchased it. At first she collected Italianate instruments for her music room in Orange Mountain, New Jersey, but her hobby became all-consuming, and her collection of early instruments grew to 276 items by 1889. It was too large for a music room, so she presented the collection to the Metropolitan Museum of Art in New York City. Even there her collection continued to grow, comprising more than 3,500 pieces by 1906.[13]

In Washington, D.C., the instrument collection of the Smithsonian Institution was officially recognized in 1879, when Dr. G. Brown Good, assistant secretary in charge of the U. S. Museum, reorganized the collections and classified musical instruments as sound-emitting devices. In 1892 he added European instruments that he had personally selected, but it was to be the Washington piano dealer Hugo Worch who developed an outstanding collection of keyboard instruments. Worch gave his first keyboard instrument to the Museum in 1914; subsequently he gave nearly 200 items.[14]

The Leslie Lindsey Mason Collection in the Museum of Fine Arts, Boston, was presented by William Lindsey in memory of his daughter, who was lost in the sinking of the *Lusitania* in 1915. This collection of 564 instruments, 317 of them European, had been assembled by Canon Francis W. Galpin of England. Keyboards did not figure prominently, but there were two spinets, a virginal, two clavichords, and a fine 1798 Joseph Kirckman double harpsichord.

Not all of these early collections were on the East Coast. Frederick Stearns, a drug manufacturer from Detroit, presented his collection of musical instruments to the University of Michigan, Ann Arbor, in 1899, expressing the hope that his gift would inspire other successful businessmen to use their financial resources for furthering worthy pursuits.[15] Several keyboard instruments were included in the collection, including Italian harpsichords of 1693 and 1702.

Early in the twentieth century George F. Harding of Chicago began collecting many sorts of art objects: Italian primitive paintings, armor, and musical instruments. Sixty-one instruments, chiefly keyboards, made up his collection. Among the most famous were a Jan Ruckers mother-and-child virginal of 1623, several regals, and various spinets. These and pianos that had belonged to Liszt and Chopin were exhibited for many years in the Harding home at 4853 South Lake Park, until the building was razed in 1965.[16]

Of course, many other Americans collected instruments as objects of fine art; they, as well as European enthusiasts, kept several prominent restorers and dealers busy. Charles Fleury and Louis Tomasini, both of Paris, were active in this field, and Tomasini might be considered an early harpsichord revivalist, for he made several copies of an eighteenth-century French harpsichord.[17] The acquisitive urges of collectors also paved the way for successful chicanery; the workshop of Leopoldo Franciolini, established in Florence in 1879, sold forged or composite instruments—nineteenth century fabrications of older component parts—to unsuspecting purchasers.

The American instrument collections were important to the renaissance of interest in the harpsichord, for through them the public became aware of the old instruments as works of art. As musical instruments, however, they were almost worthless, for there was little opportunity for any of them to produce the glorious music for which they were intended. Performance *was* encouraged at the Brussels Conservatoire, where the collection was especially large, having been started as early as 1846.[18] When the musicologist J. F. Fétis, director of the Conservatoire, died in 1871, the Belgian government purchased both his library and his instruments. Some of the instruments were restored to playing condition and were used in concerts by Conservatoire faculty or by visiting artists, such as Diémer from Paris. This sounding collection and the concerts presented by the Brussels Conservatoire were to have a far-reaching effect on the revival of the harpsichord, for they sparked an interest in old music in the young Arnold Dolmetsch.

CHAPTER
2

AN EXPLORER ARRIVES
Arnold Dolmetsch

TOWARD THE "GREEN" HARPSICHORD

Eugène Arnold Dolmetsch was an unlikely candidate to play the part of the prince to the harpsichord's "Sleeping Beauty." As an adult he was barely five feet tall, although portraits show him to have been darkly handsome. He was attracted to women and they to him: three marriages attest to that.

Both music and craftsmanship were in Dolmetsch's family background; his father had been apprenticed to an organ builder and married into a music shopkeeper's family. Arnold was born in Le Mans, France, in 1858. His early piano lessons proved to be a disaster. He preferred the violin, and it was with this instrument that his musical studies were advanced.[1] He learned careful shop techniques from his grandfather, and piano repair and tuning became Arnold's trade.

Arnold's first marriage was to Marie Morel, a widow ten years his senior. The couple was forced to elope since Dolmetsch's family refused to give the required permission for the union. A daughter, Hélène, was born on 14 April 1878 in Nancy, and the couple was married in London on 28 May of that year. Shortly after their marriage Arnold and Marie made their first trip to the United States:

> On landing, they travelled to the town of Louisville [Kentucky], doubtless attracted by its name, and established themselves in a boarding house. The cuisine was novel and they were frequently regaled with wild turkey and cranberry sauce, which they thought delicious. Madame Arnold Dolmetsch gave piano lessons and her young husband worked up a round of piano-tuning and regulation and found himself warmly welcomed in the outlying farms.[2]

The actual length of their stay is unknown, but this trip adds a surprising footnote to Dolmetsch's biography and is necessary knowledge if one is to number his American sojourns accurately.

After returning to Europe the young family moved to Brussels, where Dolmetsch studied violin with Henri Vieuxtemps and later enrolled at the Brussels Conservatoire. Concerts of "ancient music" and exposure to some of the instruments in the Conservatoire collection aroused Dolmetsch's interest in music of the past. The director of the Conservatoire at this time was François Gevaert, a scholar who had recently written a book on older music; he was interested in the problems of ornamentation and the proper instrumentation of that music.[3]

Dolmetsch completed his studies in Brussels in April 1883, having done excellently in all subjects. His next move was to London, where he planned to attend the newly established Royal College of Music. Here he completed five terms of study with such well-known figures as Sir George Grove, C. Hubert H. Parry, and Frederick Bridge. Through the good offices of Grove, Dolmetsch was added to the staff of Dulwich College as a part-time violin teacher. He published his first editions of violin music with Novello's and haunted antiquarian bookstores and junk shops, where he began to find the old books and instruments that formed the basis of his own collection. By this time Dolmetsch had come to a decision as to his life's goal: the authentic interpretation of the music of the past on appropriate instruments. Grove warned him of the difficulties ahead, but assured Dolmetsch that the service to music would be invaluable.[4]

With his wife and his daughter as partners, Dolmetsch formed a consort for the performance of early music. He found an old spinet in a junk shop, and wishing to replace the square piano that had been used as keyboard instrument for his group, Dolmetsch inquired at Broadwood's about restoring the spinet. Here he met Alfred Hipkins, who did not have time to do the work for him, but suggested that Dolmetsch do it himself. This suggestion was the right one: his background of shop work and his experience at rebuilding a square piano in Brussels stood him in good stead. Dolmetsch resolved never again to ask another person to do restoration work for him. The work on the spinet took considerable time, but the result made him extremely happy. By the end of 1889 he had done further work on keyboard instruments, having restored a large Kirckman harpsichord, an Italian virginal, and a large clavichord.[5]

Lectures illustrated by musical examples; concerts that attracted a growing number of interested persons; professional musical contacts with Hipkins, the pianist and sometime harpsichordist John Fuller Maitland, and his former teachers Grove, Parry, and Bridge; and a fortuitous meeting with the young and supportive music critic George Bernard Shaw allowed Dolmetsch to pursue his chosen way. He became a well-known figure in the musical life of London. On the personal side, his increasing immersion in work led to his separation from Marie in 1893.

A new house in West Dulwich afforded Dolmetsch something he had wanted for some time: a large music room for his subscription concerts. Among visitors to these concerts were two leading figures in the art world, Edward Burne-Jones and his friend William Morris. The result of this contact was the promise of a publication by Morris's Kelmscott Press and the eventual suggestion from Morris that Dolmetsch build a new harpsichord for exhibition. He had already been commissioned to build a clavichord for Fuller Maitland, the first of four copies

Dolmetsch made of the fine large clavichord in his own collection.[6] It was completed by July 1894 and evoked these perceptive comments from Shaw:

> He has actually turned out a little masterpiece, excellent as a musical instrument and pleasant to look at, which seems to me likely to begin such a revolution in domestic instruments as William Morris's work made in domestic furniture and decoration, or Philip Webb's in domestic architecture. I therefore estimate the birth of this little clavichord as, on a modern computation, about forty thousand times as important as the Handel Festival.[7]

The second copy of the clavichord was purchased by Sir George Grove for the students of the Royal College of Music, the third went to a museum in Italy, and the fourth remained in Dolmetsch's possession.[8]

When the divorced wife of his younger brother Edgard joined the household, Dolmetsch gained a fine keyboard player as well as the woman who was to become his second wife. Although no marriage could occur until Arnold's divorce from Marie became official, Elodie Dolmetsch already bore the family name, and most visitors to their home were unaware of the true marital status of the couple. For the artistic improvement of the consort, it certainly did not hurt that Elodie had prodigious dexterity at the keyboard. John Runciman gave the first appreciative review of her playing:

> Mrs. Elodie Dolmetsch played some harpsichord pieces by Couperin with daintiness of colour, piquancy of rhythm, and quite remarkable freedom from the nervous scrambling that ruined the playing of some of Dolmetsch's previous harpsichordists. The only fear we have now is that there may be a craze for these old instruments. Mr. Dolmetsch's price for a clavichord is, we believe, only one quarter the price of a piano of equal quality, and now that his workshop is conveniently situated on the classic ground of Queen Square[9] we are much afraid that every West-End dame with the smallest pretentions to culture will run thither to complete the furnishing of her drawing-room.[10]

In June 1896 Mabel Johnston wrote to Dolmetsch; although he did not plan to take on new pupils at this time he answered her letter. Mabel was "taken-on," not only as a pupil in violin but also as an apprentice in instrument making. In the latter capacity she moved into the Dolmetsch household. Her first major assignment was to assist in finishing the harpsichord for the Arts and Crafts Exhibition, scheduled for October. She was responsible for shaping the fronts of the keys, while the special decoration was entrusted to the artist Helen Coombe, then engaged to art critic Roger Fry. The instrument was never quite completed (the outside, painted in flat green paint when there was not enough time to complete the decoration, led to the instrument's enduring identification as the "Green" Harpsichord.[11]

It was this harpsichord that Dolmetsch played for the performances of *Don*

Giovanni at Covent Garden conducted by Mancinelli in July 1897, and of Purcell's *King Arthur* in Birmingham, conducted by Hans Richter in October of the same year. At both events he was joined by Elodie playing a second harpsichord.[12]

An only slightly disguised description of Dolmetsch at this time survives in the novel *Evelyn Innes*, by George Moore, a subscriber to Dolmetsch's concerts:

> The thin winter day had died early, and at four o'clock it was dark night in the long room in which Mr. Innes gave his concerts of early music. An Elizabethan virginal had come to him to be repaired, and he had worked all the afternoon, and when, overtaken by the dusk, he had impatiently sought a candle end, lit it, and placed it so that its light fell upon the jacks. . . . Only one more remained to be adjusted. . . .
>
> His face was in his eyes: they reflected the flame of faith and of mission; they were the eyes of one whom fate had thrown on an obscure wayside of dreams, the face of a dreamer and propagandist of old-time music and its instruments. He sat at the virginal, like one who loved its old design and sweet tone, in such strict keeping with the music he was playing—a piece by W. Byrd, "John come kiss me now"—and when it was finished, his fingers strayed into another, "Nancie," by Thomas Morley. His hands moved over the keyboard softly, as if they loved it, and his thoughts, though deep in the gentle music, entertained casual admiration of the sixteenth-century organ, which had lately come into his possession, and which he could see at the end of the room on a slightly raised platform. Its beautiful shape, and the shape of the old instruments, vaguely perceived, lent an enchantment to the darkness. In the corner was a viola da gamba, and against the walls a harpsichord and a clavichord. . . .[13]

Perhaps more than a literary description of Dolmetsch at this time in his career may exist: Mabel mentions some wax cylinder recordings of Dolmetsch's late nineteenth-century concerts made by music publisher Robert Cocks.[14] Unfortunately none have been located.

Life continued to be active for Dolmetsch and his consort: concerts, many in his subscription series; several trips to Italy; new musical discoveries; wars with the press and with other musicians, less understanding of the styles of early music than he. Several instruments, including three Beethoven pianos, came from his workshop. His divorce from Marie having become final, he married Elodie in Zürich on 11 September 1899.

A nonmusical business transaction brought upheaval to the Dolmetsch family in 1901. Having sublet one of his residences to an Italian who turned the place into a brothel, Dolmetsch was brought to court as an accomplice. Found guilty and fined heavily, Dolmetsch was forced to file for bankruptcy. Through these actions he lost his instrument collection and library.[15] All unpleasantness, however, was soon to be left behind, as the Dolmetsch consort embarked on an adventure: a trip to the "new world." On 27 December 1902, Arnold, Elodie, and Mabel Johnston sailed for the United States to begin a two-month concert tour.

DOLMETSCH IN AMERICA

The first American concert by the Dolmetsch ensemble was given at 3:30 on Tuesday, 6 January 1903 in New York's Daly Theatre; it was the first concert in impresario Sam Franko's series Concerts of Old Music. The program included Johann Sebastian Bach's *Concerto* in D Major for harpsichord, flute, and violin with string accompaniment (Elodie as soloist, assisted by "Mr. Charles Kurth and Mr. Dolmetsch"); Johann Christian Bach's *Symphony* in G minor; as well as works by Marc-Antoine Charpentier and Antonio Sacchini.[16] Not surprisingly the theatre was packed, for the debut had created much interest among the public. W. J. Henderson, the influential critic of the *New York Sun,* had devoted two full columns to the forthcoming event in the Sunday edition of the paper; and critic Richard Aldrich wrote,

> The harpsichord sounded at first, to ears attuned to the resonance of the modern pianoforte, like a far-away tinkling. But it soon took its place in the right perspective and compelled admiration and liking for beauty and qualities of tone all its own. Mrs. Dolmetsch played on an old English instrument by Kirckman, a maker famous in his day. . . .[17]

Other critical reaction was mixed, many critics disliking the period costumes of the performers as well as the archaic sounds of the old instruments. It must have been a strange occurrence for most of the audience, as well as for the critics; all the works on the program were listed as "heard for the first time in America."

During their American tour the ensemble gave fourteen concerts throughout the state of New York and one at Steinert Hall in Boston.[18] The program for Dolmetsch's first Boston concert bore this notation:

> Messrs. M. Steinert & Sons Co. have arranged with Mr. W. N. Lawrence for the appearance, at Steinert Hall, on the evening of January 28, [1903] of Mr. ARNOLD DOLMETSCH, famous throughout Europe for his rendering of old music on archaic instruments. Mr. Dolmetsch makes his American debut this season and his coming has long been looked forward to. Mr. Dolmetsch is a unique personality in the musical world, having devoted his life to restoring to their pristine condition old-time instruments. His knowledge of musical antiquities is unsurpassed, and his collection of archaic instruments is rich in interest. Of Mr. Dolmetsch's standing as an artist the praise of the foremost critics of Europe is sufficient testimony.

An unsigned review reported on one of the New York concerts:

> Mr. Dolmetsch and his concert of old music are a big success. One can pick flaws in his deductions and his theories ad libitum, but he, nevertheless, manages to interest us. The tiny tinkle of the instruments he has brought over with him made one rub his eyes in astonishment. The Prelude and Fugue of Bach, played by Mr. Dolmetsch on the clavichord—the instrument for which Bach wrote his well-known

Preludes and Fugues—was listened to with great attention and, perforce, in an almost breathless fashion. It was marvelous how the small sounds penetrated to the farthest corner of the theatre. . . .

The most interesting number to musicians was the Bach Prelude and Fugue on the clavichord. After a careful hearing most of us, I think, came to the conclusion, that although Bach is good on the clavichord, he is decidedly better on one of our modern grands. Mr. Dolmetsch, of course, would consider this rank heresy, and in a certain sense, no doubt the music Bach wrote for the clavichord should be played on the clavichord, but there are those of us who having known it only on the pianoforte, find Mr. Dolmetsch's reading faint, musty and even dry.[19]

Perhaps the most intriguing appearance of this series was a private soiree at the home of a newly married granddaughter of society doyenne Mrs. Jacob Astor:

For the occasion, the entrance hall and corridor were profusely decorated with masses of long-stemmed crimson roses which, according to Dolmetsch's agent [W. N. Lawrence], cost a dollar apiece. The musicians duly settled in the corner appointed to them and commenced their programme with a couple of ensemble pieces. Then, as Elodie began to play the opening notes of a Scarlatti sonata, the sound was completely swallowed up by a burst of melody from a Hungarian string quartet installed in the opposite corner. The rest of the evening's entertainment resulted in a series of strange musical contrasts, with considerable misunderstanding as to whom should play and for how long: a procedure unaided by the fact that it was conducted almost entirely in Hungarian.[20]

One might think that this was a scene created by Richard Strauss's librettist Hugo von Hofmannsthal as an extension of the musical mixups in *Ariadne auf Naxos!*[21]

The Dolmetsches sailed for England on 7 February 1903 aboard the *Mauretania* (but having caught on in America, they were not to be absent for long). On 24 February, his forty-fifth birthday, Dolmetsch received a copy of Couperin's *L'art de toucher le clavecin,* the gift of Mabel Johnston. This volume was to prove most valuable as a tool for his researches into the interpretation of early music. He also received Mabel Johnston as his third wife, another acquisition that was to prove relatively imperishable (she outlived him) and invaluable. Mabel and Arnold were married on 23 September 1904, four days after Arnold and Elodie were divorced (in Zürich). As property settlement, Elodie received the Kirckman harpsichord. Her departure from the Dolmetsch circle left a vacancy for a harpsichordist. It was filled by a young woman named Kathleen Salmon, who had never played the harpsichord before, but who learned very quickly under Dolmetsch's teaching.

The next American tour, embarked upon in November 1904, was to have far-reaching effects for the harpsichord revival on the west side of the Atlantic. Arnold, Mabel, and Kathleen Salmon arrived in New York City just in time for their first concert at the Manhattan Theatre on 9 November. After a second concert in New York, they traveled to Springfield, Holyoke, Northampton, and Boston; to Providence; south to Baltimore; then inland to Pittsburgh, Indianapolis, Ann Arbor, and Chicago. Originally planned for seven weeks, the tour kept expanding because of successful concerts and added engagements. With requests for concerts coming from music clubs in many cities, Dolmetsch decided to make the United States his home. From the Virginia Hotel in Chicago, Dolmetsch wrote to poet W. B. Yeats, "I shall return to America [after a short trip to England] for an indefinite period alas! They are willing to support me here, whilst in England they let me starve. . . ."[22]

Dolmetsch returned to England with Kathleen Salmon, He was faced with putting all his affairs in order, finishing several instruments, and packing all his family's goods, musical and otherwise. But, on 1 July 1905 he sailed from England aboard the *Minnehaha* with a daughter, Cécile (born in the spring of 1904), her nurse, and forty-one cases of personal effects, weighing 3,500 pounds.[23] Mabel gave birth to a second daughter, Nathalie, shortly after Arnold's return.

Concerts and providing music for several plays kept the Dolmetsch music productions active. Then, in the winter of 1905, Dolmetsch signed a contract with Chickering and Sons of Boston, the well-known piano manufacturers. He was engaged to establish a department of early keyboard instruments, viols, and lutes. "These farseeing and generous people offered me a good salary, a choice corner in their factory, the pick of their eighteen hundred workmen, every facility and freedom to carry out my ideas. Needless to say, I gladly accepted and made some eighty instruments there under ideal conditions. . . ."[24]

The importance to the American harpsichord revival of his work at Chickering's would be difficult to overestimate. Not only did Dolmetsch produce some of his most beautifully crafted instruments there, but also the dissemination of these instruments provided the necessary vehicles for the introduction of early music in various American cities. During the years he worked for Chickering's, Dolmetsch and his workmen made thirty-three clavichords, thirteen two-manual harpsichords, and a few virginals and spinets. Among the purchasers of these keyboard instruments were Arthur Whiting; E. B. Dane of Chestnut Hill, Massachusetts; Henry Gideon of New York City, who "gave many concerts and lectures using his harpsichord"; Frank Taft of Montclair, New Jersey; E. F. Searles of Methuen, Massachusetts; O. G. Sonneck of the Library of Congress, Washington, D. C., who purchased a clavichord; John Wanamaker of Philadelphia; E. P. Warren of Liverpool, England; composer Ferruccio Busoni of Berlin; and Smith, Wellesley, and Vassar colleges.[25] Another purchaser of a harpsichord (in 1908) was the collector Belle Skinner; she also purchased a 1784 Hoffman clavichord from Dolmetsch at the same time.[26]

BOSTON AND WASHINGTON: SHOP AND SOCIETY

The flavor of Dolmetsch's work in the factory was well captured by Jo-Shipley Watson in a vignette published in 1912:

Arnold Dolmetsch at Chickering's, 1907. (Courtesy of Dr. Carl Dolmetsch.)

Arnold Dolmetsch at Work on the New Old
Clavichords

We were walking through the show rooms of a huge modern piano factory. "Now let me show you something which I'm sure, you have never seen before," said our guide, as he threw open the doors leading into an adjoining work room.

A man with soiled hands and rolled-up sleeves was bending over a fragile instrument that was poised as lightly as a butterfly; he was patiently clipping the pins that held the tiny wires.

As we entered he looked up interestedly, and shaking aside his long brown hair, tinged with grey, said, "Oh, I'm glad to meet you. You are interested in harpsichords and clavichords? Yes, we are working here on one. You have never heard the clavichord? Well, I'm here, the clavichord is here, you are here, so why not hear it now?"

He drew up a chair and placed it before a vermilion lined clavichord; then he pushed his sleeves still higher and said, "Now I'll play; but first let me shut out some of this terrible American noise."

After pulling down all the windows and closing all the doors he tried again. "Now we shall try, but you will not get the best effect; it is far too noisy here. Yes—the clavichord must be played in a quiet place. It has the most delicate tone in the world, dainty, tremulous tones, dripping melodies. Have you heard Bach on the clavichord?"

He then played Bach's first *Prelude* in the *Well-Tempered Clavichord* [sic], then without stopping he played the second *Prelude and Fugue*. It was Bach as I had never heard it before; not the tremendous, thunderous Bach of modern pianism, but a musical, wistful, appealing Bach. It sounded like a really usable, home-like kind of everyday Bach.

"Yes, this is the most beautiful instrument in the whole world. It will stand anything; it will wear. The harpsichord? Ah, that is another thing; it will not stand everything. I would not advise it for a damp climate.

"But the clavichord any tuner can fix, or you can fix and tune it yourself if you have a good ear; it is quite simple. Then again it is so easy, so very easy and the most delightful and helpful instrument to play. It improves your technic as nothing else can. It gives the most delicate pianissimo effects; no matter how hard you have worked these out on the piano you will not obtain the result you do on the clavichord. Ah, you get a most delicate touch, Madame.

"We are not making these for profit. No, it is simply to create an interest that we make them. These cases, they are all mine, my own design, my idea. I make them to please myself, and not the trade.

"These you see are in cream and gold; now this one I have made black and gold, a very striking design. I have several in cream and vermilion, and one in old English. Each one, you will notice, bears an inscription, and the keys are all made by hand."

There they stood, poised like the wings of gay butterflies on the floor of this huge, busy piano factory.[27]

Dolmetsch, the performer, continued to entrance new audiences with his music. For four seasons Chickering and Sons sponsored a series of three Dolmetsch Concerts at Chickering Hall in Boston. The first program, on Wednesday, 27 February 1907, consisted of English music from the sixteenth and seventeenth centuries for a chest of six viols, lute, virginals, violins, and treble and bass voices. For the second program, on 13 March, French music of the seventeenth and eighteenth centuries held the stage, with a consort of viols, viola d'amore, viola da gamba, harpsichord, lute, and voice. The third program, on 27 March, devoted to music by Johann Sebastian Bach, included a harpsichord concerto and a cantata. During this series a new performer's name appeared on the programs: Charles Adams at the harpsichord.[28]

In 1908 Dolmetsch became the first musician to play an "ancient" musical instrument in the White House. Through the advance work of Mabel's brother, the explorer Sir Harry Johnston, who was invited to visit President Theodore Roosevelt because of their mutual interest in big-game hunting, Arnold received this letter, addressed to him at the Cosmos Club, Washington, D. C., dated 14 December:

My dear Mr. Dolmetsch,

Indeed, it would give Mrs. Roosevelt and myself great pleasure if you could come to the White House on Wednesday at 2:30 and let us hear the clavichord. It is most kind of you to make the offer. I heard much of you through Mr. Harry Johnston and of course entirely independently know much about your work in introducing the harpsichord and clavichord at least to the American world of music.

Sincerely yours,
THEODORE ROOSEVELT

The President and his party entered the room exactly at 2:30.

The President introduced Mr. Dolmetsch to Mrs. Roosevelt and other members of the party and then viewed the clavichord and listened to the playing of several of Bach's Preludes and Fugues and one little selection by Galuppi.

"I never saw such close attention in my life," said Mr. Dolmetsch, "as was paid by those in that room Wednesday afternoon to my playing. I have played to many distinguished people and members of royalty abroad, but I never met a man who so impressed me as did the President. As a gentleman he is quite the equal of any member of the royalty or other dignitary of European countries and he is far more clever than many of them. He is really a most superior man and it was the greatest pleasure to me to play for him."[29]

The clavichord used for this unique demonstration was the one purchased by O. G. Sonneck, Music Chief of the Library of Congress. Dolmetsch made good use of his time in the nation's capital; he played continuo harpsichord for the Washington Choral Society's production of Handel's oratorio *Judas Maccabaeus,* doubtless another first for the history of music in Washington.

AT HOME IN CAMBRIDGE

The Dolmetsch family had lived quite happily in Boston at 16 Arlington Street, which was close to easy public transport to the Chickering factory in Cambridge. With the birth of a longed-for son, Rudolph, in November 1906, Dolmetsch must have turned his thoughts again to larger quarters for the expanding family. In the autumn of 1907 he sketched a design for a house with the requisite large music room.

The site chosen was a back lot adjoining the house of Cambridge poet James Russell Lowell, whose heirs still lived on the property.[30] The architect was a young French Canadian named Luquer, who incorporated several special features in the design:

The front door is purposely unostentatious: a brass plate gives the name; the letter-box awaits your pleasure, should you wish to leave a note; if you wish to go further, you ring a bell. Then you are ushered into a vestibule, after which, perhaps, you may go up three steps into the hall, and so to the music room. For the owner is a musician, and his house is built first for his own pleasure, then for the pleasure of those who listen to his music. The room, 15 × 30 feet, has walls stained a soft green, and long French casement windows on three sides. A clavichord and harpsichord stand in opposite corners, and on the wall hang fine old viols, lutes, and theorbas [*sic*]. Conventional figures of these instruments are seen on the balustrade of the staircase, with the signs of the bass and treble clef beneath, and a "pause" appropriately placed on the landing.[31]

This staircase was especially designed by Dolmetsch to have a landing every four steps: thus, in case of an accident a child would fall no further than this short distance. Moreover, all the downstairs rooms could be opened up to make one large space, just right for the Dolmetsch concerts.

For its time the Dolmetsch house, twelve rooms on three floors, must have been the ultimate in luxury. Mabel's brother Alex wrote in December 1907, "The automatic, instantaneous water-warmer, however, sounds too good to be true in this imperfect world. If patented widely in America it should certainly stimulate emigration to that country!"[32] The address in Cambridge, originally 11 Elmwood Avenue, later became 192 Brattle Street. When the house was sold, its next owner, Simon Marks, placed a codicil in the deed forbidding any change to the special staircase. The house still stands, presumably with this feature intact.

Dolmetsch was quick to make use of his fine facility: in 1909 he began giving concerts in the new house. "These concerts brought together some of the most intelligent music lovers, and one was sure to come in contact with persons of rare learning and culture and knowledge of the best in the arts. At the intermission of each concert the dining-room doors were opened and a buffet supper was served; then more music in the music room."[33] Evidently these concerts were a success, for shortly after the first series took place, Dolmetsch published another announcement:

Mr. Arnold Dolmetsch announces a Second Series of Three Concerts of Intimate Music, to be given in his Music Room on Tuesday Evenings, April 13, 27, and May 11, 1909.

As in the First Series, the Programmes will consist of Vocal and Instrumental Music of the sixteenth, seventeenth and eighteenth centuries, performed upon the instruments for which it was written: the Lute, various kinds of Viols, Harpsichord, Clavichord, and other instruments.

The music will begin at 8.30 punctually. It is expected that no one will come late or leave early, as there should be no disturbance during the evening. The music will not last more than one hour and twenty minutes, which, with an allowance of twenty minutes for refreshments and conversation, will bring the close of the evening to ten minutes after ten.

The price of single tickets is $4, with the privilege of subscribing to the Series for $10.

The number of tickets is limited to thirty.[34]

BUSONI AND THE HARPSICHORD

One of a fairly large group of distinguished visitors to the Dolmetsch house in Cambridge was the pianist and composer Ferruccio Busoni (1866–1924), with whom the Dolmetsch family had been acquainted in London. As Mabel Dolmetsch recalled,

> When he came to visit us in Cambridge . . . he seemed to relax and to enjoy our company and surroundings. At tea, after admiring my set of old Somerset china cups, he looked round with a sigh and said, *"Everything* is beautiful here."* He reminded me of how I had once played to him on an enormous instrument (the violone); and then turned with interest tinged with humour, as though examining some outmoded object, toward Arnold's latest achievement, the fourth "Beethoven Piano."* He had, to my thinking, become somewhat tactless; for later on, while Arnold was demonstrating the clavichord, he thought it very funny to strike some notes on the piano! What he really did appreciate was the latest harpsichord . . . and when he expressed his fervent admiration of this fine instrument, the open-handed firm of Chickering made him a present of it.[35]

That Busoni's interest in the harpsichord was more than polite afternoon talk is evident from this letter to his wife:

BOSTON, 12 APRIL, 1910

> . . . I have just come back from a motor drive from Cambridge where I and Mr. Byrn [from Chickering's] visited DOLMETSCH. He looks like a little faun, with a handsome head, and lives in the past. He builds pianos, Clavecins and Clavichords. The Clavecin (the English harpsichord) is magnificent. I made capital out of it at once and first, of all, brought the instrument into [my opera] the *Brautwahl* (when Albertine accompanies herself on it) and, secondly, begged for one to be sent to Berlin. They are beautiful outside too. . . .[36]

Mabel Dolmetsch continued,

> [Beyond making a present of the instrument to Busoni, Chickering's] sent Arnold to join [Busoni] in New York for a week, in order to initiate him into its intricacies. There Arnold was lodged in a splendid suite at the Waldorf Astoria, which suite was furnished with rich carpets, a china-closet, multiple electric lights (including some which shone in the wardrobe, when its door was opened) and immense vases of flowers. Here he and Busoni met daily, and no doubt, did at least as much talking as playing.[37]

Dolmetsch reported Busoni's progress to his wife:

30 April 1910, Hotel Astor, New York

Busoni had a good lesson yesterday and another one this morning. He is very intelligent and very enthusiastic. . . . He asked me, "Are you happy with your pupil?" I said that he needs to have more lessons. He replied "No one has ever given me lessons. I have learnt everything myself." I replied "One is not able to teach anything to anybody." He said, "This is true, but what about the pupils? One needs the pupils."[38]

Busoni's opera *Die Brautwahl* (The Choice of Bride) occupied the composer between 1908 and 1910. The libretto was based on a story by the German Romantic poet E. T. A. Hoffmann (of *Tales of Hoffmann* fame). The completed work was first produced in Hamburg on 12 April 1912. The harpsichord was heard onstage at the beginning of the second act. One wonders how effective Busoni's week with Dolmetsch had been, for the writing is pianistic in the extreme.

A more successful use of the harpsichord, and the only other appearance of that instrument in the catalog of Busoni's compositions, was the *Sonatina ad usum infantis pro clavicimbalo composita,* completed in 1915. The third of Busoni's six sonatinas, this work "for the use of children" was the only one to be designated for harpsichord. The score[39] bears the inscription "ad usum infantis Madeline M.* Americanae," the only time the composer concealed the name of a dedicatee for one of his works. Among Busoni's papers found in Berlin after his death was a photograph dated New York, 1918, with the name "Madeline Manheim" pencilled on the back. This young lady, apparently about eighteen years of age at the time of the photo, has been identified as a friend of Busoni's elder son, Benvenuto, and may be the mysterious lady of the Sonatina.[40] The five short movements of the work are musically attractive, particularly the third, *Vivace alla Marcia,* which is reminiscent of Prokofiev in its sarcasm; and the fifth, *Polonaise: un poco cerimonioso,* obviously a favorite creation of its composer, who used it again as an important musical idea in his comic opera *Arlecchino.*[41]

THE END OF A BEGINNING

In addition to the concerts at home in Cambridge, the continuing series of Chickering concerts kept Dolmetsch active in the Boston area. There was touring, too, as Mabel Dolmetsch's memoirs attest:

The years 1909 and 1910 were for us thickly strewn with concerts, including two Bach festivals in Montclair, New Jersey. . . .
It was enjoyable during this period to improve our acquaintance with the pleasant city of Philadelphia, where we gave a series of concerts in a hall attached to Messrs. Wanamaker's stores. . . . Here we were joined by an attractive singer, named Mrs. Sheridan, who had a voice of unusual quality. . . .
[On] one such occasion . . . the New York branch of Wanamaker's store engaged

us to give a grand concert in order to herald the opening of an extension of their already large premises. Our group this time consisted of Arnold, Mrs. Sheridan . . ., Charles Adams and myself; and the concert was held in the Wanamaker firm's capacious hall, possessing most flattering acoustical properties. Despite the fact that it was filled almost to suffocation, the music, which seemed to take on a dreamlike, ethereal charm, quite captivated the audience.[42]

From the end of 1910, however, unpleasantness began to encroach on this idyllic existence in America. Chickering's fell victim to the economic depression widespread in the land, and, to avoid further financial drain, the firm joined a consortium of five piano manufacturers. Instead of the luxury of fine workmanship and artistic (but unprofitable) endeavor, the emphasis of the new partnership was on increasing sales and decreasing the time required for the production of instruments—hardly an atmosphere conducive to the work of Arnold Dolmetsch.

Although Chickering's offered Dolmetsch alternative employment in the manufacture of pianos, Dolmetsch decided that it would be better, at the conclusion of his original contract, to return to Europe. To that end he embarked on a scouting trip to see what might be available there. Although he was now fifty-two, he turned to his search with enthusiasm. In the autumn of 1910 he journeyed first to England and then to France, where his contacts with all three of the leading Paris piano manufacturers—Érard, Pleyel, and Gaveau—gave him a choice of positions. He eventually chose employment with Gaveau, where he was, once again, to have his own department devoted to the manufacture of early stringed instruments and keyboards.

Back in America, Dolmetsch prepared for his last U.S. season of early music performances: his 1911 announcement, dated 2 January, read,

The Annual Series of Concerts of Intimate Music which I usually give early in the season had to be postponed on account of my journeys in Europe and the west of this country. I intend to give them during next February.

The music will consist of Vocal and Instrumental Compositions of the 16th, 17th, and 18th centuries performed upon the instruments for which they were written: Lute, Viol, Harpsichord, Clavichord, etc.

I have been fortunate enough to acquire recently a number of precious old music books from which several pieces will be played.

A very beautiful new Harpsichord will be introduced. Beside the three sets of strings of 4-foot and 8-foot tone of my former instruments, it has another set of strings of 16-foot tone which, extending downwards to the lowest note of the keyboard, reaches the F of 24-foot pitch. The depth, grandeur, and variety of colour of its tone are wonderful.

Harpsichords of this kind were occasionally made in the 18th century. J. S. Bach had one which he prized highly.[43]

One further picture of Dolmetsch at home in Cambridge has survived in the writings of William Lyman Johnson:

Mr. and Mrs. Dolmetsch were particular about the manner in which their food was prepared. All roasts were cooked on the turning spit. When the weather was warm enough, luncheon and dinner were served on the veranda which faced the lovely garden. Sometimes in summer I arrived there in time to do weeding, also to collect the bleached romain, escarolle, endive. Then came a delightful dinner with equally delightful talk relative to music and the allied arts.

Then to the music room. With all cares of the day done at the Chickering factory, Mr. Dolmetsch rested in a large easy chair for a short time, and then made his way to either the clavichord or the harpsichord and did his practicing, not by playing scales but by playing the works of the masters. There was the true artist, and in a few minutes he evidently forgot I was present. From whichever instrument he chose to play there came forth great compositions masterfully performed.

In that quiet end of the music room, shut in from the noises outside by the garden wall and at the hour of tender eventide, there was a quietness which allowed the floating tones of the clavichord to be heard in all their loveliness. At a certain period in his practicing, when the spirit moved him to play Bach, he lovingly made the gentle clavichord caress the thirds and the sixths in the *Andante espressivo* of the Preludio XII in F minor [*WTC,* II]. He made much of using just the right speed of vibrato on those thirds and sixths and they gave out a haunting loveliness of sound.[44]

Dolmetsch's final project in the United States was a series of twelve lectures for Harvard University, given in the old Fogg Museum. The topic, "Early Music and Its Instruments," covered music at the court of Henry VIII, Elizabethan music, the works of Purcell, the music of J. S. Bach, and the music of Franz Joseph Haydn—familiar topics to Dolmetsch followers through the years. According to Mabel Dolmetsch,

Our broken consorts now, for the first time, included the recorder. . . . It was played by [Dolmetsch's] first recorder pupil, namely, the Harvard Professor Peabody, a distinguished anthropologist who was, besides, a skilled amateur flautist in his moments of recreation.

. . . The whole series of lectures was a brilliant success, the hall on each occasion being crowded to the limit. The musical illustrations were performed by ourselves, assisted by Charles Adams, Professor Peabody, and our usual company of string players and singers, augmented by certain talented young Harvard students with their clear fresh voices. Having the whole twelve lectures to provide with adequate musical illustrations, Arnold adroitly rang the changes among the members of this galaxy of performers, using all to the best advantage.

I look upon this final outburst as the very pinnacle of his pioneer work in America. It originated in the minds of two of his particular friends, James Muirhead (a partner in Baedeker's European Guide Books), and his enterprising wife, Helen. This gracious lady was a lavish entertainer of all the European visiting professors; consequently, her suggestion of the lecture course was enthusiastically accepted by the Harvard authorities. Our last concert in America took place at the house of Professor Peabody and holds a special place in my recollection on account of [our daughter] Cécile, (then celebrating her seventh birthday), having taken part as treble viol player in Morley fantasies and seventeenth-century English consort pieces. An auditor confided to me that a lump had risen in his throat as he watched that innocent child playing her part with such calm assurance.[45]

William Lyman Johnson wrote, "When Mr. Dolmetsch returned to Europe, the making of the old instruments, also the playing of viols and most of the enthusiasm he had created, declined, so that from about 1912 to 1931 there was no professional interest from any source in Boston."[46]

From France Dolmetsch himself wrote on 29 June 1911 to Simon Marks, the Cambridge man who had bought the Dolmetsch home:

> We miss our old house very much. However, we are quite happy here, we find that it is quite possible to do without electric light, bathrooms, and ice cream, or even plain ice. We get over it some other way!
>
> From the artistic point of view, the surroundings are incomparably more congenial here than in America. I am one among a number of people who work on lines similar with mine, whilst in America I was alone, preaching in the desert![47]

But the seeds had been planted; there were to be, for early music, arid years and arid spaces in this huge land, but the Dolmetsch legacy would be put to use. Early music's voice may have become less eloquent following 1911, but it was not completely stilled.

CHAPTER
3
DOLMETSCH'S
AMERICAN LEGACY

Players of keyboard instruments were not the only ones who benefited from the efforts of Arnold Dolmetsch. At a New York recital in 1918, soprano Margaret Namara used the harpsichord:

> In a group of medieval airs, sung to the tintinnabulations of a harpsichord kindly loaned by Henry Symons, Mme. Namara established at the very outset the atmosphere she had sought to create. And when she sat down at the ancient instrument to accompany herself in an encore, and, warned by a few tinkling chords that her memory might not be quite reliable, called into the wings for the music, she put herself into even closer touch with her audience.[1]

Namara (who was in subsequent years a "one-name" artist) usually managed to do the unusual. And this interest in the harpsichord was not a passing fancy; she prized, throughout her long and exciting life, a spinet built for her by Dolmetsch. Visiting her in the 1960s, critic John Ardoin described the instrument as having a "clear, bright sound . . . something between that of a harpsichord and a clavichord. . . . [She] often used it to accompany herself in Spanish songs, which were flung out in a raucous chest voice."[2]

Slightly less colorful but more far-reaching in its presentations of early music was the Société des Instruments Anciens of Paris. New York critic Richard Aldrich described a typical concert by this group:

NEW YORK, JANUARY 29, 1917

> The Friends of Music acted as hosts yesterday afternoon to a most interesting and delightful organization of artists, the Society of Ancient Instruments. This organization is at home in Paris, and it is understood to be now in America because it has been sent here by the French Government to make propaganda for French music and musicianship.
> . . . The Society comprises Henry Casadesus, who founded it, and plays the viola d'amore; [players on the quinton, the viola da gamba, bass viol]; and Mme. Regina Patorni, who plays the harpsichord.

. . . The four string players are artists of uncommon skill and fine artistic feeling. . . . Even more valuable in contributing to the results they gain is their appreciation of the elusive element of style, and the essential qualities of the music to which they devote themselves. Mme. Patorni . . . stands on the same artistic level; a brilliant and facile performer, who has thoroughly mastered the peculiar style of the instrument, different in many ways from that of the pianoforte. She played on a modern harpsichord [Pleyel] that yielded an astonishing variety of timbres and colors through its two manuals and its stops controlling plectra of different materials and sets of strings of different lengths.[3]

During the First World War and the years immediately following, the Société des Instruments Anciens toured extensively in the United States. It had been founded in 1901 (one of its former harpsichordists had been the Italian composer Alfredo Casella). The group was first heard in America in 1914, as it returned to France from a world tour, via Japan. Three long winter tours in the years after 1918 took the group to many places, including "Boston, Baltimore, Cincinnati, Detroit, Ypsilanti, Cleveland, Philadelphia, Chicago, Washington, St. Louis, and Toranto [*sic*]."[4]

American-born players of the harpsichord also built on the foundations laid by Dolmetsch during his American residency. In a letter to the editor of the *New York Times,* Daniel Gregory Mason (1873–1953) included a list of these American artists:

Harpsichord Pioneers

Those of your readers who are interested in music for the harpsichord will be rather surprised at the statement in a letter of Mme. Wanda Landowska in your issue of Sunday, January 3, [1926] in which she says: "I have succeeded in giving the harpsichord, after much struggling, the position it deserves."

This hardly does justice to the achievements of other artists of the harpsichord, such as Diémer, Dolmetsch, Henry Casadesus, Regina Patorni, and Violet Gordon [Woodhouse] in Europe, and in our own country Arthur Whiting, Miss Pelton-Jones, Miss Van Buren, Lewis Richards, and others.

Mr. Richards, who has played the harpsichord throughout Europe as a member of the Société des Instruments Anciens of Paris, was, I believe, the first to appear as a harpsichordist with orchestra (Minneapolis Symphony Orchestra) in this country, and contributed much to the interest of Mrs. F. S. Coolidge's festival in Washington last autumn.

Mr. Whiting has been an indefatigable pioneer in cultivating interest in ancient music among us through his recitals at Harvard, Yale, Princeton, Bryn Mawr, and New York. It is possible that many in our present day audiences have been prepared to appreciate Mme. Landowska's art through Mr. Whiting's deep knowledge and tireless energy through all these years.

DANIEL GREGORY MASON
NEW YORK, JANUARY 11, 1926[5]

Landowska's forceful personality and her artistry at the harpsichord made immense impressions wherever she went. The United States welcomed this superb harpsichordist in 1923; but Professor Mason's letter tells many truths about the slow progress of harpsichord consciousness in this country following the departure of the crusading Dolmetsch family.

ARTHUR WHITING

Foremost among the keepers of the flame for early music was Arthur Whiting (1861–1936), who was performing solos at the harpsichord by 1907. Whiting came from a musical Boston family; his first musical venture was in that city, as organist for a black church. "He resigned this position, not so much because his salary was hopelessly in arrears, as because the negro minister insisted on praying for him at the morning service whenever he gave violent expression to his desires for remuneration."[6]

At this time foreign study was obligatory for an American who wished to be taken seriously in the musical professions, so Whiting went to Germany for several years. During his time in Munich he had one arm rendered useless by neuritis. Shades of Schumann! His lack of keyboard facility led him to study harmony and composition more vigorously than might have been the case if his plans to be a piano virtuoso had materialized. Upon his return to America, his first important orchestral work was played by the Boston Symphony, with the young composer conducting.

Whiting recovered the use of his arm and gave a Pianoforte and Harpsichord Recital at New York's Mendelssohn Hall (113 West Fortieth Street) on Wednesday afternoon, 11 December 1907. The reviewer for the *New York Times* had very intelligent things to say about this performance:

Interesting Performances of Old Music on a
Modern Harpsichord

Arthur Whiting's Piano and Harpsichord Recital

Mr. Whiting gave a recital yesterday afternoon, appearing as pianist (as he has been long-known in New York City) and also as harpsichordist in a Gigue and Rigaudon by Rameau; two Sonatas and a Minuet by Scarlatti; and Bach's English Suite in G minor.

The instrument he used is a modern one, a skillful reproduction of the old models and their qualities of tone. These qualities, by the use of stops and of two manuals, can be largely varied in tonal color and effect; and so, though the harpsichord does not admit of gradual changes of dynamics or of accent by the player's touch, as does the piano, it nevertheless affords striking and subtle variety. The instrument is a delicate and intimate one, with great possibilities of charm and of suggestive detail. The old music played thus seems animated by its true spirit, clothed in its rightful garb; and it gains in significance, in grace, and suavity. This is especially true of the 18th-century compositions that are by the men essentially of their time, as were Rameau and Scarlatti. Yet it is in large measure true also of this English Suite of

Arthur Whiting. (Collection of the Library of Congress.)

Bach, who was a man of all time, and who often reckoned little with the means immediately at his disposal and wrote quite untrammeled by their limitations—often, indeed, in a way that seems to need all the sonorities of the modern pianoforte.

Mr. Whiting has put himself into the spirit of this music, and has acquired a command of the harpsichord by which he makes it speak its own voice. His playing of it was clear, beautifully phrased, and skillful in "registration," if that term may be used to denote the employment of the different timbres that the instrument affords. It may be that listeners of the 20th century cannot hear with the ears and the taste of the 18th, but it is something more than a mere gratification of curiosity to hear this music played as it was played by those who composed it, sounding as it sounded to those for whom it was first composed. The performance gave a real artistic pleasure of an individual kind, and it was not without its valuable suggestions. It is something that might well be made less of a rarity in music. . . .[7]

Whiting's harpsichord was, of course, a Dolmetsch-Chickering; and his artistry must have been considerable. Whiting's understanding of his instruments (he owned a clavichord as well as a harpsichord) is further evidenced by his writing in a twenty-eight-page promotional pamphlet, *The Lesson of the Clavichord,* published by Chickering's. Whiting described the construction and tone qualities of early keyboard instruments, as well as the artistic conventions needed for playing them. His prose was eloquent and apt, displaying the communicative capabilities for which he was so well known.

> The pianoforte player will find the Clavichord as difficult to manage as a canoe at the first venture, in fact, it has much in common with that wayward little craft. It demands, at all times, a light and sympathetic touch by which, with a free wrist and forearm, its fullest and sweetest voice may be called forth. It refuses to respond to anything but a pressure stroke, and if that is not elastic, the upper notes of the instrument become unpleasantly sharp.[8]

Where had Arthur Whiting learned so much about his instruments? From the instruments themselves, of course, and from their maker. Mabel Dolmetsch described Whiting's early encounter with the clavichord:

> Arthur Whiting, who specialized in the music of Brahms, became by way of contrast enamoured of the clavichord and its music. Having developed a forceful style in his Brahms repertoire, he was at first inclined to be too violent with the gentle clavichord, which avenged such treatment by producing discordant intervals. Turning to Arnold (who had undertaken to familiarize him with its technique) he complained, "This instrument is all out of tune!" Arnold replied triumphantly, "It isn't the *instrument* but *you* who are out of tune." Whiting appeared scandalized, but was at last convinced of his error, and worked hard to acquire the necessary delicacy of touch. In after years he gave up the piano entirely and devoted himself to the ancient instruments, touring the country to give performances which he entitled "Dolmetsch Concerts". . . .[9]

In the end, Whiting demonstrated remarkable understanding of the musical capabilities of early keyboard instruments: "The emotional quality of [the clavichord's] tone signifies further that the playing of Bach was highly flexible and expressive, and thus opposes the theory that his compositions should be delivered with academic rigidity."[10] In discussing the harpsichord, Whiting wrote:

> Because gradations of tone and accent on these instruments of the plectrum family are so slight as to be almost negligible, the Clavichord players and the pianist, who are trained to regulate the quality and quantity of each note by a special impulse of the finger, are at first constrained by the apparent unresponsiveness of the keys, but

they later learn to use a light touch at all times, even when the music is weighty and impassioned. As the essential notes of a phrase cannot be accented, emphasis is made by dwelling on them, as in organ playing. By robbing the non-essential notes of their full value of time, the regularity of the rhythm is preserved in the average and the principle of *tempo rubato* is demonstrated.[11]

Illustrated with photographs of Dolmetsch's modern instruments, Whiting's monograph made a strong statement concerning the importance of Dolmetsch's work: "It is no exaggeration to say that the reproduction of [these instruments] is as important to the present-day students of keyboard music as are some recent discoveries of the antique to archaeologists. Excavation and rehabilitation bring to light a beauty which was unsuspected and which disturbs our certainty of superiority to the past. . . ."[12] Dolmetsch had certainly found in this Bostonian a worthy and articulate disciple!

Whiting gave chamber music programs as well as solo recitals. Indeed he had asked Mabel Dolmetsch to tour with him at one time; she declined, pleading "domestic responsibilities," but in tandem with her husband she gave several recommendations to Whiting. Eventually it was Paul Kefer who joined him as a performer on the viola da gamba; the association was fairly short-lived, though, as each thought the other a "dull fellow."[13] Constance Edson, violinist, and Georges Barrère, flutist, were other players who joined Whiting in his educational concerts of early music.

Mason's *New York Times* letter mentioned Whiting's university recitals. A description of one of these events at Princeton holds some surprises:

> I was dining at one of Princeton's luxurious upper-class clubs one evening when my host, a typical Princetonian athlete, leaned across the table and asked a clubmate, "Are you going to the Yale basketball game tonight?" "It's been postponed," was the answer. "There's a Whiting recital scheduled."
>
> "A Whiting recital? Oh well, I guess I'll go to that, then."
>
> That a recital of any kind should cause the postponement of an athletic event in Princeton was such an unheard-of proposition that it almost took my breath away.
>
> "And what, pray, is a Whiting recital?" I gasped.
>
> It's an educational musicale given by Mr. Arthur Whiting," said my host solemnly. "He tells us a few things about classical music in such a way that you forget you are being educated, and then illustrates his point by having various pieces presented by soloists or by himself. . . ."
>
> . . . Seated later on in the beautiful, softly-lighted music-room of McCosh Hall, I received a new and even more remarkable impression of Mr. Whiting's popularity with the students. A rather slight, gray-haired man, with a serious and scholarly face, stepped upon the stage and was greeted with a storm of applause. Princeton students are unstinted in their ovations, and it was several minutes before there was a cessation of the clapping, cheering and stamping of feet. But when Mr. Whiting came forward to speak, the sudden silence was just as marked as the applause had been.
>
> "He doesn't try to be a high-brow and talk over our heads," my friend whispered to

me. "He puts things so that you can understand them, and he makes you feel that there is other music besides rag-time, after all."[14]

With such evangelistic abilities for music it was no wonder that Arthur Whiting's name cropped up in every description of harpsichord playing in the United States during the first two decades of the century. It would be pleasant to report that Whiting composed music for his harpsichord and clavichord, but a look through his manuscripts in the Boston Public Library and a search of the card catalog of the New York Public Library have failed to uncover any such works.

THE HYPHENATED HARPSICHORDIST

Frances Pelton-Jones (1863–1946), born in Salem, Oregon, attended the New England Conservatory in Boston and studied organ with Dudley Buck and William C. Carl. As a prominent biographical dictionary put it, "[she] became interested in harpsichord playing and attained considerable proficiency at it."[15] The reviews of her playing generally concentrated on cosmetic details, leading one to believe that she was most likely one of the "club ladies" of music. Typical of her press is this amusing article:

Miss Pelton-Jones Explains Clever Details

"A new gown—fancy, I am getting it to go with the harpsichord," such was the laughing remark of Frances Pelton-Jones to a *Musical Courier* representative the other day.

Miss Pelton-Jones, the "hyphenated harpsichordist," as one of her recent flattering press notices terms her, is just now a very busy person indeed. In addition to playing ten or twelve concerts in the past few weeks, she is booking a long list of engagements for next season (being her own manager), and last but not entirely least, is considering the subject of her wardrobe.

"But why must your gowns match the harpsichord?" naturally asked the amazed interviewer; surely here was an anomaly—for who ever heard of an artist choosing clothes to suit his or her instrument?

"Well, you see," explained Miss Pelton-Jones, "my harpsichord, although a very beautiful replica of the original eighteenth century models, is something of a 'chef d'oeuvre' on the stage and must be 'played up to,' so to speak. At any rate, Arnold Dolmetsch, the great musical antiquarian, allowed his fancy rather free scope in the way of decoration, which means that I must exercise some slight discretion in selecting shades that harmonize with the color scheme, else my audiences might suffer artistic indisposition. But then I really enjoy that side of my art; nothing pleases me more than to plan a whole stage picture, where artists, instruments and accessories in the way of furniture and scenic [*sic*], all combine to form a congenial, consistent and inspiring whole. On my tours it often surprises me to see how, with a little study, even a college or conservatory platform can be transformed into a sixteenth or seventeenth century salon with a 'real atmosphere' of the renaissance."

That this visualization of art has not been a mistake is attested by the numerous brilliant engagements of Miss Pelton-Jones during the present season. At Mrs. Stuyveysant Fish's entertainment for the Duke and Duchess of Manchester, Mrs. Reginald de Koven's Elizabethan fête, the "Vigée le Brun" salon at the Vanderbilt Hotel, the chronological concerts in the Wanamaker Auditorium and numerous smaller engagements, the picturesque charm of her stage presence has been mentioned in connection with her superior artistry. It is no wonder she is in demand from one side of the continent to the other.[16]

The "club lady" image of this durable harpsichordist was reinforced in a short article, "The Harpsichord, A Veritable Musical X-Ray (Unique Work of Miss Pelton-Jones)":

One very interesting type of program given by Miss Pelton-Jones, which has achieved great success before "Rubinstein," New York; "Matinee Musical," Philadelphia; "Pacific Musical," San Francisco; "Tuesday Musical," Pittsburgh, and other prominent clubs, is where the day centers around the harpsichord, Miss Pelton-Jones appearing as soloist (in celebrated classics of great interest to piano students) assisted by artist club members in old repertoire (early art songs of Italy, England, etc.) sung to harpsichord accompaniment.

The program thus rendered is one of indescribable uniqueness and charm and has aroused the greatest enthusiasm wherever presented.[17]

Yet there was a serious, even scholarly side to Pelton-Jones. A response to the Landowska—Mason newspaper correspondence presented additional information about harpsichords to the general public:

May I be permitted a few words on a subject, current interest in which is attested by recent correspondence to *The Times?*

No list of famous harpsichords and their exponents would seem complete without mention of the very remarkable collection owned by Miss Belle Skinner at her Colonial country home at Holyoke, Mass. Nowhere in America outside possibly of a few art museums are so many rare and valuable antique instruments assembled. Three Ruckers, one of which is a double spinet (of which type only two more examples are in existence); a royal Italian harpsichord purchased at a fabulous price, and an exquisitely wrought spinet owned and played upon by Marie Antoinette— these number only a few among this almost priceless collection—triumphs of European seventeenth and eighteenth-century art.

And why should America not be a fitting house for the harpsichord, when our own Francis Hopkinson (first American composer and a signer of the Declaration of Independence) not only was a skilled harpsichordist, appearing in many Colonial concerts, but also invented an improvement to the instrument, afterward (late eighteenth century) adopted in Europe . . .? (The invention referred to was a type of quill now difficult to procure, but adding much of beauty to the tone quality.)

FRANCES PELTON-JONES
NEW YORK, MARCH 1, 1926[18]

Frances Pelton-Jones. (Drawing by Jane Johnson.)

Richard Aldrich reviewed a Pelton-Jones offering in the *New York Times* for March 22, 1918:

> Frances Pelton-Jones, assisted by Louise MacMahan, soprano, gave a harpsichord recital yesterday at the Princess, an afternoon of quaint pieces from the various Bachs, from old English William Byrde and Dr. John Bull, the classic Frenchmen Couperin and Rameau, even a folksong of Grainger. . . . An artistic stage was decorated with a single glowing lamp and one flower stand in Japanese simplicity.[19]

Pelton-Jones continued her concert career until advanced age; the last of her concerts to be reviewed in the *New York Times* was apparently that of 5 January 1937. The complete review reads, "Frances Pelton-Jones, harpsichordist, gave the first of her two recitals of the season yesterday afternoon at the Hotel Plaza. The assisting artist on the program was Harold Haugh, American tenor."[20] These New York concerts at the Plaza Hotel ballroom, known as Salons Intimes, had lasted twenty years. Although the reviewers did not take the concerts very seriously, the performances at least kept the harpsichord before the public at a time when few other artists were playing the instrument.

A PRESIDENT'S GRANDNIECE

Time magazine for 19 August 1935 devoted half its music page to a concert in Connecticut:

> The program listed eight artists, performing works by composers from the 9th century (Notker Balbulus) to the 18th (Grétry), but the busiest person at a concert given last week in Deep River, Conn. was an earnest lady in a brown evening dress named Lotta Van Buren. She delivered explanatory remarks. She plucked twangy notes with a crow's quill on a monochord. She strummed on a psaltery which looks like a large, shallow cigar-box with strings. Standing up, she tinkled on an octavina. Sitting down, she bowed away on a viol, played a virginal. She blew into a black wind instrument called a recorder. Lotta Van Buren had so performed twice a week since July, would continue through September. She organized the Deep River Festival of Music, furnished the old instruments, trained her young performers to play old music, much of which she had dug up in the Library of Congress. . . .[21]

Lotta Van Buren (1877–1960) was the most professional of the early music performers to succeed Dolmetsch in America. She was a native of Wisconsin; her father, Martin Van Buren, was a nephew of the nation's eighth President. Upon her graduation from the State Normal School in Madison in 1896 the Board of Education granted her a license to teach even though she was only nineteen, and thus under the legal age for teachers.[22] Van Buren taught school for three years, during which time she realized that she would rather specialize than teach general classes. In 1900 she moved east to enroll for courses in art and piano at the Pratt Institute in Brooklyn. One year later she decided that piano teaching would offer her a better opportunity for making a living. In her year at Pratt she had used up most of her savings, but during the summer she managed to sign up enough piano students to enable her to live. So she rented an apartment at 207 West 98 Street in New York, where she established her studio with a rented piano. After only two years she had saved enough money to buy a Steinway baby grand.

Her own studies continued with local pianist Eugene Heffley; and then with Harold Bauer, with whom she worked in New York, in Paris (summers of 1907 and 1909), and Vevey, Switzerland (summer of 1912). After these weeks in Switzerland, Van Buren went to Germany to do research on the life and works of Wagner. She returned home by way of England, where she spent some time with Arnold Dolmetsch learning how to repair the clavichord she had purchased from him some time earlier.

Van Buren's successful teaching led her to the concert stage through a special sidelight of her lessons: "June 6: Miss Van Buren gave a young people's piano recital at her residence-studio, showing what they have accomplished during the past season. A feature of the program of twelve numbers was the playing of motifs from 'Rheingold' and 'Parsifal'. . . ."[23] Her manner of teaching was progressive: Van Buren did not burden beginning students with scales and technical exercises but had them play favorite and familiar melodies by ear. She gradually introduced them to the fundamentals after they had become interested in making music; and, given her great interest in the music of Wagner, what more satisfying route than to let his music contribute to this process?

These methods were so successful that interested young students soon attracted interested adults. Van Buren gave a series of lectures on Wagner and his music dramas at the Brooklyn Institute of Arts and Sciences. She also devised a series of lecture-recitals for children featuring seventeenth- and eighteenth-century clavichord music linked to specific historic events or personalities: the British troops evacuating New York City, 25 November 1783 (program of Saturday, 25 November 1912); the Marquis de Lafayette (20 January 1913); and the Adams family—the untitled nobility (17 February 1913). These recitals were given at the historic Abigail Adams House in a ballroom once graced by Lafayette.

At one of these Adams House concerts Van Buren came to the attention of the manager Catherine Bamman. During the 1913 season Bamman arranged for Van Buren to present a number of lecture-recitals on Wagner; although in 1922 these programs shifted to clavichord and early music concerts, Bamman remained Van Buren's manager throughout her career. The first clavichord recital that was reviewed was held downtown, at 212 West 59 Street:

> Lotta Van Buren gave a clavichord costume recital with candle light and appropriate features, at the American Institute of Applied Music on January 9. She sang songs of the last three centuries which came from England, France, Germany and Italy, along with many dances and lyrics by Bach and four of his sons. It was most artistically carried out and muscially very unusual and satisfactory. A crowded house attended.[24]

Her interest in the clavichord and its music led Van Buren to restoration work, which became an important part of her subsequent career. Dolmetsch encouraged her, for he had found her an apt and clever pupil. He welcomed her to his workshop in England during the summers of 1923, 1924, and 1925, realizing that many of his own instruments in the United States would need her care. She also was a guest of Lady Astor, "whose activities in Parliament have made this former American woman a leading figure in British politics."[25]

Lotta Van Buren in period costume. (Van Buren Collection,
Brigham Young University.)

Lotta Van Buren and some forerunners of the modern piano became nationally
known both in print and in film. A lengthy illustrated article appeared in the *Musical
Courier* for 29 May 1924, and the film company Pathé engaged her to pose with her
instruments for an educational film entitled *What Do You Know About the Piano?*
This ten-minute silent film, shot in her studio and in the Cooper Union Museum,
proved most successful. As Van Buren's manager, Catherine Bamman, reported,
"It is the easiest that I ever had to sell, and I sold it two to one on everything else on
a recent trip I made."[26] Six stills from it, published in *Musical America,* showed the
scope of Van Buren's collection. In costumes corresponding to the period of the
instruments featured, the artist was photographed with her portable octavina, which
might have been used in Renaissance Florence; with a virginal from the court of
Queen Elizabeth and a double-decker virginal used in England in the seventeenth

century; with a French spinet from the time of Marie Antoinette; with a Dutch clavichord of the seventeenth century; and with the Jenny Lind piano that the Swedish singer and P. T. Barnum brought to Castle Garden.

Van Buren also played the harpsichord, but it took some time to obtain an instrument from Dolmetsch. She had had one on order for several years, and finally the old man returned her deposit. She was then able to purchase Busoni's harpsichord, which had been returned to Chickering's, Boston, after Busoni's death in 1924. The concerts, many with a soprano, continued for several more seasons:

> Lotta Van Buren, clavichord player, spent the summer in England with the famous Dolmetsch family—the greatest present-day authorities of old instruments and all that pertains to them. Arnold Dolmetsch has been selecting the programs to be used by Lucy Gates and Lotta Van Buren in their combined programs, and some rare classics which for centuries have not seen the light o' day will be given.[27]

In a contemporary management brochure one may read press reactions to several concerts. From the *Cleveland Plain Dealer:*

> It was a quaint sort of recital that Lotta Van Buren offered an interested audience last night. She played curious old music on curious old instruments, and she commanded a remarkably large repertoire of the former and evidently knows all there is to know about the latter. Miss Van Buren's researches have been extraordinarily extensive. She has the zeal and enthusiasm of the indefatigable collector.
>
> She played pieces by Byrd, Farnaby, Rameau, Couperin and other ancient music makers, closing with some Preludes and Fugues by Bach played as the composer intended on a "Well Tempered Clavichord."
>
> The recitalist's opening group was especially intriguing. Her playing is crisp, clear and facile. And I take it that she knows the traditions of this archaic music if anyone does. She will play again tomorrow at the Museum of Art.

And from the *Providence* (Rhode Island) *Tribune:*

> In a dainty little old fashioned gown Lotta Van Buren looked very delicate and "fetching" when she stepped before her audience in Memorial Hall last night and stood before her Octavina, her Virginalls, and her Clavichord, the old time instruments which preceded the piano.
>
> For a while she talked about these instruments and so well did she picture them and how they were made that the attention was absolute.
>
> With this preface she proceeded to give her program, using all three of the instruments. After the concert the audience proceeded almost in a body to the stage to inspect the instruments and talk with the artist.

At the end of the 1920s there was a change in Van Buren's address and in her career:

There are so many little places in our city which we often pass without pausing to investigate or think about. Perhaps they are happiest in being forgotten, happy at being released from the rush and bustle of our modern lives. POMANDER WALK, which lies between 94th and 95th Streets, just a stone's throw from Broadway, is like that. You have only to walk through its narrow gate to feel yourself in a leisurely Dickensian atmosphere. Looking at those two rows of tiny brick houses—with the narrow street separating them, and the diminutive gardens before each door—you feel that skyscrapers and motorcars just aren't real. And if you're fortunate enough to step over the doorsill of Number Fifteen you will be certain that just a few paces have carried you back several centuries.

In Miss Lotta Van Buren's candlelighted living room you will see two clavichords, two harpsichords, a lute, some recorders, and a chest of viols. All these ancient instruments are in good playing condition because they have been transformed by the touch of an expert and loving hand. And yet there is no magic in the touch of Lotta Van Buren. Everything that she does is based on careful, patient research, and upon sound knowledge gained through years of study and practice. Lotta Van Buren is gracious, smiling, and keen-eyed, but in her calm manner there is a touch of the repose of a day that has vanished. I am sure this is because she has synchronized the rhythm of her life to the old instruments to which she has devoted so much time and care.

Miss Van Buren's specialty is so unusual that I asked her how she began this work. She was a serious student of the piano, it seems, and longed to hear the music of Bach, the master, played as he intended that it should be played. Realizing that the modern piano—unknown to Bach and his contemporaries—could not fulfill her wish, she went . . . in search of a clavichord. . . .

Of course this old instrument and others like it needed certain restoration to keep them in proper playing order. And as all those who had tried to repair ancient instruments with modern materials and by modern methods had succeeded only in spoiling the ones on which they had worked, Miss Van Buren set about learning how to restore these precious relics to their original condition. . . .

. . . First, Miss Van Buren studies the materials used in the original building of each instrument entrusted to her—and she faithfully keeps to these same materials although the finding of them may cost her endless time and trouble. She would never desecrate an old keyboard instrument by using modern felt hammers. Instead, buckskin and handwoven wool—of not only the same texture but of the original color—are used. At first it was quite a problem to find handwoven wool of the correct shade of green, but now the workshops of the "Lighthouse for the Blind" supply her with just what she needs. She has the pride of every real artist in doing a perfect job.

During Miss Van Buren's so-called "restoration period" she gave no concerts. . . .[28]

Van Buren made a major commitment to Yale University, which culminated in this announcement:

The Officers of the School of Music of Yale University invite you to attend an exhibition of the recently restored musical instruments in the Morris Steinert Collection; in the President's Room, Memorial Hall, Tuesday Evening 29 January 1929, at half after eight o'clock. Miss Lotta Van Buren, of New York, who has been in charge of the restoration of the instruments will play informally.

An amplified description of Van Buren's work appeared in *The Yale Alumni Weekly:*

> The Steinert Collection of Musical Instruments, after being closed for more than a year, is again open to the public. Cleaned, freshened, repaired with devoted patience and expert skill by Miss Lotta Van Buren, the instruments make a very attractive exhibit. Every one of the fifty pieces has been renovated and put into condition for preservation; viewed as antiques their present state leaves nothing to be desired. Four specimens, representing four types, have been put into playing condition, becoming, thus revived, no longer mere relics of the past but true instruments of music. At an opening reception in January these four instruments were played for the first time in many years. The donor, Morris Steinert, took the greatest pride in the fact that he had succeeded in bringing his instruments back to their actual living state where the music of the great eighteenth-century composers could be played upon them.
>
> The playable instruments are a clavichord, a spinet and two harpsichords. . . . Miss Van Buren has also put in order the collection of viols. . . .
>
> Aside from its importance to the student of musical history, which is, of course, its first reason for being, there are several other points at which the collection awakens interest. As examples of design and workmanship the objects are instructive both on the mechanical and on the artistic side. Their cases show a wide range of taste in cabinet-making—finely proportioned outlines, woodwork attractively finished and decorated, ingenious application of ornament. Most of this work is in remarkably good taste, though a few of the pieces have an amusing touch of the bizarre. There were years of experiment before the action of the pianoforte reached its present development; in a long series of instruments from the hands of various makers we have a record of the devices adopted and discarded in the process of evolution. To their collector, himself a manufacturer of pianos and the inventor of a system of action, this mechanical interest was not the least important aspect of the collection.
>
> . . . Museums are no longer regarded as mere collections of curios to be gazed upon by more or less idle sight-seers. The modern museum, of whatever kind, is put to use in numberless ways to arouse interest, to raise standards of taste and to help in original work. Taken in this spirit the Steinert Collection has a place of its own in the musical equipment of the University. . . .
>
> Since January Miss Louisa Bellinger ('26 Music) has been acting as curator. Miss Bellinger is a thorough musician and is doing all she can to add to the attractiveness of the collection and to promote interest in it. . . .[29]

After Yale, Van Buren did restoration work for the Cooper Union Collection, the Joline Collection at Barnard College, and for John D. Rockefeller's Colonial Williamsburg in Virginia.

Fortune magazine for August 1934 reported fascinating doings in the world of early music:

Clavichord Boom

For a while this year it looked as if the bugbear of overproduction would reach even the clavichord and harpsichord business. Arnold Dolmetsch of Haslemere, Surrey, England, was going strong. John Challis of Ypsilanti, Michigan, had three or four pieces in his shop. And then Lotta Van Buren of New York announced that she was going to break open the low-priced or Ford field with a $300 clavichord. Other modern clavichords sell for $500 and up. But this industrial crisis seems postponed. For word has come from Surrey that hard times and Arnold Dolmetsch's eccentricities have finally discouraged his backers. . . . His big Haslemere workshop is shut down and his old workmen have been dismissed.

. . . Miss Van Buren, the lady who will offer clavichords for $300 (she is building two now) is one of the foremost authorities on old instruments in the country and is the best and busiest American restorer of them. She is extremely scrupulous about matching old materials and catering to the whims or fashions of the old harpsichord makers. For instance, only the bristles of a Siberian boar will do for a part of the harpsichord quill and for certain springs, only bloxate, the hair of a whale's jawbone.[30]

Depression times did not lend themselves to the mass production of obsolete instruments, so this venture into commercial production did not go very far.

Lotta Van Buren resumed giving concerts, most of them now with her Van Buren Players of Old Instruments. The Deep River Festivals, sponsored by Pratt, Read, and Company, manufacturers of piano keys, actions, and ivories, took place in an auditorium at their factory.

Touring, private concerts, lecture-recitals, and the Williamsburg work continued until Lotta Van Buren's retirement in 1940. A concert sponsored by the New London (Connecticut) American Association of University Women for the benefit of its scholarship fund presented a typical late program: At the octavina, Van Buren played *A Toye* and *Mother Watkins' Ale* (anonymous, sixteenth century) and *Dances in the Form of a Suite* (D'Andrieu). On the virginalls she played *Pavana and Gaillarde* (William Byrd), *Suite* (William Croft), *Menuet* (Lully), and *Musette* (Rameau). The second half of the program was played on the clavichord: *The Story of David and Goliath* (Kuhnau), *Dances and Lyrics by the Bach Family,* and "Prelude and Fugue in F minor from *The Well-Tempered Clavichord [sic]*" (J. S. Bach).[31]

In 1940 Van Buren moved to California and married a friend of many years, Henry Bizallion. When they sold their home in 1955 the collection of papers, music, instruments, and costumes went to Brigham Young University, a result of Lotta's concerts, many years earlier with Lucy Gates, a descendent of Brigham Young.

CHAPTER
4

THE INCOMPARABLE
WANDA LANDOWSKA

> We Americans, when we have thought of the harpsichord at all, have usually
> thought of it as the chattering instrument of a pedantic preciousness. . . . Now there
> comes to us a supple and undulating lady out of Poland, by way of Berlin, and of
> Paris, and lo! in a trice all our preconceived notions and prejudices vanish in thin air!
> The sorcery of her mind and spirit, the prestidigitation of her fluttering, skimming
> hands—but hands of steely strength and temper—in their infallible response, and
> what is the magical result? The quaint and pretty fossil for antiquarian collections
> lives again.[1]

Wanda Landowska made her American debut with the Philadelphia Orchestra on
16 November 1923. As she was the world's best-known exponent of the harpsichord, her engagement marked a new excitement about the instrument, an excitement lacking since the departure of the Dolmetsch ensemble twelve years earlier.
The news magazine *Time* was also making its debut in 1923. Its first mention of the
harpsichord occurred in the issue for 26 November:

In Philadelphia

> Philadelphia's Stokowski, orchestra leader, triumphed gloriously when he brought
> forward Wanda Landowska to make her American debut. Mme. Landowska plays
> the harpsichord, instrument of an older time and more fastidious taste. She played the
> Handel Concerto in B-flat for harpsichord and orchestra and then the Bach Concerto
> for harpischord [*sic*] unsupported, and finally the Mozart Concerto in E-flat for piano
> and orchestra. Four recalls gave convincing evidence of her triumph.

Landowska was born in Poland in 1879. Even as a child she had a feeling for
"old" music. She began to study the piano at the age of four with a kindly teacher,
and soon she discovered the C major *Prelude* of Bach. But a stricter teacher made
her practice technical exercises by Kalkbrenner and Thalberg instead of her beloved
gavottes and bourrées, so she made a vow that, when she was grown up, she would

play a program devoted entirely to the music of Bach, Rameau, Haydn, and Mozart—on the piano, of course.[2]

After discovering old instruments in museums and trying her "old" music on the few available Pleyel and Érard copies of harpsichords, Landowska was convinced that the music she loved sounded best on the instrument for which it was originally written—the harpsichord. Aided by her husband, Henri Lew, an ethnomusicologist, she continued to search out instruments in museums and private collections. Dissatisfied at first with the copies at her disposal, Landowska persuaded Gustav Lyon of Pleyel to make a grander instrument with a sub-octave set of strings—the 16-foot register, found in only a few early instruments. This instrument, introduced at the Breslau Bach Festival in 1912, became the standard Landowska harpsichord.

After various successes all over Europe (including Russia, where she played for Tolstoy), Landowska added post-war America to her triumphs. As she said, "I arrived like a lion tamer, dragging along four large Pleyel harpsichords."[3] She was not unknown in the United States, for in 1905 the popular musical journal *The Etude* had published an article by Robert Brussel stating,

> This new epoch of the harpsichord, which is largely due to Madame Landowska, will have the effect that it deserves. These harpsichord works revived in their proper conditions will prove that emotion is not only to be associated with grandiose masses of sound. Today, music is somewhat weary of the sublime on a large scale. It is weary of routine pianistic literature, and conscious that it is impossible to go farther in brutal effect without sacrificing the very nature of music itself; it is tentatively searching other horizons. The present re-awakening of interest in the harpsichord, and the hearty reception accorded Wanda Landowska seem to accord perfectly with our new artistic necessities.[4]

Four days after her Philadelphia debut, Landowska was heard in New York City, when Stokowski and his orchestra performed in Carnegie Hall for a sold-out house. The repeated program produced a less-positive reaction from the critic of the *Musical Courier:*

> The twangy and guitarish tone of [the harpsichord], while it pleased audiences in the days of Bach, seems to have outlived its usefulness at the present times. However, it may perhaps be better suited for solo works, and that in a smaller hall, or rather in more intimate surroundings. With the orchestral accompaniment (. . . Stokowski used one-third of the players), the harpsichord lost its charm, because of its weak and non-carrying quality.[5]

Audiences evidently did not agree with this criticism, however. Landowska gave a series of solo performances in New York during that season, the first one at the David Mannes Music School on 21 December. As usual, she played on two instruments: Handel's *Air and Variations* from *Suite* in E major, Bach's *Partita* in C minor, several Scarlatti *Sonatas,* and her own *Bourrée d'Auvergne* at the harpsichord; and the *Sonata* in A minor by Mozart and the *Sonata* in C major by Haydn at the piano. It was reported that she gave half a dozen encores at the harpsichord.[6]

On the following Sunday David Mannes introduced Landowska's program at the Metropolitan Museum of Art, describing the workings of the instrument for the audience. Of course the opening sentence of the *Musical Courier's* description of the events on 16 January 1924 was not entirely accurate:

> Mme. Landowska appeared at her first solo recital in New York at Aeolian Hall . . . before a good sized audience that was evidently extremely interested in the work of this unique artist and exceedingly liberal in its applause. On the harpsichord she played Handel's Passacaglia and Bach's Capriccio on the Departure of a Beloved Brother, a group of pieces by Scarlatti and a closing group of compositions by Pasquini, Daquin, Rameau and [Couperin] le Grand. On the piano she played a Mozart Sonata in D major and a Haydn Sonata in E minor.
>
> Mme. Landowska is an excellent pianist. Her technic is beyond cavil and she plays with beautiful tone, warmth, and understanding. All this is true also of her harpsichord playing, and in addition one must remark the special effects which she achieves on this obsolete instrument. Particularly notable was the effect of the Bach. It is, on the piano, rather an ordinary affair, but with the special coloring given to it by the harpsichord it stands out as the miniature masterpiece that it really is. The smaller pieces by ancient masters acquired for the first time their true significance upon this instrument and under the delightful musical treatment which she gives them. It was a pleasure not only to listen to her on the harpsichord but also to see the perfection of her technic.[7]

Indeed Landowska's influence on the musical scene seems to have mushroomed, if one is to believe the next printed encomium:

> The harpsichord has come back and Wanda Landowska is the artist who has restored it. Following the great success of Mme. Landowska, no less than three other harpsichordists suddenly appeared in New York within a week [Whiting, Pelton-Jones, and Lewis Richards]. The position of the harpsichord as "ruler of the orchestra" has been re-established. Mme. Landowska has "ruled from the harpsichord" over the Philadelphia, Philharmonic, New York Symphony, Boston and Detroit orchestras, and she will be heard with the Chicago Symphony on March 13 and 14.[8]

And what a debut in Chicago!

> Could anything in the whole realm of music be more delightful than the playing of *The Harmonious Blacksmith* on the harpsichord as done by Wanda Landowska at Orchestra Hall last Saturday night?
>
> We doubt it.
>
> Mme. Landowska played other solos on the same instrument which were good, too, as also a Handel Concerto, and she played a Mozart Concerto on a grand piano

of the present moment (not so well, however, as at least one Chicago pianist in the audience would have done it), but these were not comparable to *The Harmonious Blacksmith* which was at once novel and convincing.

The orchestra cut out one number because the walking back and forth of Mme. Landowska in acknowledgement of applause took so much time, but still played numbers by Grétry and Debussy which were beautiful. The Symphony of Bax (A-flat Major) we hope never to hear again. It is monstrously ugly and terribly monotonous.[9]

The Chicago correspondent of the *Musical Courier* gave these impressions of Landowska's first appearance in his city:

> Wanda Landowska's performance on the harpsichord of the Handel concerto and the three solos . . . was a novelty well deserving place on one of this season's programs. The harpsichord, a musical instrument of other days, has been happily replaced by the piano, as the candle has been replaced by oil, then gas and now electricity. The harpsichord has a metallic sound such as the banjo, the guitar, and the mandolin, but under the fleet fingers of Mme. Landowska the instrument revealed many unforeseen possibilities. Her touch is so lovely that she makes the instrument talk in a most pleasurable manner, and it speaks with fine delicacy of tonal quality and responds to her demands in a most astonishing way, and by the use of added devices made less thin than otherwise would be possible. Mme. Landowska is not only a great harpsichordist but also a very fine pianist. All the beautiful qualities revealed in her playing of the Handel, Bach and Scarlatti selections were disclosed anew in the Mozart concerto for piano. Here is a true Mozart interpreter, a pianist whose delicate touch brings out all the beauties of the composition and whose interpretation of the classics disclosed the learned student. At the harpsichord and at the piano, Mme. Landowska is a mistress of her art and the big success she scored at the hands of a delighted public presages many returns to this city.[10]

In addition to such distinguished orchestral appearances and solo recitals, Landowska made her first recordings, at the RCA Victor studios in Camden, New Jersey, during her first visit to the United States. The repertoire included the highly praised Handel Variations from her concert appearances; Mozart's *Rondo alla Turca;* Scarlatti's *Sonata* in D, Longo 465; and her own *Bourrée d'Auvergne* No. 1.[11]

With all her critical acclaim and a full schedule of offers for the following season, there was no question that Landowska would return. In only a few months her artistic impression on American audiences had been extraordinary.

INTERLUDES AND TRIUMPHS

A rare glimpse of Landowska back home in Paris is provided by the American pianist Arthur Shattuck:

The Unpredictable Wanda Landowska

One summer in the 1920s, on one of their holidays, Ernest Urchs, New York director of the concert department of the Steinway firm, arrived in Paris with Mrs. Urchs and their daughter, Nita. That arrival was celebrated by a memorable dinner which Mr. Urchs gave at the select and elegant restaurant, Escargot, in honor of Fanny Bloomfield Zeisler. Our host had engaged a private dining room for the occasion, and the guests, all pianists, had assembled, all but one, and the maitre d'hotel stood ready to set things in motion. We waited fifteen minutes, twenty, a half hour; then our host gave the signal to begin.

Ten minutes later the doors were thrown open and the tardy guest, Wanda Landowska, entered smiling. It was an impressive entrance, effected entirely without excuses. Mr. Urchs jumped up and met her halfway and escorted her to her place. The Escargot's famous snail course was already being served. La Wanda eyed the strange objects on her plate, and Mr. Urchs said, in German, "Mme. Landowska, I presume you are sufficiently Parisienne to be snail-minded." She replied, "To tell the truth, I don't know what they are nor how to eat them," wherewith Mrs. Urchs got up and showed her how to extract the minuscule animal from its domicile. The famed harpsichordist was an apt pupil at the trick. Grasping the tiny instrument with her thumb and index finger, she proved expert at the game, as though she were executing a series of Couperin ornaments. She gave her unstinted approval of this new and exotic food.

The dinner was elaborate and successful, and before we separated, Wanda, in a moment of expansion, invited all of us to her Montmartre apartment the following Thursday, for lunch. Wanda lived with her mother and two able secretaries, Elsa and Trudie, in a top floor walk-up apartment consisting of several small rooms, more or less thrown together to give space for harpsichords and pianos.

The repast offered us was a Polish masterpiece. We all wondered by what magic it had been created. One course followed the other in ordered succession, and each bringing undreamed surprises. When we had finished, the tables were spirited away to give room for circulation.

Wanda's mother was living then. Uncommonly intelligent, she was a conversationalist of exceptional brilliance. This rare art Wanda inherited from her. Wanda was equally at home in Polish, French, and German.

My personal experience with the Poles was always pleasant. I had unlimited admiration for the brilliance of their minds and for the aristocracy of their manners.

Leschetizky shared my opinions with reservation, although he was a Pole himself. He had among them devoted friends and students. He maintained that the Poles had no innate rhythmic sense, and rhythm was one of the things he found generally lacking, even in Paderewski.

During the luncheon at Wanda's apartment, remembering what Leschetizky had told me, I asked Mrs. Zeisler how she explained the impeccable rhythm of our hostess. I said, "She's Polish; no getting around that."

Mrs. Zeisler said, "Oh, but she is a Jew. She merely happened to be born in Polish territory. That accounts for her perfect rhythm."

As we talked, we were standing next to the Pleyel piano on the top of which was placed an exquisite little clavichord of the sixteenth century. It was open and displayed a painting of a landscape on its inside cover. Mrs. Zeisler was gently touching its keys as we discussed our gracious, rhythmic hostess.

Wanda Landowska. (Pencil sketch by Arthur Shattuck,
dated Paris, 27 September 1923.)

Presently the unpredictable Wanda slithered up and passed behind us muttering aloud (with obvious intention that we should hear it): "Mais quel blasphème, voyons!" [Good heavens, what blasphemy!]

She never could tolerate strangers' fingers touching her clavichord or harpsichord. Later that afternoon she cornered me and asked, as though she didn't know, "Quelle est cette femme là?" [Who is that woman?] I said, "Don't you know? She is America's greatest pianist."

I expected contrition on her part, for her remark regarding the clavichord incident, but she shrugged her shoulders and said, "Connais pas." [I don't know her.] If proud Mrs. Zeisler could have known that![12]

An even more outrageous vignette of Landowska appears in George Painter's biography of Marcel Proust:

The new gaiety of the 1920s had begun, in time for Proust to glimpse a new age which he found too incongruous to insert in *À la Recherche*. At the Princesse de Guermantes's last matinee the music is still a dying echo of the Vinteuil Septet; but the evenings of 1922 were danced away to the unfamiliar syncopations of tango and ragtime, which to survivors of a past epoch seemed to symbolise a dislocation not only of rhythm but of morals. "And what do they do after they've finished dancing?" enquired a great lady, after watching with deep interest a couple interlocked in the first tango she had ever seen. . . . [Proust] attended the Ritz ball on 15 January, and received a promised demonstration of the latest steps from Mlle d'Hinnisdael—"even when indulging in the most 1922 of dances, she still looks like a unicorn on a coat of arms!" He admired the chaste chivalry with which Morand, dancing with a lady in mauve, succeeded in disengaging his portliness from her person; he was introduced to the harpsichordist Wanda Landowska, "just when she was in the act of biting Mlle Vacaresco in the buttock"; and then he fled to his private room upstairs and devoured a leg of lamb.[13]

Life in the United States for a cosmopolitan artist such as Landowska, was doubtless less exciting than life in Paris. But Landowska confided to at least one interviewer that she "adored New York," especially because of its beautiful sunshine.[14] The American season of 1924–25 began for Landowska with a concert in New Brunswick, New Jersey, on 6 November. Her first New York engagement came on 10 November at Aeolian Hall, a program of harpsichord and piano music entitled "Bach and His Beloved Masters." As the *Musical Courier* reported, "In the short time she has been here, [Mme. Landowska] attracted a large following, enough in fact to nearly fill [the hall]."[15]

Other concerts were further afield: Philadelphia; Toledo; Washington, D.C.; Lancaster, Pennsylvania; Cincinnati, with the orchestra conducted by Fritz Reiner; Dayton; Detroit; St. Louis; Lawrence, Kansas; Chambersburg, Pennsylvania; Cleveland and Oberlin, Ohio; and Pittsburgh. These programs contained music for both piano and harpsichord and usually consisted of a selection of smaller works: the ubiquitous *Coucou* of Daquin, a Scarlatti sonata (the "hunting-horn" E major was particularly popular), a Telemann bourrée. The Aeolian Hall program had been a heavier one, including several pieces that through the years became Landowska specialties: the Vivaldi–Bach *Concerto* in D, Bach's *Chromatic Fantasy and Fugue,* and his C minor *Partita,* the last played, however, on the piano.

The public was not ready to accept an all-harpsichord program. The prevailing attitude about programming is revealed in a review of a New York recital by the pianist Harold Samuel: "An all-Bach program is a rare and alarming event. To attempt such a thing shows moral heroism and crowning self-confidence. To attempt it successfully shows an amazing talent, a masterly technique. . . ."[16] To expand such limited horizons education was an absolute necessity. Landowska had already distinguished herself in various teaching capacities: from 1900 to 1913 she had taught harpsichord at the Schola Cantorum of Paris; from 1913 until the end of the First World War she had been on the faculty of the Berlin Hochschule für Musik, as the first "modern-day" professor of harpsichord anywhere; in the summer of 1925 she began her School of Ancient Music at her newly acquired home in the Paris suburb of St.-Leu-la-Forêt; and, beginning with the fall of 1925, she undertook a famous series of lectures on early music at the Curtis Institute of Music in Philadelphia, which began its second year of existence on 1 October of that year. These lectures were for the entire student body, not just keyboard players, and they covered the aesthetics and repertoire of Bach and his predecessors.

Expanding horizons in another direction, Landowska appeared in the League of Composers presentation of Manuel de Falla's *El Retablo del Maese Pedro,* the puppet opera commissioned by the Princesse de Polignac and first performed at her salon in Paris on 25 June 1923, with Landowska as harpsichordist. The American première took place in New York on 26 December 1925. Writing about highlights of the season, critic Pitts Sanborn declared, "This production proved to be one of the unforgettable events of the winter. . . . Conductor Mengelberg and the playing by Mme. Landowska of the harpsichord (which figures prominently in de Falla's fine and individual orchestration. . . .)"[17]

Landowska herself commented on this production in a letter to the editor of the *New York Times:*

I read the following sentence in your article of December 27, referring to the League of Composers' production last Tuesday night of "El Retablo":

"It has been stated that this is the first modern composition which enlists the aid of the harpsichord. The statement is erroneous. Fritz Delius, to mention only one modern composer, has written pieces for the harpsichord."

There seems to be a slight misunderstanding which it would be a good idea to clear up.

It is evident that ever since I have succeeded in giving the harpsichord, after much struggling, the position it deserves, the interest in that instrument has been much increased. It is evident, too, that many a composer has attempted to revert to olden times by imitating the old style of music, more or less felicitously. Not Fritz Delius alone, whom you mention, but many other contemporary composers, such as Rontgen, Kochinski, Buts, Drischner, &c., have composed music for the harpsichord. I receive constantly "Gavotte Rococo," "Souvenir de Versailles," "A la Grâce de Pompadour," with inscriptions by their authors. But this does not alter the fact that the harpsichord for the first time lives a new life, a modern life, in de Falla's work.

Why? Because de Falla is the first to have attempted and succeeded to understand fundamentally the harpsichord, which is a very intricate instrument; he has worked a long time with me, fathomed the character and the climaxes of that instrument and studied the thousand possibilities of fioritura, without trying to reproduce the effects or manners of the ancients. De Falla is the first who, by studying the harpsichord, discovers in it fresh and unexplored sources of modern inspiration.

The concerto which he is finishing now and which has been composed for me, and which I will play next season, will be a most eloquent testimony of it.

There is one manifestation which it is particularly interesting to observe: the music of the seventeenth and of the eighteenth centuries and the instruments of the epoch have a very great influence on the younger school. The Group des Six are of my good friends. Thus we should not be astonished to see, soon, blossom out a whole school of very modern music which will have taken birth in the ever fresh though ancient source of the music of our ancestors. And Manuel de Falla will have started the movement.

WANDA LANDOWSKA
NEW YORK, DECEMBER 29, 1925.[18]

Traveling with an instrument the size and weight of the Pleyel harpsichord was not as easy as packing one's piccolo and setting out for the train station. Nevertheless Landowska continued to introduce the harpsichord to towns and cities all over the eastern third of the United States and into Canada: her 1926 dates found her in Wooster, Ohio; Cooperstown and Utica, New York; Erie, Indiana, and Scranton, Pennsylvania; Newport, Rhode Island; and Toronto.

An all-Bach program *was* essayed during this year, albeit not one with harpsichord alone: appearing with the cellist Evsei Beloussoff allowed the program to have a variety of textures, including the cello alone: the *Suite* in G; cello with harpsichord: *Sonatas* in G and D; and harpsichord alone: the *Italian Concerto*.

> The joint recital was interesting not alone for the high quality of musicianship displayed by both principals, but also because the production of the Bach music approximated in some respects its first introduction to the world, a fact made possible by the newly revived popularity of the harpsichord. Mme. Landowska played with that felicitous charm which has been a motivating influence in re-creating public favor for this instrument of an older day. Beneath her agile fingers the instrument attained a delicacy and tone that at once revealed the master technician and the consummate artist.[19]

Among the many programs played during this third season in America, a particularly fascinating one was given for the Normal Concert Course in Ypsilanti, Michigan on 8 April 1926. Not distinctive for any repertoire unusual to Landowska, the program included the by-now customary Vivaldi *Concerto,* the "bird pieces" of Rameau and Daquin, the E-major Scarlatti *Sonata,* the Bach *Italian Concerto,* and a Pachelbel *Magnificat* at the harpsichord, plus the Mozart A-major *Sonata* at the piano. However the concert was intriguing for the fact that the young John Challis must have been in the audience, as it was his teacher, Frederick Alexander, who arranged this concert. In less than a decade Challis would become America's first native-born professional harpsichord maker.

Landowska had still more music to introduce to the United States this season; *Time* reported another first:

K.P.E. Bach

> To a very musicianly audience in Manhattan, harpsichordist Wanda Landowska proved last week that there was more than one Bach worthy of mention. On the occasion of her appearance as soloist with the Flonzaley Quartet she played for the first time in the United States K.P.E. Bach's (son of the great J.S.) *Concerto in G*

minor for Harpsichord and String Quartet, scored by herself from the manuscript parts found in the sale of Krieger's collection at Bonn. Said critic Lawrence Gilman of the *New York Herald Tribune,* "The whole of it is vital and distinguished music, but the slow movement, the Largo, is not only an exquisite piece of writing, but it is charged with a depth of feeling, a poetic beauty, a musing, tenderness. . . ."[20]

Manuel de Falla's *Concerto,* a major piece of chamber music for harpsichord and five solo instruments—flute, oboe, clarinet, violin, and cello—occupied the composer for three years. It finally received its première in Barcelona on 5 November 1926, with Landowska as soloist, Falla conducting. The initial impression was not favorable. The parts had been transcribed quickly and, in some spots, inaccurately; the players were underrehearsed; Falla's conducting lacked incisiveness.

When Falla asked Landowska to repeat the *Concerto* for its Paris première, she was able to plead a prior engagement (in London). Falla himself was the soloist, playing the work twice—once at the piano and once at the harpsichord. Landowska did play the work on two subsequent occasions: she gave its American première with the Boston Symphony, conducted by Serge Koussevitzky, on 31 December 1926; and the same program was repeated in New York on 6 January 1927. The *New York Times* critic reported, "The concerto is in three movements. The work follows loosely established forms, but there is considerable freedom in tonal relations and harmonic effects, which ill conceal the cloven hoofs of Igor Stravinsky. . . . The harpsichord was at times barely audible and seldom effective in the spaces of the big auditorium [Carnegie Hall]. . . ."[21] Landowska also played the work in Philadelphia, with Stokowski conducting.[22]

> Wanda Landowska was soloist with the Philadelphia Orchestra at its concerts of January 7 and 8. . . . After the intermission, the soloist appeared . . . in a Concerto . . . by De Falla. The orchestral parts were played by the "firsts" of the respective instruments. While interesting as a novelty, this modern composition seemed strangely out of place on the old time instrument. Of course the performance of the composition was excellent as each player is an artist on his own instrument. Possibly it would have been more pleasing had it been heard in a smaller room. Mme. Landowska, as is her custom, wore a gown made in the style of the period which the harpsichord represents—this time it was a rich green velvet. Many recalls were accorded her. . . . Dr. Stokowski, with his right arm still in a sling, conducted for the harpsichord concerto and for the final orchestral number. . . .[23]

Landowska was not to play the Falla *Concerto* again after these concerts. The use of solo players from the orchestra did not make this work a particularly efficient one for an orchestral program, and the rhythmic difficulties presented to the ensemble required considerable rehearsal time. But it was the large stretches in the harpsichord part that really made Landowska decide not to play the work: it caused her intense physical discomfort to practice and to play the piece.[24]

Landowska continued her usual full schedule during the first months of 1927—recitals, concerts with orchestra, teaching. She sailed for Europe on 13 April.

Although she was not listed on the Arthur Judson concert artists' roster for 1927–28, she was apparently back in New York for at least one concert on 18 December 1927 at the Guild Theatre, where she appeared in a Christmas program with the English Singers, a madrigal group.

> Mme. Landowska maintained and added to her high reputation as a star on her favorite instrument, setting forth Elizabethan music with Wolsey's Wilde by William Byrd, a Gigge by Giles Farnaby, and Les Bouffons and The King's Hunt by John Bull. In her second group were Noel by Pierre Dandrieu, Les Sauvages and La Joyeuse by Jean Ph. Rameau, and J. S. Bach's Allegro from his D Major Concerto. Persistent applause brought delightful encores from her extensive repertoire.[25]

After her fifth visit to the United States, Landowska

> sailed early for Europe, having been obliged to cancel her final New York engagement in order to be able to reach Berlin for her scheduled concert with the Philharmonic Orchestra. She went to her chateau in France for a few days en route, and, following the Berlin engagement will tour the Continent and England until May. Her itinerary will include seven concerts in seven consecutive days in Italy, and appearances in Leipsic, Milan, Switzerland, Belgium, Poland, England and the Scandinavian countries. Mme. Landowska is not planning to return to the United States next season for the year has been entirely booked abroad, Egypt even having been included in the countries she will visit. However, she is planning to return to this country the year following.[26]

Despite these optimistic words, she was not to return for fifteen years. The main reason undoubtedly was that her work at home, at St.-Leu-la-Forêt, became more absorbing and more fulfilling with the opening on 3 July 1927 of her own concert hall, a "honey-colored temple seating about 200 auditors . . . nestled amidst the flowers and greenery of Landowska's own garden."[27]

SAINT LEU

> Yearly, after her American tour, Mme. Landowska goes to St. Leu, France, where she has established a "little Bayreuth." Her courses—intimate talks in her library, rich in books and manuscripts of bygone centuries, illustrated either at the piano, the harpsichord or the clavichord—draw from all quarters instrumentalists, singers and others eager to embark upon a profound study of the technical and aesthetic principles of interpretation. She guides them along the path of two voices, music which conducts to the kingdom of polyphony. They pursue the principles of the older style not like book-worms who feed on musty treatises in the shadow of some old spinet, but like artists who strive to refashion by an anxiously pondered and soundly directed interpretation the very life of the music of a bygone period.[28]

Landowska attracted students from all over the world, including, of course, a number from the United States. Some sense of what she had to impart and how she did it can be gleaned from this description of some public teaching at the Salle Pleyel:

> The students . . . were on a platform grouped around this teacher . . . each called upon one by one to play the pieces on the program, Mme. Landowska permitting each one to determine the best interpretation. Then she would criticize this interpretation and require the pupil to defend his own point of view, after which she would show him in what way his idea was defective, playing certain passages herself.
>
> It was a masterpiece of intelligent pedagogy. Of course I shall not be relating anything new when I declare that Mme. Landowska is a marvelous exponent of the music of the eighteenth century. What I did not know was that this artist was endowed to such a degree with the gift of initiating others into these mysteries which long and patient studies have revealed to her.
>
> Therein, precisely, lay the interest of this course. Such lessons do indeed teach how the music of the past must be played. But their especial value is found in the love they engender for such music. I never realized how much I cherished Bach, Handel, Scarlatti or Couperin until I was present at one of Wanda Landowska's lessons. I loved these masters instinctively, but today I know much better why I love them. Furthermore, I have also become very much aware why so many people do not love them. It is because they have never heard them in their living and creative state. . . .
>
> Nothing could be further from stupid and narrow fanaticism than this artist's manner of teaching. In no wise does she disdain the modern piano and employs it frequently in the interpretation of the older music. Never has she maintained that Bach can be played only on the instruments of his time. She claims, on the other hand—and her contention is unassailably logical—that when the piano is used for the performance of this music the player must effect a kind of adaptation and bring to the piano a sort of interpretation based on a study of the original instrument.
>
> The vibrant life which animates polyphony is the third great truth that Wanda Landowska's teaching brings to light. All polyphonic music—even that written for the keyboard—is governed by the laws of song. Taking this principle as a point of departure she bases her study of such music upon the two-voiced Inventions, which offer the key to the interpretation of all music whatsoever written for several voices. Therein she only follows the example of the old masters of composition who grounded the entire study of their art on an understanding of two-part counterpoint.[29]

A particularly astute description of life for a student of the School of Ancient Music is found in the memoirs of the German harpsichordist Eta Harich-Schneider:

> But back to the year 1929. Professor Springer knew Landowska quite well and counseled me to try to study with her. "You will get to know a very nice but very conceited lady. And if she says something that doesn't please you, don't argue with her!" From Springer and Johannes Wolf I already knew the Landowska saga: her extravagant success in Berlin, her tragic marriage with the Communist Lew, the tales of love and scandal about her and her female students, her eighteenth-century manners: "Permit me to introduce my husband, Monsieur Lew, and Madame So-and-so, my husband's mistress"—a much laughed-at scene. Further her beginning at the

Hochschule, finally Lew's murder by right-wing terrorists in 1919 and Wanda's move to Paris. "Watch out for your chastity," laughed Johannes Wolf significantly as I took my leave.

A hot Paris summer, dust and noise in the Gare du Nord, joyful, excited anticipation, and then the pleasant country surroundings of Saint-Leu-la-Forêt. Elschen Schunnicke, Wanda's German confidant and secretary, received me talkatively, showed me photo albums of Wanda's harpsichord courses and was not reserved in talking about the intimate acquaintance with prominent persons. Then, for a moment, I was permitted to listen in on a private lesson in the Music Room. I was amazed: the Goddess sat like a comfortable little mother, small, a little bent, glasses on the gigantic nose, pencil in hand next to the harpsichord and corrected fingerings, exactly like my piano teacher Alma Martin in Frankfurt-am-Orkus!

Finally I was called into the presence. Wanda's private workroom contained a Pleyel harpsichord and a library of harpsichord literature from the seventeenth and eighteenth centuries in original editions as well as the relevant literature on the subject in five languages. The furnishings were Louis XVI. On the table stood a vase with large opened light red roses. I brought Wanda pressed leaves from the grave of Lew [her husband]. She was pleased by my eagerness for a study of "sources." Then she turned at once to examining my hands and went through some finger exercises with me. It was the purest ballet school. She stated that my hands were first-class, and if I were to devote myself seriously to the harpsichord, she would take care that I should become her representative in Germany, "because there is *no one* there," said she pointedly.

She kept her word. Already after the second course she wrote to Leo Kestenberg and recommended me as her successor for the harpsichord professorship at the Berlin Hochschule. Kestenberg managed to obtain my appointment to that position through the director, Professor Georg Schuenemann.

I was totally amazed at Landowska. She was one of those rare women who had built her career totally alone, without money. Because of this she was also shot at like the holy martyr Sebastian. The groups of players from the *Jugendbewegung* and from the *Hausmusik* groups would not leave alone a single hair of her head, and accused her of stylistic ignorance. She was, however, very well read and far ahead of them both in sources and knowledge. In everything she was very stubborn, but so were the others, only they had less talent!

"She was sweet as a mother and strict as a ballet master," it says in my diary. Certainly she knew how to place herself in a stage picture! She came to class by a garden path reserved only for her; it ran behind the great lawn where her Polish gardener, Cadzin, worked; she would greet him with a relaxed word and he would fly to kiss her hand; then through her private entrance she would enter her small Sanctum Sanctorum behind the concert hall, and would stand suddenly on her stage—we would all rise silently. "Seat yourselves, my children."

Her relationship to Germany was ambivalent; a certain love-hate. I believe that she had never given up the wish to return to her position in Berlin. . . . The "BB," the Prussian Staatsbibliothek, she missed greatly. In the five years I studied with her I often sought references there for her, work which I was later to use for my own source material. There lay, certainly, an air of the emigré around the costumes of her German secretaries and their mania for wearing sandals. We all were permitted to approach the harpsichord only in sandals. . . .

Wanda's students lived entirely dependent on her, as planets circle a sun. The discipline was first class, the atmosphere rather pretentious. Professional critiques of Wanda's interpretation, teaching methods, or choice of literature I never heard, but in her absences bitter complaints about her injustices, whims, intrigues—an atmosphere of jealousy like that of a twelfth-century court.

The class ran only in summer and ended with a costume ball and a champagne reception. I remember especially the one from September 4, 1932. The loveliest was Wanda as "Royal Mistress" with her long hair in great Louis XV style, off-the-shoulder gown of heavy yellow silk. She looked bewitching. Her shoulders were still perfect and snow-white. Madame Nef came as a German sailor in my sailor suit; Ruggiero Gerlin as Madam Verdurin, and a large Belgian girl as "young Greek," with headband and white linen shift: by Zeus she looked like a fat girl in a nightgown. . . .

I wore an Etonian tie and riding costume with red jacket; Isabelle Nef acknowledged me, "His royal majesty, the Prince of Wales." Wanda greeted me with a deep courtly bow. I danced a lot with the girls because all the men were such bad dancers. Wanda was very amused: "Eta has outdone us all." She seated herself at the piano and played popular songs and old waltzes . . . she could do this too.

Through a chance experience I saw Wanda once entirely without mask. From that experience I know that her famous hardness, her mistrust, her intrigue, her pride were only protective coverings created by a deeply musical person in order to withstand the difficulties of life. I was walking in October 1932 in the evening twilight through the woods toward Taverny, through the rustling colored leaves which covered the ground. Coming the opposite direction was a tiny, insignificant, bent woman. She saw me just as she saw everything else, but she did not recognize me, for she was not wearing her glasses. And I recognized her, also, only in the split second of passing, so private was Wanda "La Victorieuse." I saw a shy, enthusiastically lively face, lost in dreams, from which two large eyes pierced the evening darkness.[30]

American harpsichordist Ralph Kirkpatrick was another of the students at St. Leu. His comments give a certain balance to Harich-Schneider's view of Landowska's school, for it is well known that Kirkpatrick and Landowska did not see eye-to-eye through most of his career.

Wednesday, October 14, 1931: Thursday afternoon I took the train out to St. Leu-la-Forêt to see Landowska. While she was engaged with lessons, her secretary took me around and introduced me to some of the hocus pocus and some of the pupils. "Yes," she said, "Wanda Landowska is a truly wonderful person. She can do anything. Yes, she even planned this garden. You've heard about the concert hall. We call it the Temple, devoted to old music," etc.

"Holy jumping cats," I thought, "what am I getting into." My amazement increased when we entered the hall and found a perfect Negro mammy, Landowska's chief pupil in costume having his picture taken. There were a number of women, one the kind that gives you a finger instead of a whole hand, and a number of old harpsichords obviously chosen for decorative rather than musical effect, in a very nice room with two Pleyel harpsichords and two Pleyel pianos ensconced on a little

Costume Ball at St. Leu, participants identified by Putnam Aldrich. First row, seated: Ruggiero Gerlin (Italian), dressed as Landowska; Dr. Caroli of Paris; Régine Hoerée. Second row, seated: Rebecca Davidson (American); Ethel Preston (American); Jeanne (Landowska's cook); Lipnitzki's niece; Jean Christie (Australian); Amparito (Spanish); Incarnasion (Spanish); Anyla (Polish). Third row, seated: Miss Offheimer (American); Carmen (Spanish); Lipnitzki (Russian photographer); Elsa (Landowska's companion from Berlin). Fourth row, standing: Julietta Goldschwang (Argentinian); Madeleine Cohn; Mme. Sacerdoce (Nelia's mother); Nelia (Argentinian); Landowska; Arthur Hoerée (Belgian critic); Clifford Curzon (English); Trudy; Putnam Aldrich; Momo Aldrich. At the top: Aimé (the gardener). (Courtesy of Momo Aldrich.)

raised platform. I was somewhat alarmed by the hocus pocus-ness of the atmosphere and the general spirit of "Isn't this old music just lovely. And nobody can play it but Landowska!"

Some time later came a hush, and Landowska entered. She is a sort of combination of Mrs. Landowsky, the pawnbroker's wife, and Wanda, daughter of Henry VIII, sister of Mary and Elizabeth. I shook her hand, which she withdrew quickly, and said, "Oh, be careful. My harpsichord hand!" However, she was very nice in a sort of come-into-the-parlor-Red-Riding-Hood way.

Then she and pupils rehearsed some music for two harpsichords, and as she was very tired, and as I was a bit swamped in hocus pocus, I was not much pleased with her playing, which seemed rather dry, resembling nothing so much as a wellbred typewriter, rather than a well-tempered clavichord. I found her registration quite contrary to the structure of the music, and her phrasing the exact opposite of anything

I had found out about Bach's phrasing. I began to wonder what I was going to do. . . .[31]

Kirkpatrick began to change his initial harsh opinion of the virtuosa on subsequent visits:

> I went back on Saturday to her class. . . . There I was considerably more favorably impressed, particularly with the rhythmic precision and clarity of her technic and her specifically harpsichord touch, and I realized what much needed benefit I would derive from a thorough grounding of technic, although I did not approve of many details, and although one must question her interpretations constantly for historical accuracy and stylistic consistency. She made me play for her and told me that I was very talented and had a good hand, but needed technic.[32]

The young Kirkpatrick met Eta Harich-Schneider that very evening; she was to have a major influence on him and become a friend and helper to his career.

By the weekend Kirkpatrick's capitulation was nearly complete: Landowska's performance with Gerlin of the Mozart *Sonata for Two Pianos* elicited these words:

> I have only once heard Mozart playing that even approached the precision, brilliance, and delicacy of hers, and the way she could turn and mold the phrases and simply take you straight to heaven in the slow movements. . . . Her harpsichord registration is often very effective, as well as her playing, although frequently unsound stylistically. She is a much greater musician than I first thought her.[33]

Kirkpatrick was not the only American student at St. Leu. He mentioned as one of his best colleagues "American harpsichordist Lucille Wallace."[34] Pianists such as Frank Bishop, a "Miss Hutchison," and the Boston teacher Lillian Paige attended the summer classes. Perhaps most important to American harpsichord students in later years was the apprenticeship of Putnam Aldrich, who arrived at St. Leu with his old friend Miss Paige in the summer of 1929.

CHAPTER
5

LEWIS RICHARDS, AMERICAN HARPSICHORDIST

Wanda Landowska's successor as harpsichord soloist on the roster of Arthur Judson Concert Management was the American harpsichordist Lewis Richards. No mere successor to the doyenne of early keyboardists, Richards had actually scooped Landowska by being the first to perform a harpsichord concerto with a major orchestra in the United States. That occurred on 4 November 1923, when Richards played the Haydn D-major *Concerto* with the Minneapolis Symphony, Henri Verbrugghen, conducting.[1]

Born in St. Johns, Michigan on 11 April 1881, Richards studied piano during his formative years. In 1902 he went to Belgium to study with Arthur De Greef at the Royal Conservatory of Music in Brussels. He won a first prize with distinction in 1905, the first American pianist to attain that honor. He taught for three years in the United States before returning to Europe, where he became very well known as a pianist. His interest in the music of the past led Richards to take up the harpsichord, and eventually he was invited to join the Société des Instruments Anciens of Paris as a harpsichordist.

Richards was living in Belgium in 1914, when the First World War broke out. Through his friends Brand Whitlock, a United States minister in Belgium, and Hugh Gibson, secretary of the American Legation, he met Herbert Hoover and was invited to join Hoover's London-based war relief organization. Because of his superior executive ability, Richards became the assistant director of the program. The administrative experience and the friendship with a man destined to become President of the United States were to have a major impact on Richards's later career.

Richards returned to the United States shortly before his Minneapolis debut in November 1923, bringing his Pleyel harpsichord with him. In addition to the Haydn *Concerto* he played (in the style of orchestral concerts of the 1920s) three harpsichord solos: *Rondo* by Rameau, *The Brook* by Ayrlton, and *Gigue* by Desmaret (the last two from manuscripts provided by Henri Casadesus of the Société des Instruments Anciens). Evidently this appearance with the Minneapolis Orchestra was a success, for Richards was at once re-engaged for the following season.

Richards made his New York debut as harpsichordist on 22 January 1924, when he played a recital at Aeolian Hall, assisted by flutist Georges Barrère. In addition to ensemble sonatas by Bach and Handel, Richards played a prelude and fugue, gavotte, and musette by Bach and works by Rameau, Ayrlton, and Desmaret.

> All ancient music, all classical, all genuine—this is the sort of program that is proper for such recitals, and, it must be added, it was played in a way that is proper for such music. That is to say, there was no pomp and circumstance attached to it, no affectation, no fancy costumes, no attempt to play to the gallery. This recital was in no sense of the word a vaudeville stunt given with the object of disguising technical limitations and of gaining cheap notoriety. Mr. Barrère is already known as a great musician and a great artist, and Mr. Richards lacks none of the essentials of his art and might very well succeed as a pianist were his passion not for the harpsichord.
>
> The harpsichord is, in other words, not a mere makeshift in this case—a fact that it is necessary to stress for the reason that so many artists take to it or to something similar simply because they find it impossible to meet competition along ordinary lines. Mr. Richards is not of that class at all, but a real artist and a real enthusiast of the harpsichord. His virtuosity is of the first order and he plays the harpsichord not as a piano but as a harpsichord, which is not at all the same thing.
>
> And this instrument thus played will entertain all genuine music lovers. It is quaint and curious, of course, and one understands why it has been superseded by the more robust piano. But one understands, too, the marked difference between the music that was written for it and the music that was later written for the piano. And harpsichord music is as unsuited to the piano as is piano music to the harpsichord.
>
> Let us hope that Mr. Richards will be widely heard, as he deserves to be. His work is of historical and educational significance, and is entertaining as well.[2]

The impact of Landowska's recent debut in New York evidently was still with the reviewer of the *New York Herald-Tribune:*

> Lewis Richards, harpsichordist gave a concert yesterday. Once upon a time Domenico Scarlatti who was a famous keyboard wizard of his time, went to visit at a house where, as he entered, he heard the gentle tones of a harpsichord. He listened a minute and then exclaimed: "This is either Handel or the devil!" Hereafter those whose ears are saluted by the sounds of an unseen harpsichord admirably played may exclaim: "That is either Landowska or Lewis." . . . Richards displayed a finely wrought touch and an airy agility of finger. He was discreet in the matter of dynamics, in which pianists are so often tempted to exaggeration in playing the harpsichord. He presented all his music in a style combining swiftness with delicacy, clarity, and smoothness, and, in short, the correct qualities of his art. His style was that of fastidious student and ardent enthusiast.[3]

From the *New York Times* came these kind comments:

Lewis Richards interested a large audience yesterday afternoon at Aeolian Hall in a scholarly recital of music for the harpsichord. His program was more simply and sincerely presented by the young American than is sometimes done by revivers of antique art, who emphasize the antiquity at the expense of the art that has thus endured.[4]

And from the *New York Sun and Globe:* "It must be confessed that Mr. Richards did absorbing things with his two groups of solos. He achieves plaintive romance when he wills."[5]

Clearly Richards could make music at his reconstructed antique instrument, a gift that is borne out by his several recordings. For the Brunswick-Balke-Collender Company he made a disk of Ayrlton's *The Brook* and Rameau's *Musette en Rondeau,* and one of Handel's *The Harmonious Blacksmith* coupled with Mozart's *Rondo all Turca.*[6] A royalty statement of 25 May 1926 shows that they sold extremely well: between May 1925 and 31 March 1926 the Handel–Mozart disk sold 4,255 copies. Richards received $.0315 per disk, for a total of $134.03!

Richards gave three recitals with Georges Barrère in January 1926 at Steinway Hall, New York, but the most interesting program must have been the private concert given with Arthur Whiting at the Century Club on 14 January:

a recital for harpsichord and clavichord. . . . It is unfortunate for lovers of old instruments and their music that this was a private recital, because it was the first time since the days long before the invention of the piano that two harpsichords have been played together. . . . In his concerts with Georges Barrère he delighted his audience with the performance of unpublished pieces, and his recital with Arthur Whiting was no less a treat for the small number of privileged hearers.[7]

Another highlight of 1926 was certainly Richards's appearance at Carnegie Hall with Walter Damrosch[8] and the New York Symphony Orchestra on 26 November.

A goal which he established as a boy of twelve was reached by Lewis Richards, American harpsichordist. . . . Richards lived in Detroit before that city had its own symphony orchestra and the visits of the New York Symphony, with Mr. Damrosch, were events long looked foward to by the twelve-year-old boy. He always attended these concerts and it became his ambition to play some day with the Symphony.

Later, as a student at the University School of Music at Ann Arbor, Michigan, Mr. Richards often had the opportunity of hearing Mr. Damrosch and the orchestra when they came to Ann Arbor to appear on the Choral Union Scries which always presented the biggest attractions. . . .

The harpsichordist, who is considerable of an explorer in the field of music, was prepared when the great opportunity came and his long ambition was to be gratified. He had copied the Haydn Concerto in D major, which he played with the Damrosch organization, from the original copy in the library of the Royal Conservatory of Music in Brussels. At that time he took note of the number of instruments originally intended to accompany the harpsichord solo and it was with these same instruments that Mr. Damrosch presented the work.[9]

Lewis Richards at his Pleyel harpsichord. (Courtesy of Elsa Richards.)

The ambition realized produced another fine critique for Richards:

> Lovely music, because of the absence of any crass modernistic outbreaks, marked the Friday evening concert of the Walter Damrosch band. Lovely playing, too, made the occasion completely enjoyable. . . . Lewis Richards, an American, played the harpsichord, and did so with refined taste, finical musicianship, and unfailing technical skill. He won warm and prolonged applause.[10]

A full house with four hundred standees in the rear of the Lyric Theatre greeted Richards when he played the same concerto with the Baltimore Symphony in December. The hall had been sold out ten days in advance.[11]

Lewis Richards may be credited with yet another first for the harpsichord in

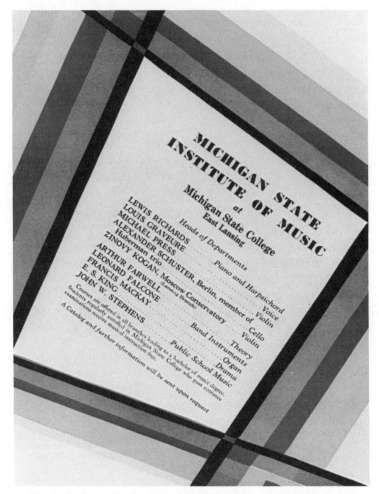

America's first collegiate harpsichord department? A Michigan State College advertisement in the short-lived periodical *Artistique*, 1929.

America: He was the first in modern times to play the instrument in the White House. (When Dolmetsch played there in 1908, he used a clavichord.) No doubt because of his friendship with Herbert Hoover, now serving as secretary of commerce in President Coolidge's cabinet, Richards was invited to perform on Thursday, 10 February 1927, on the same program with the soprano Elisabeth Rethberg. In addition to his recently recorded pieces Richards played *A Gigge (Myself)* by John Bull and a *Rondo* by Rameau. In keeping with a claim in his brochure that he "never had an engagement without a return invitation" Richards played again at the White House on 7 October 1929, following the dinner given by President and Mrs. Hoover for British Prime Minister J. Ramsay MacDonald and his daughter Isabel.

The short program consisted entirely of music by old English composers, including the "rollicking tune, Dr. Bull's Myselfe, by John Bull."[12]

Richards had two other engagements in Washington, both at the Library of Congress. In 1925 he appeared with the English Singers and several string players.[13] Then, on 9 October 1929, as part of the Elizabeth Sprague Coolidge Foundation Chamber Music Festival, he and harpsichordist Frank Bibb joined Leopold Stokowski in an orchestrated arrangement of Bach's *The Art of Fugue*.

Artistique, a new magazine "dedicated to the arts in Michigan," appeared in October 1929. It was scarcely an auspicious time in the American economy to launch anything, let alone an esoteric magazine, and the new venture lasted for only one issue. Nevertheless it announced still one more Richards "first": inside the back cover he was listed as "Head of the Departments of Piano and Harpsichord" at Michigan State Institute of Music, Michigan State College, East Lansing—probably the first harpsichord department in any American institution of higher learning.

Although Richards was the only solo harpsichordist listed in the roster of artists for Community Concerts in 1930[14] (Stephanie Wall and Fern Sherman were listed as a "costume recital with harpsichord"), his playing career occupied less and less of his time. His duties as director of the Michigan Institute, which he had assumed in 1927, expanded, and his wife's illness may also have kept him from performing. He died in East Lansing on 15 February 1940.

CHAPTER

6

LANDOWSKA'S AMERICAN CIRCLE

While Landowska was not the only harpsichordist to have a following in America, she remained the most famous and eventually the most recorded. She must be considered the most influential when one counts the number of players who studied with her and who emulated her playing style and her choice of the Pleyel harpsichord.

PUTNAM ALDRICH

Among the early leaders in the Landowska school, Putnam Calder Aldrich (1904–1975) had the most far-reaching influence on the succeeding generation, for he was noted not only as a fine player but even more as a fine teacher.

Aldrich completed his baccalaureate degree in French literature at Yale University in 1926, and as he was also a gifted pianist, he went to London to study piano with Tobias Matthay for two years. When the critics commented on his beautiful piano tone but lambasted his poor technique at his New York Town Hall debut, he came to Landowska not to study harpsichord, originally, but for her help in technical matters.

> Early in June 1929 he sailed to Europe, planning to spend his vacation in Italy and France. Wishing to catch a glimpse of North Africa on the way, he disembarked at Gibraltar to stay a little while in Morocco. There, he met the Viscount of Mamblas, who was then the Consul of Spain at Tangier.
>
> When, in the course of the conversation, the Consul discovered that Putnam was a pianist, he told him of his friendship with José Iturbi. Putnam responded by exclaiming "Oh, I wish I had his technique." Well, then why don't you study with him?" suggested the Viscount. "Let's ask him if he would be willing to give you some lessons."
>
> Iturbi answered that he was not interested in teaching but proceeded to explain that he had acquired his technique from Wanda Landowska. In his youth he had won a

Putnam Aldrich playing for Landowska. (Photograph by Lipnitzki, Paris; courtesy of Momo Aldrich.)

scholarship to study in Paris and, at the time, was fortunate enough to have had some piano lessons from Landowska. Putnam, he suggested, could study with her at [St. Leu.][1]

Momo Aldrich, Landowska's personal secretary, described the nature of the classes at St. Leu:

Wanda worked with a limited number of students in turn. The classes dealt with all the technical problems of the piano and the harpsichord. The strength and independence of the fingers were stressed, but, more importantly, the result of those technical exercises was applied to actual performance. The classes dealt also with the reconstitution of the ornaments, which involved analytic study of their genesis, as well as comparative study—finding the analogies which exist between them. In addition, the classes delved into varieties of touch and phrasing, as well as the characteristic features of the music (and musical "laws") of the different periods.[2]

It took only one summer of study with Landowska for Aldrich to become so enamored of the harpsichord that he decided to switch from the piano to the older keyboard instrument. He spent three years with Landowska, which he remembered as "very trying times."

> "She was a terrible tyrant," he said.[3] "Most Americans studying with her just couldn't take it. Ralph Kirkpatrick, for example, lasted only six weeks. I found it best to act like a little child and just take the abuse she heaped on. Finally, I got to understand what she was doing."
>
> While studying with her, Aldrich ran out of money and was unable to pay for his lessons. So she put him to work doing her research in return for the lessons. This involved many hours poring over old manuscripts and annotating the music.
>
> "I worked on countless scores but I always made my own copy of everything I did, and I ended up with reams of material no one even knew anything about at that time," Aldrich said. "When I came back to Harvard I used this material to get my Ph.D. in music. That's how I happened into musicology—it was quite accidental. I got the Ph.D. only to use the material—not to get a job."[4]

It was at St. Leu that Aldrich met Madeleine Momot. "Forget the Madeleine," said Landowska, who nicknamed her "Momo Momot." Putnam married Momo in 1931 and took her home to New England. "That upset Madame very much and it was ten years before she ever spoke to me again," he recalled. Author and lexicographer Nicolas Slonimsky wrote of that summer of 1931, "We [Slonimsky and his wife, Dorothy] had lunch with several of Wanda's girls and a young harpsichord player, Putnam Aldrich, who subsequently abducted one of Wanda's girls to America. (Wanda never forgave him.) They were soon married, and had a daughter, Allegra."[5] Perhaps Landowska's displeasure was not as great as it was reported to be, for in actuality Momo and Putnam were married in Paris, with Putnam's brother David, at that time a student in architecture classes at Fontainebleau, as witness for the groom, and Wanda Landowska, herself, attending Momo as witness.[6]

Aldrich's unique position as harpsichordist in Boston was described by Elizabeth Borton in the seventeenth installment of her series "Talking It Over With Unusual Bostonians":

> Putnam Aldrich is the only person in Boston with a working harpsichord. Now this is not only a distinction but a responsibility. A working harpsichord, by the way, is an instrument in good working order, as contrasted with a museum piece which emits but a feeble tinkle when furtively and unlawfully touched by a passerby. . . .
>
> But "Put" Aldrich's harpsichord brought by him to this country, at such terrific expense (as musicians count expense) that he scarcely dares permit it out of his sight for a moment, has a clear loud voice, two manuals, and plenty of personality. . . .

Nicolas Slonimsky, Wanda Landowska (effectively shaded by her parasol),
Putnam Aldrich, and Momo Aldrich at St. Leu, May 1931.
(Courtesy of Momo Aldrich.)

"The trouble with the harpsichord is that it's so delicate," says Mr. Aldrich, a little bitterly. He looks delicate himself—small, dark and slender as he is, with nervous hands and overbright dark eyes. But then, he is certainly less delicate than his harpsichord, for no one must trail him with a satchel full of loose parts, to be hastily screwed on when he falls apart—and that is what he has to do with his harpsichord.

When he walks out on the stage to play a concert, he brings not only his music, but his emergency bag full of new plectrums, wrenches, hammers and whatnot. The wretched harpsichord keys get stuck once in a while, and notes refuse to sound. They are always important notes. Then Mr. Aldrich has to make his excuses to the audience, roll up his sleeves and get out and get under.

"I can't allow any one to touch it but myself," he says, "because then I have to work weeks putting it into shape again. It's like a fountain pen, you know. It gets used to a certain touch."[7]

Aldrich was active as a harpsichordist in the New England area while completing his doctorate in musicology at Harvard. In 1935 he played the Bach *Brandenburg Concerto* No. 5 with the Boston Symphony under Koussevitsky. In 1938, together with Alfred Zighera, he founded the Boston Society for Ancient Instruments, which presented nine subsequent seasons of concerts. He played continuo in Boston and at Tanglewood for the Bach *Mass in B minor, Suite* in B minor, and *Magnificat,* all conducted by Koussevitsky. He also served as a music critic for the *Boston Herald* during this period. In this capacity he reviewed the playing of another Landowska student, Alice Ehlers, to whom he loaned his harpsichord for her recital in Cambridge on 18 February 1936.[8]

As soon as Aldrich received his Ph.D. he was offered a teaching position at the University of Texas in Austin. "I had never taught a day in my life, but I took the job anyway and ended up staying two years."[9] He then returned to Boston to continue his playing career. One notable event was a performance of Bach's *Concerto for Three Harpsichords* on the Boston Symphony Chamber Concert Series of 1944; the other soloists were Sylvia Marlowe and Daniel Pinkham.

This pattern continued as Aldrich taught for two years at Western Reserve University in Cleveland and then went back to concert life in Boston. Next came two years at Mills College in Oakland, and a tragicomic performance of the Bach *Brandenburg Concerto* No. 5:

In 1949 the San Francisco Symphony Orchestra, in recognition of the growing interest in baroque music, instituted a series of "Classical Interludes—Monteverdi to Mozart." I was engaged to play the solo harpsichord part in Bach's Fifth Brandenburg Concerto. The conductor, Pierre Monteux, guaranteed that this was to be an absolutely authentic performance; he conducted from the Bach-Gesellschaft Edition. At a preliminary rehearsal with the flute and violin soloists, I began straightway realizing the figured bass of the opening *tutti*. The conductor interrupted: "What are these chords you are playing? Bach wrote no chords here!" I tried to explain that the figures under the cembalo part stood for chords, but he said, "If Bach wanted chords he would have written chords. This is to be an authentic performance. We shall play *only* what Bach wrote!" And in an aside to the other musicians he said, "You see, musicologists have always their noses in books and forget to look at what Bach wrote." At any rate in the opening *tutti* it is not too serious, since the harmony is quite complete in the instrumental parts. But in the second movement, scored for three solo instruments, the effect of the harpsichordist's playing one note at a time with the left hand only was nothing short of ludicrous. Even Monteux began to suspect that something was wrong. At the dress rehearsal he said to me in a whisper, "In this movement you may add a few discreet chords."[10]

To counteract such strange ideas about Baroque music, Putnam Aldrich spent the rest of his career at Stanford University, where he developed a program in performance practice of early music. The beginning of Stanford's doctoral program in music coincided with his arrival, and a distinguished group of students studied with him. The first was George Houle, who later went on to direct the New York Pro Musica. Many others took the gospel of early music to colleges and universities across the land: among them were Natalie Jenne, Margaret Fabrizio, Irene Bostwick, Newman Powell, Don Franklin, Meredith Ellis, Elizabeth Hays, Peter Hurd, and Erich Schwandt. Arthur Lawrence recalled that Aldrich had a set method of teaching harpsichord: everyone had to begin with Bach's *Two-Part Invention* in E major. There were three touches to be perfected in this piece. Since Lawrence worked on it for a semester and never got it right, for his second semester he transferred to Margaret Fabrizio, who was also teaching at Stanford.[11]

Aldrich wrote several important studies, two major ones being *Ornamentation in Bach's Organ Works* (1950) and *Rhythm in Seventeenth-Century Italian Monody* (1966). He continued to play the harpsichord: yearly faculty recitals at Stanford always played from memory, and orchestral appearances. He was known for his performances of the Poulenc *Concert Champêtre;* the Haydn *Concerto* in D major (with cadenzas by Wanda Landowska), which appeared on the San Francisco Symphony series of 1958 (Enrique Jorda conducting); and the Bach *Concerto* in F minor.[12] Finally, the teaching and writing took over entirely, and there was no time to practice. Just before Aldrich retired from Stanford in 1969, an interviewer reported: "Putnam Aldrich studied his Pleyel harpsichord for a moment, then looked down at his hands and flexed his fingers several times as if to limber them up. 'Now I will be able to play again,' he said with a smile. 'It's been a long time.' "[13]

PHILIP MANUEL AND GAVIN WILLIAMSON

Despite a penchant for cute and trendy prose, *Time* magazine offered a great deal of information in an illustrated article about America's first harpsichord duo:

Musical Antiques

One night last week Chicago's elegant Goodman Theatre was packed to its heavy oak doors. What drew this throng was no thunder-rousing maestro or pudding-fed diva, but a pair of pale, genteel young men who plunked softly on 18th-century-model harpsichords. Before a silver backdrop, gently lit by amber lights, they joined in deft pluck-a-pluck duets by Mozart and Bach. Occasionally they were joined by two lush lady harpsichordists in 18th-century lace and velveteen. To all this harpsichordery their audience listened reverently, applauded with loud smacks. For they were listening to the No. 1 harpsichord team of the U.S.: Chicago's famed Philip Manuel and Gavin Williamson.

The harpsichord, which looks like an incubator-baby-grand piano and sounds like a choir of mandolins, was once the most important of concert instruments. Before it was ousted (at the beginning of the 19th century) by the louder and more flexible modern piano, composers like Bach and Handel wrote sheaves of compositions for it. Even Beethoven turned out a batch of sonatas for the harpsichord. Today, harpsichord playing occupies the position that falconry does in the field of sports. And most early harpsichord music is now played on modern instruments like the piano. But today's handful of harpsichordists point out the undeniable fact that only they can make this 18th-century music sound the way it did in the 18th century.

When they are not giving concerts, Chicago's Manuel & Williamson tinkle their harpsichords in privacy in a handsome old grey-stone house on the South Side. Its 14 large, high-ceilinged rooms are filled with obsolete instruments, antique pictures, books about music of the long ago. Inseparable bachelors, they act, talk, think alike, have identical handwriting, birthdays within 24 hours of each other (June 29 and 30). Though they have toured the whole U. S., they have never appeared in Manhattan because Manhattan concert managers insist that they hire their own hall.

> To Manuel & Williamson all music written since the 18th century has come a long way down hill. Occasionally, for relaxation, they visit the concerts of Frederick Stock's Chicago Symphony, consider the ponderous 19th-century classics they hear there as comparative fluff. Last month when they heard Harpsichordist Yella Pessl play a lick of swing on a harpsichord broadcast, they turned away their dial in horror. Asked why they prefer 18th-century to all other music, they reply: "It makes us feel spiritually spick & span."[14]

An earlier published anecdote gave a folksy account of one person's reaction to the curious sounds of the harpsichord. The iceman who serviced the Lake Park Avenue studio apartment in which the duo lived and practiced knocked one day and inquired about the music coming through the windows. He introduced himself as a saxophone-playing music lover and expressed an interest in hearing some more of the "funny music." His reaction to Manuel and Williamson's performance of Bach was enthusiastic. "Say, gents, that's certainly the swellest music I ever listened to—got the saxophone beat a mile. What did you say the name of them things was?" "The harpsichord." "Well," he said as he departed," all I gotta say is that the harpsichord is one swell piece of machinery, and I bet that as soon as the musicians all over the country get onto 'em, pianos 'll be drove right out of the market."[15]

Philip Manuel (1893–1959), born in Canton, Minnesota, studied piano with itinerant teachers, at a military school, and at Grinnell College, Iowa. His first professional association with Boston-bred Gavin Williamson (born in Canada in 1897) was as tenor singer to Williamson's piano accompaniment. These concerts were announced under the management of Harrison and Harschbarger for 1923. Both young men performed from memory—"a point which makes for intimacy and individuality of performance."[16]

> The manner in which Manuel & Williamson first became interested in . . . old instruments is curious and interesting. . . . They were scheduled for a duo-piano recital at Bloomington, Ill., and on the way both pianos were smashed by trucks. What to do? The town was scoured for pianos and finally, two, about half the size of the modern concert grand were unearthed. They were taken to the hall and quickly put in condition and the program played. The first number was a Mozart Sonata, and so exceptionally did the smaller pianos with their thinner tone, project the Mozart music that Manuel and Williamson thought of the greater charm there would be in playing Mozart, Bach, and their forerunners on the instruments for which their music was written.
>
> Then began some extensive research work on the part of the two artists, during which they went to Paris, spending several weeks at the famous Pleyel factory, where they made arrangements for two harpsichords. "It is like the passion for antiques," said Manuel, "wherever we find one of these old instruments, not to mention their lesser sister, the clavichord, we feel we must purchase it. Consequently our collection is increasing to such an extent that we have been forced to move from one place to another to find space for each additional instrument we acquire. The more one studies the harpsichord the more fascinating it becomes, for the tone has much more resonance and variety than the piano."[17]

Manuel and Williamson studied with Landowska in New York. In addition to instruction on the harpsichord, her lectures at the Curtis Institute were also important to the duo. They would ride with her on the train from New York to Philadelphia so she could rehearse the lectures for them in order to practice and correct her English.[18]

As with all the artists of the "Landowska connection," Manuel and Williamson played harpsichords by Pleyel. "Grand Harpsichord Number 1" (the first Pleyel with the 16-foot stop) dated from 1912, and the firm numbered its harpsichords consecutively through the year 1929. Instrument number ten (probably 1922) belonged to Alice Ehlers; eleven through fourteen to Manuel and Williamson; and number fifteen to Putnam Aldrich. Pleyel's production of harpsichords, which seemed to permeate the entire harpsichord revival, really proceeded at the pace of one instrument per year.[19] Two of the harpsichords owned by Manuel and Williamson had especially beautiful decoration: the motto on one (from 1926) read "Omnis spiritus laudet Dominum," while the jackrail of another carried an inscription from the French poet LeJeune.[20]

With multiple harpsichords available it was natural to turn to the Bach repertoire for multiple keyboards. The duo appeared with the Minneapolis Symphony on 25 November 1927 playing Bach's *Double Concerto* in C major. On 27 December 1932, for the first of their four appearances with the Chicago Symphony, they played Bach's *Concerto No. 3* for two harpsichords, "the first-known tune for two quilled instruments" by Giles Farnaby, C. P. E. Bach's *Adagio* for two harpsichords and strings, and Mozart's *Rondo* from *Sonata* in D for two harpsichords.

> Philip Manuel and Gavin Williamson, who made a stir at their first appearance as soloists with the Chicago Symphony Orchestra earlier in the week returned for the December 29 and 30 concerts in a program different from the one presented in the Tuesday afternoon series (!) The harpsichord has two able champions in these young men, and there was reason to rejoice in their performance of the Mozart Concerto in F. It was interesting also to hear them play two pieces by Couperin [Le Juillet and Musète de Choisi] and Bach's Allegro from the Concerto [in C major]. Messrs. Manuel & Williamson are, as far as we can ascertain, the only pair of harpsichordists touring the country.[21]

At Ravinia the duo triumphed again. The headline read "Ravinia Festival Opens: Sir Adrian Boult wins Chicago; Manuel & Williamson, harpsichordists, play Bach."

> The obvious drawing power was the announced appearance of Philip Manuel and Gavin Williamson, harpsichordists, who played the Bach [Concerto in C minor] for two harpsichords with strings, and won an ovation. There is widespread interest in the exquisite music of the harpsichord and no-one in America is doing as significant a work in this field of music as these two gifted artists, who, incidently, live and work right here in Chicago.
>
> There is a spirit and flowing line to their Bach that is buoyancy itself, while

impeccable attention to detail and complete respect for the composer's intention make it possible for you to hear in their work (and especially since it is played on harpsichord) exactly what Bach wanted heard—with no superficialities of what some might *think* he wanted. The small string accompaniment was properly delicate, restrained, and perfectly balanced. The audience was insistent in its applause—and wanted more—but the length of the program apparently did not permit of any extra numbers.[22]

Manuel and Williamson were associated with Community Concerts, Inc., directed by their old friend Dema Harschbarger. They toured extensively with four instruments: two harpsichords and two Steinway pianos. While that seems to be a monstrous task, it was not so complicated in the days of an efficient railway express. Sturdy crates for the instruments allowed them to be packed securely; the movers picked them up in Chicago and delivered them to the various halls—in many respects it was simpler than trying to move a harpsichord today.[23] A typical itinerary was that of 1928, with concerts starting in early November in El Paso, Texas, for Mrs. Hallett Johnson's Twilight Musicales; the following day, the opening of the Junior Artist series in Ogden, Utah; then on to Denver, Colorado Springs, and Boulder, Colorado; Marshalltown, Iowa; Fond du Lac, Wisconsin; Evanston, Illinois; Ashland, Kentucky; Raleigh, North Carolina, and a tour of the southern states.[24] For the American première of Bach's *Concerto for Three Harpsichords* in Chicago on 7 April 1929 Manuel and Williamson were joined by their student Margaret Davies. Eventually the duo went on to form a larger harpsichord ensemble, and with Dorothy Brown and Dorothy Lane they were able to present even more unusual works to the American public.

> Equipped with the most extraordinary specimens of the harpsichord-builder's craft, and associated with an outstanding artistic personnel . . . Manuel and Williamson offer musical experiences heretofore unknown in this country. The four harpsichords in their sweep across the stage are a spectacle in themselves. . . .[25]

Landowska was not especially pleased with the success of her friends. "These children are taking the food out of my mouth," she complained at dinner with Arthur Judson's submanager. Her ire was raised because the duo, not Landowska, had been engaged for a concert in Milwaukee. Later she canceled a European engagement (the Bach triple concerto under Furtwängler) because the duo dealt directly with Pleyel in buying its second pair of harpsichords, and she resented the lost commission.[26]

Although Manuel and Williamson were reported to be aghast at "modern" music, they did play a two-harpsichord arrangement of Poulenc's *Concert Champêtre* for a concert in connection with an exhibition of tapestries at Chicago's Art Institute. The working-out of the arrangement was done with the composer's help.

"Past Masters," their series of radio broadcasts for NBC's Blue Network, was the most far-reaching result of their years of research and study. It was an immensely

Philip Manuel (left) and Gavin Williamson playing a radio concert.
(Courtesy of Gavin Williamson.)

popular program, even eliciting a telegram from some steelworkers who heard the end of a broadcast while waiting for a prizefight to begin! The duo was touched that these men would chip in ten cents each to send a congratulatory word to two classical musicians.

Echoes of these elegant programs were captured by Musicraft Records in four albums: the Manuel and Williamson Harpsichord Ensemble play Bach concertos for two harpsichords and strings, the *Violin Concerto* in A major and the *Pastorale* in A of Vivaldi, Handel's *Oboe Concerto* in G minor and *Harpsichord Concerto* in F, and the Bach C-major *Concerto for Three Harpsichords*. The original 78 rpm recordings have never been reissued; they might be found in antiquarian shops or in the archives of historical sound recordings in the Sterling Library of Yale University, which holds the collection of Samuel Puner, founder of Musicraft.[27]

ALICE EHLERS

"Do come in and sit down! Madame Ehlers is going to play the harpsichord." With these words in William Wyler's 1939 film *Wuthering Heights,* the harpsichord was ushered into the motion picture era. Ehlers's nimble performance of Mozart's *Rondo alla Turca* was heard by more people than had any previous harpsichord performance. Popular on late-night American television, the movie continues to present her playing to modern audiences.

It was fitting that it should be Alice Pauly Ehlers (1887–1981) who filled the screen, for in many ways she had always seemed "larger than life." She was born in Vienna and went to the Hochschule für Musik in Berlin in 1909 to study piano. In 1913, when Wanda Landowska was appointed to the faculty as the first twentieth-century professor of harpsichord, Ehlers became her first harpsichord student and began a five-year association with the famous artist. Thus Ehlers was the first member of a second generation of revival harpsichordists.

The relationship with Landowska was a difficult one: a true love-hate story. Throughout her long life, Ehlers maintained an admiration for Landowska's artistry but resented her self-centered personality and her overwhelming identification with the instrument they both played. To questions about Landowska, Ehlers would respond, "Why are you so interested in *her?*" She would then tell the story of her own harpsichord debut in Berlin: how she was scheduled to play Bach's *Concerto* in F minor but how her teacher upstaged her and put Ehlers in an unfavorable situation by playing the same concerto (to be reviewed by the same critics) only a few days before the scheduled debut.[28]

"We didn't talk much in lessons, but I *listened* to her playing," Ehlers reported in later years.[29] She was not impressed with Landowska's pedagogical abilities, especially her work with her untalented students. She remembered that there were not many with talent, perhaps the only other one being the organist Max Drischner.) Eventually Ehlers functioned rather as a graduate assistant for Landowska, taking over the instruction of some of the other students at Landowska's plea, "My child, work with them."[30] Many years later Landowska still figured in an apocryphal tale of Ehlers's lesson with student Malcolm Hamilton, who had had the temerity to add a trill to the subject in a fugue by Bach. When Ehlers stopped him, he explained, "I heard a recording by Landowska and she put a trill there." Ehlers snorted, "Wanda Landowska was a genius; you and I, Malcolm, we are *not* geniuses—'spaacially you!"

During these student years in Berlin, Ehlers had access to several Pleyel harpsichords: those belonging to Landowska and one purchased by the Hochschule only to be sold again as soon as Landowska's master classes ended in 1918. Ehlers, too, owned a Pleyel instrument early in her career. Her first instrument was the harpsichord Mahler had purchased for the Vienna State Opera. It had been relegated to the basement after his tenure there. Ehlers disliked its "sour tone."[31] She preferred the instruments of Johann Georg Steingräber, a Berlin builder who had begun his work as a restorer of antique instruments. His instruments were constructed entirely from wood, with no metal framing. "All wood-constructed instruments have a wonderful advantage of resonance and vibration all through, but also this disadvantage [of expansion and contraction]," Ehlers remarked some years later.[32] Steingräber worked slowly and carefully, producing only a small number of instruments.[33]

Ehlers had access to a Dolmetsch-Chickering harpsichord at this time, which may have helped to shape her liking for Steingräber's metal-free instruments:

> Busoni was, strange as it might sound, a lover of the harpsichord. He had a small harpsichord in his house in Berlin, and sometimes called me to come over and play for him. I felt so stupid, me, *nobody,* going to play for Busoni. But he couldn't handle the harpsichord with his big hands, and being used to the sound of the piano, he wanted to get the same sounds out of the harpsichord. . . .[34]

At the conclusion of her Hochschule study Ehlers was the co-recipient of a high honor, the Mendelssohn Prize, which she shared with pianist Wilhelm Kempff. She was engaged to succeed Landowska as teacher of harpsichord at the school, where she remained until 1933. During these years her concert career blossomed, with trips throughout Europe, to South America, to Russia (where she met Otto Klemperer in Leningrad[35]), and, especially, to Italy, where she gave lecture classes at the Milan Conservatory and toured as far south as Palermo. There were concerts with her friend Paul Hindemith, who had made realizations of six of the Biber *Mystery Sonatas* for them to perform as a viola-harpsichord duo. South of Rome, "they liked only light things. They could cry ten times for ten times my playing *Il Coucoula; il coucoula, coucou* by Daquin. Finally Hindemith said, 'If you play that once more I will take the next train home.' Ehlers, 'What should I do?' Hindemith, 'Come out and smile, bow, but *don't* play!' "[36]

In 1927 Ehlers appeared on a Beethoven centenary concert in Vienna. Carl Engel was impressed with her playing and reported his opinion to Elizabeth Sprague Coolidge, who invited Ehlers to perform at the Library of Congress in 1936, three years after Ehlers had prudently decided to leave Nazi Berlin and make her home in London. "I am Jewish," she declared triumphantly.

During her first visit to the United States, in 1936, Ehlers gave several concerts. Putnam Aldrich reviewed her appearance in Boston:

> Alice Ehlers, harpsichordist, gave a recital at Paine Hall, Cambridge, last night, under the auspices of the division of music of Harvard University. Miss Ehlers played the following program: Fantasia in C minor, Chromatic Fantasy and Fugue, Italian Concerto, Bach; The Bells, Byrd; Fugue on the Magnificat, Pachelbel; Harmonious Blacksmith Variations, Handel; The Battle Between David and Goliath, Kuhnau; Les Vendangeuses and La Bandoline, Couperin; La Poule and Le Rappel des Oiseaux, Rameau; three Sonatas, Domenico Scarlatti.
>
> Miss Ehlers wisely selected a program composed largely of works which are familiar to the concertgoer. The three compositions by Bach are frequently performed at piano recitals, as are Handel's "Harmonious Blacksmith" variations.

Kuhnau's "Battle" is offered by every course in the appreciation or history of music as one of the early examples of program music. The listener at last night's concert was therefore prepared to make direct comparison between the piano and the harpsichord as medium for the interpretation of these works. One need not be a rabid purist to recognize the superiority of the harpsichord for this purpose. Broadly speaking its advantages are greater precision and distinctness and the possibility of obtaining variety of tone color.

The clear, precise tone of the harpsichord was particularly grateful, last night, in Bach's Chromatic Fugue, since one's understanding and enjoyment of such a work is almost entirely dependent upon one's ability to follow several melodies simultaneously. Similarly the highly ornamented pieces by Rameau, Couperin and Scarlatti acquire a new meaning when their filigree is traced in the sharply defined lines of the harpsichord tone. Miss Ehlers played these pieces with good taste and a fine sense of style. She has a good touch, which is the first essential attribute of the harpsichordist; the heavy-handedness of the average pianist will thwart the best qualities of the instrument. Her phrasing was interesting and musical. The audience was extremely appreciative, and Miss Ehlers was called back to add several encores to her program.[37]

A week later she gave her first concert in New York, at Town Hall. The critics liked what they heard: "Throughout, Miss Ehlers gave interpretations of notable clarity, as well as digital fluency, and did notable work . . . in setting forth the fine points of color and volume," wrote Francis D. Perkins in the *Herald-Tribune*. Downes, of the *Times* went even further: "As a harpsichordist, Alice Ehlers has every desirable quality including amazing virtuosity, precision, capacity to sing a phrase, which is as conspicuous as her clean articulation, taste and temperament, which carries everything before it."[38] Ehlers returned to London following these American engagements. Her assessment of the harpsichord scene in England was typically pithy: "Harpsichordists were utterly nonprofessional in every way. I was the first professional [there]."[39]

Two years later, in 1938, she gave a summer class at the Juilliard School in New York City and later went to see her daughter Maria, a film actress, in California. This visit led to Ehlers's making the United States her home. While visiting Maria, Ehlers met director William Wyler, and the following year she and the harpsichord made their motion-picture debut.[40]

Her American career flourished: Ehlers appeared twice with Bing Crosby on his radio hour. Then she was offered a teaching position by Dean Max Krone of the University of Southern California. When Ehlers told her daughter the news, the younger woman thought her mother must have had a heat stroke. "Mother, come have an ice cream!" was her reaction.[41] Thus began Ehlers's twenty-six-year association with the Los Angeles university, where her harpsichord class was to include Malcolm Hamilton (of anecdotal fame), Bruce Prince-Joseph ("Enormously talented and a born showman. I liked him very much—warm-hearted, talented, impulsive"[42]), John Gillespie ("my first student"[43]), Harold Chaney, and John Hamilton. Her popular class on Baroque interpretation attracted students Charles

Alice Ehlers as she appeared in William Wyler's film *Wuthering Heights*.
(Collection of the Library of Congress.)

Hirt, Roger Wagner, and Michael Tilson Thomas among conductors-to-be, as well as singers Marilyn Horne and Carol Neblett.

Ehlers became the prominent figure in early music on the West Coast. She played many solo and chamber music concerts, appeared with her old acquaintance Otto Klemperer in the Bach *Brandenburg Concerto* No. 5 with the Los Angeles Philharmonic, and was heard with Eugene Ormandy in Philadelphia and New York. In addition to her tenure at USC she held a Walker Ames Professorship at the University of Washington, the first Brittingham Professorship of Music at the University of Wisconsin, honorary doctorates from Lewis and Clark College and the University of Cincinnati, a merit award from the University of Southern California Alumni Association, and the distinguished service medal of the German Republic (bestowed during her eightieth year).

For more than fifty years Ehlers played the same Pleyel harpsichord. It was an unusual-looking instrument painted vermilion inside, and, at the urging of her sculptor-artist husband, green on the outside (since the original mahogany did not go well with the brillant red lid). The instrument was Pleyel's tenth of the Landowska 16-foot models; it was constructed in 1922.[44] Although Ehlers was aware of the superior sounds produced by period instruments with nonmetal frames, years of concert playing utilizing a colorful style of registration made the Pleyel instrument a comfortable one for her. "I'd rather have it with the metal frame!" she explained. "Wood cracks, [creating a] danger for instance which I have gone through, travelling in all the different climates. I don't think an instrument built in the old way could have taken it."[45]

CHAPTER
7
MADE IN AMERICA
Harpsichords?

JOHN CHALLIS

"A Dolmetsch of the Middle-West: the story of John Challis and his Clavichords" was the title of a lengthy article that appeared in 1932. After tracing the changes of fashion that led to the supremacy of the piano, it focused on its subject:

It is not generally known . . . that in our own country there is a young man, a native American, who is skilled in building and playing these early instruments. John Challis, of Ypsilanti, Mich., is a worthy successor to those master craftsmen who lived and worked before the machine age. True to their tradition, his clavichords and harpsichords are fashioned entirely by hand, every detail as perfect as skill and devotion can make it.

In his studio-workshop above his father's jewelry store one morning last summer, Mr. Challis laid aside his tools to tell me something of his life and the events leading up to his present work. His story is one that many modern parents might well pause to consider.

With gratitude he looks back—and not very far back at that, for he is but 25—to a boyhood when childish wishes were not gratified as quickly and easily as they were expressed. Instead of having the objects of his desires bestowed upon him forthwith, he received opportunities to earn money to buy tools and *make* the things he wanted. Thus early and unwittingly was laid a foundation for his career as a craftsman. At thirteen he began repairing clocks in his father's jewelry store; at sixteen he graduated to watches—all of it invaluable preparation for handling the delicate tools which were to become a part of his profession.

About the time he took over the watch repairing he made his first venture in the line of musical instruments. Details of this episode were told me by Frederick Alexander, director of the Normal Conservatory in Ypsilanti, whose part in the whole story is of rather more importance than appears in the present narrative. John wanted an organ, and to his mind the logical way of getting one was to build it. So he acquired a small reed organ and rigged it up with a set of pedals—or perhaps one should say half a set, for he played the pedals with one foot and pumped with the other. Mr. Alexander, with his lively interest in all young persons, and particularly in imaginative ones like John, admired the effort but mentioned the fact that it is customary to use both feet on the pedals.

Nothing daunted, John took the information as a suggestion, and before long Mr. Alexander was invited to view the organ again. This time it was equipped with a complete set of pedals playable with both feet, the wind being supplied from the family vacuum cleaner. Needless to say the noise of the vacuum cleaner rather overwhelmed the music, but the principle was there, and it worked!

John enrolled for piano and organ lessons in the Conservatory, meanwhile continuing his watch repairing and his high school work. At the Conservatory he had an opportunity to investigate the beautiful Dolmetsch clavichord owned by Mr. Alexander. At once he conceived a new desire. He had always hated Bach, particularly Bach *Inventions*. Now for the first time he glimpsed the true possibilities of the master. He must have a clavichord. Obviously the thing to do was to build it. And this he did, entirely without assistance except for the Dolmetsch instrument which served as model and guide. True, his clavichord was crude but, like his organ, it worked—and he could play Bach on it. From this beginning his interest in the early keyboard instruments and their music grew apace.

Unquestionably the one place to continue his work was with Arnold Dolmetsch at Haslemere. Eventually fortuitous circumstances opened the way, and John at the age of nineteen found himself on the way to England. He was set to work at once to test his ability. He assisted in building various instruments, but his musical studies were confined to the recorder and viola da gamba with no chance at the harpsichord and clavichord which he loved. All this, however, was but a period of preparation, a chance to learn the delicate principles of the instruments and to *hear* old music day in and day out until the style and proper rendition of it became second nature. Then when he was finally permitted to take up the study of keyboard instruments the results were gratifying—so much so, in fact, that he received, at Mr. Dolmetsch's request, the first scholarship awarded on the Dolmetsch Foundation. Thus was his study at Haslemere assured. In all he remained in England four years, during which time he played in the Haslemere Festivals and appeared with the Dolmetsch family at their concerts in London and elsewhere.

Meanwhile Mr. Challis was collecting for himself a library of seventeenth- and eighteenth-century music, a fascinating undertaking in itself. Sometimes second-hand copies were available, sometimes valuable reprints of early editions; otherwise it meant copying by hand or reproducing photographically old prints and manuscripts now almost priceless.

Upon returning to America his first commission was a large two-manual harpsichord which he built for the Normal Conservatory. This instrument has four sets of strings, each with a different tone quality and all controlled by pedals so that they may be used separately or in combination. Two of the four sets are tuned to regular pitch, one an octave higher, and one an octave lower. What a wealth of tone color an instrument of this kind afforded the composers of polyphonic music! It gives to each contrapuntal voice an individuality and clarity of outline that the modern pianoforte cannot even suggest.

Mr. Challis is now engaged in building a lovely one-manual harpsichord for Miss Madge Quigley of Detroit, who also owns a clavichord that he made in Haslemere. For himself he has built a small but exquisite clavichord. It stands in an inner room back of his studio, where protecting doors can be closed when he plays, for its delicate tone would be drowned by street noises. Such instruments were built for gentler days than ours. . . .

. . . Just what the future may be for this field of work Mr. Challis does not attempt to predict. Interest at present is naturally limited to a small field of serious musicians, but there are many music lovers who, given an opportunity, would appreciate the individual charm of these instruments and their music. It is to be hoped that in the course of time harpsichords and clavichords will cease to be regarded as museum pieces and will find their way increasingly into studios, to bring back to our world a beauty it forgot long ago.[1]

America's first native-born twentieth-century harpsichord maker was from South Lyon, Michigan; John R. Challis (1907–1974) remained a "Michigan builder," moving to Detroit in 1946 and working there until his property was taken as right of way for a road project. In 1966, disgusted, he moved to New York City.

That Challis built harpsichords in America was due in part to his health. He might have remained longer with Dolmetsch in Haslemere if the Surrey weather had been kinder to his always precarious constitution.

They have fourteen different kinds of rain and, once in a long time, a little sunshine. It had a very bad effect on my health. I had one continual cold from October to May every year. I was in misery much of the time. But I was doing what I wanted to do. What Dolmetsch was doing was fascinating to me and very soon, I was doing everything there was to do in the way of making keyboard instruments from start to finish.[2]

Challis's onetime apprentice William Dowd surmised that Dolmetsch's obsession with an improved "patent" action for the harpsichord might also have helped drive Challis back to his homeland.[3] It seems unlikely, however, given his continual delight in experimentation, that such an attempt to re-invent the pianoforte would have caused Challis to forsake the Dolmetsch workshop. His resistance to Dolmetsch's continual suggestions that his daughter would be a suitable bride and Challis's eventual assertion that "he was not the marrying kind" probably led to a climate in the shop that rivaled the damp and chill of the outside.[4]

About returning to Ypsilanti, Challis said,

There was no person more scared than I was. . . . I wanted to know how I could make a living making these crazy instruments. Especially when nobody over here in America knew what they were. Not even the musicians. To them, it was some kind of funny thing that Bach used to play on. I wondered what I could do.

When [my first harpsichord] was finished, I had to play it. . . . My job was not only to build it, but to play it so these people could hear it and enjoy it.

I did play it, and it was accepted. After that I was called upon to play various recitals. Once in a while someone would come up to me and say quietly "I *like* the harpsichord" as if it were something one was not supposed to say. At that time there was only Manuel and Williamson of Chicago who [were] playing the harpsichord in this country. This, of course, in addition to the three tours Landowska had made. The

John Challis at one of his first instruments. (Courtesy of Ephraim Truesdell.)

audiences were not too impressed by her tours. They were not yet ready for the harpsichord.[5]

However, the orders came: there were forty-eight names on the list of purchasers of Challis instruments between 1931 and 1945. In addition to that first instrument, 1931 brought an order from R. Sydney Sprout of Leslie (also in Michigan). Nothing is listed for 1932 and 1933, which must be years of delivery, for the Quigley harpsichord mentioned in the 1932 interview with the builder is listed as an instrument of 1934. In 1934 instruments also went to St. Louis; Washington, D. C.; and Detroit. Chicago got one in 1935. Both coasts were represented in the list for 1937: New York, where the purchaser was Blanche Winogron Beck of New York City, a distinguished player of virginal music; and California, where the instrument went to Mrs. Kenneth Brown of Claremont. In addition an instrument went to Western Reserve University in Cleveland, and other orders came from Washington, Pennsylvania, and Michigan. In 1938 the musicologist Leonard Ellinwood of Washington, D.C., bought an instrument; in 1939 another went to Illinois. In 1940 the artist Thomas Hart Benton had an instrument delivered to Kansas City, Missouri; while two went to California; one to Provo, Utah; one to Seattle; and one to Mamaroneck, New York.

Poor health kept Challis from serving in the armed forces during the Second World War, so he continued to build harpsichords. In 1941 he delivered an instrument to the University of Texas at Austin; in 1942 important purchases were made by Smith College in Northampton, Massachusetts; Baldwin-Wallace College in Berea, Ohio; Daniel Pinkham, the young Cambridge harpsichordist and composer; and jazz-great Artie Shaw. In 1943 Challis instruments went to the concert artist Ralph Kirkpatrick and to North Texas State College in Denton. Customers in 1944 were Yale University; Dr. and Mrs. Bert D. Thomas, Columbus, Ohio; Frank Shaw, director of the Oberlin College Conservatory of Music; and Mrs. Q'Zella Jeffus of Fort Worth, Texas. In 1945, at war's end, six instruments were delivered: to Oberlin College, to Arthur Quimby at Connecticut College, and to other individuals in Houston; Washington, D.C.; Berkeley; and New York City.

A photograph of John Challis at work on a set of keyboards illustrated this article from *Time* magazine's music page early in 1944:

Man from Ypsilanti

The maker of the finest U.S. harpsichords was back last week in Ypsilanti, Mich., full of happy memories. Wiry, black-haired John Challis had vastly enjoyed a holiday season of harpsichordery in Manhattan. But he was anxious to get to work.

The U.S. enthusiasts for harpsichord music are a small, fervent, growing body. John Challis is probably the only man in the world who, despite war, continues to manufacture the instrument. (England's world-famed Dolmetsch family, who made and played harpsichords at Haslemere, have long since turned to defense work.) Like most people interested in harpsichords, he is irritated by the lay notion that the instrument is a sort of Pleistocene piano. The true ancestor of the piano is not the harpsichord but the dulcimer, a more primitive stringed instrument played like a xylophone, with little hammers held in the hands. The harpsichord's strings are not hammered but plucked with quills or leather plectra (picks).

But the harpsichord was the piano's great predecessor. In the first half of the 18th Century, it was as popular as the piano is today. The finest composers of the century wrote for it prolifically. The harpsichord repertory includes a mass of rich and fascinating music.

Bakelite and Boar Bristles.

John Challis makes his harpsichords in a two-floor studio above an Ypsilanti dress shop. Two assistants, who have been with him for years, help him fit together the intricate combination of carved hardwoods, leather plectra, metal strings and frames, ivory keys and Siberian boar-bristle springs out of which a fine harpsichord is concocted. A slow, painstaking craftsman, Challis turns out only about eight harpsichords a year, at prices ranging from $400 to $2,700. So far, wartime shortages of materials have not affected his output.

John Challis, who is a first-rate harpsichordist himself, was born in Ypsilanti [actually, he was born in South Lyon] 36 years ago. . . . He introduced many improvements into harpsichord manufacture, utilized modern materials like bakelite, aluminum and nylon. "I am not an antiquarian," he explains, "my idea is simply to carry on the manufacturing of harpsichords where it left off when the instrument went out of popularity at the end of the 18th Century."[6]

Just what sort of instrument was Challis building? In appearance his harpsichords resembled those of Dolmetsch: the case exteriors of oiled wood with a thin gold molding around the lower edge,[7] slanted key cheeks, a simple trestle stand, and the same style of lettering on the nameboard. The metal frame of the instrument was a Challis invention, although Dolmetsch also used a welded metal frame to support the 4-foot hitchpin rail, and the idea may have been planted in Challis's mind during his apprenticeship.[8] Challis's original framing, developed in collaboration with an unemployed machinist, was made of welded steel. Because the metal tended to warp from the heat of the blowtorch, making strict tolerances impossible, Challis designed a cast aluminum frame. The soundboard rested on this frame—it was not built with a reinforcing plate over it as were many other metal-framed harpsichords—and all was constructed lightly enough that it was possible for the instrument to resonate. The instrument was extraordinarily stable, and so satisfied Challis's primary concern.[9]

In his first harpsichords Challis made the soundboards from Douglas fir, which Dolmetsch had been using in place of spruce since the First World War. In 1946 Challis noticed that some of his instruments were in difficulty: the glue joints of the soundboards pulled loose, although none of the other joints in the instrument gave way. Surmising that the problem had something to do with a chemical property of Douglas fir, Challis decided to use spruce, but it produced too small a tone. His next step was to use laminated soundboards, made of a spruce plywood, supplied by the Chicago piano manufacturer Kimball. Finally, largely in response to a plea for an instrument that could withstand the Florida climate (for Catharine Crozier and Harold Gleason, who had moved from Rochester, New York, to Winter Park), Challis turned, in the late 1950s, to soundboards of cast metal. The exact composition is a closely guarded secret, [10] but the later Challis instruments, thus, became largely metal harpsichords.[11]

How successful were these instruments? Wolfgang Zuckermann stated categorically, "I personally cannot tell a Challis with a wooden board from a Challis with a metal board. To me they both have the characteristic Challis tone—loud but not particularly singing, and overplucking, causing a slight tearing of the string." Plectra, originally of a thickly cut leather, were made of plastic in the later instruments. As with the soundboard, the characteristic Challis tone was little changed. "It seems that a builder's personality is sometimes so strong as to impose itself on his instruments no matter what material he uses."[12]

Stability of tuning and freedom from constant maintainance were the goals of Challis the builder. His brochure stated,

> The musician needs an instrument which will be ready to play when desired, one on which he can depend. And it should remain as beautiful with the passage of time as when it is new.
> The important things to know when buying a harpsichord are: How long will it endure? How long will it keep in tune? Will repairs be frequent and costly? These have always been problems in buying harpsichords. Mr. Challis has found that skillful designing and superior workmanship will conquer all these difficulties so that the instruments stay in tune and need little attention.

. . . The structural frames are made of cast aluminum which assures complete stability. The jacks are moisture resistant and will not stick in damp weather. The tuning pin blocks are made of materials which cannot split. Above all, the new Challis soundboards are also made of materials which will neither crack nor lose their tonal beauty through the years.[13]

That Challis achieved his goal to an extent not formerly seen in harpsichord making is indisputable. Concert artist Fernando Valenti saw his Challis harpsichord dumped into the Colorado River, bailed it out, and played a recital on it the same night.[14]

Challis set *the* professional standards for dealing with one's customers: if the instrument didn't work, Challis would fix it; if the customer wasn't satisfied, he or she could return the instrument. Challis gave real credence to the definition of a professional builder as one who would buy back any of his own work. Indeed a prospective buyer could read in the builder's brochure, "Purchase first a small instrument such as you can afford which, if used carefully, may be exchanged later, when the initial cost will be applied toward a larger instrument. In this way one may start with the smallest, and in a few years advance to a two-manual harpsichord."

John Challis was ahead of his time with his interest in a Mozart piano. His catalog listed "A pianoforte constructed especially for the music of Mozart and Haydn, having thin strings, small hammers and a light, responsive action. The tone quality reminds one of orchestral strings and woodwinds. Though the volume of tone is only half that of the twentieth-century pianoforte it has a large dynamic range."

Shortly before his move to New York City, Challis was pictured once again in *Time*. The article "The Plectra Pluckers" surveyed the burgeoning harpsichord business, giving this assessment of Challis: "Leader of the metal faction is John Challis, pioneer U.S. manufacturer of harpsichords. . . . In a shop at the rear of his huge, century-old brick house in Detroit, Challis constructs about twelve harpsichords a year (last week he was working on his 230th), grosses $30,000. . . ."[15]

Challis was also the builder of several "pedal" harpsichords—large independent instruments played by the feet, on which a double-manual harpsichord could be set—giving an organlike machine. E. Power Biggs was especially enamored of this instrument. During the national convention of the American Guild of Organists in 1960 Biggs came to Challis's Detroit residence to try the prototype instrument for the first time. Taking off his shoes, he played in his stocking feet his own solo version of the Soler *Concerto* in G major, which he had recently recorded at the organ. He was most complimentary about the instrument, subsequently purchased one, and made numerous recordings on it.[16]

Challis was never shy about offering his opinions. At a 1966 recital by Gustav Leonhardt, played on a Hubbard harpsichord at Hunter College, he expressed his view of the latest trend in harpsichord making. As the applause died away before the intermission his rasping voice was heard complaining, "If I hear one more note of quill I'm going to puke!"[17]

Blanche Winogron Beck, quoted in Biggs's obituary for John Challis, evaluated his contribution to the American harpsichord revival:

Due to the movement toward literal reproduction of the seventeenth and eighteenth-century instruments, John Challis, [a] pioneer of early keyboard building in this country, is not always accorded the honor he deserves. John had arrived at his techniques in order to make instruments suited to our climate and heated houses. Whether or not we agreed with his ideas of construction and materials we know he was a master builder. The younger generation knows and honors the newer builders. But they have little idea of how many of these newer builders John Challis helped, coached, schooled and how he led the way. Challis was a first-rate artist, artisan and craftsman, and a fine generous human being. He is fully responsible for recreating an art and an industry in our time.[18]

And this fine builder had spent his life doing what he wanted to do: " 'People are in a constant scramble . . . to produce more than will make them happy. I find that by making twelve or fifteen instruments a year, I'm happy. After all,' Challis said, fingering a series of chords on the new harpsichord to play it in some more, 'shouldn't that be the purpose of a man's work?' "[19]

JULIUS WAHL

At least one other professional harpsichord maker was working contemporaneously in the United States. An extensive article in *Musical America* reported, "The only generally known makers of harpsichords and clavichords in the United States today are John Challis of Detroit, and Julius Wahl, of Los Altos, California."[20] Wahl (1878–1955), born in Krefeld, Germany, emigrated to the United States in 1891. He began his career as a piano maker with Chickering's in Boston during the Arnold Dolmetsch years (1905–1911). It is uncertain whether he worked on harpsichords at this time, but it is easy to assume that Dolmetsch's pursuits had some influence on him. Later he served as curator of the Belle Skinner Collection of Early Instruments in Holyoke. In the late 1930s Wahl and his wife visited California and decided to move there.[21]

For the past ten years [1940–1950] Mr. Wahl has been working alone with no interest in training apprentices, on the Duveneck ranch in Lost Altos. He has produced about forty instruments—one- and two-manual harpsichords, virginals, spinets, and clavichords. His fine cabinet work and his reverence for traditional decoration can be observed. . . . Every part of a Wahl instrument, even the hinges on the cover, is made by hand.

Neither Mr. Wahl nor Mr. Challis considers himself bound by all the traditional methods of constructing harpsichords, although the basic mechanical form remains much as it was in the earliest known instrument, dated 1521. . . .

Mr. Wahl prefers to use traditional woods—boxwood from Ceylon and Madagascar for the natural keys, ebony for the sharps, spruce for the sound-board, maple for the wrest-plank; and a variety of Latin-American woods for the casing and cabinet work—primavera, de oro, and mahogany. Occasionally he uses rosewood, olive, or cherrywood for the keys and other parts, or for the often elaborately carved roses in the soundboard.[22]

Julius Wahl in his shop at Hidden Villa Ranch, Los Altos, circa 1947.
(Courtesy of Elizabeth Dana.)

Wahl built his instruments two at a time because he had discovered that to be the most efficient way to work: one instrument generally took five months to build, while two could be completed in eight. A customer's waiting time after ordering an instrument ran between four and eighteen months.[23]

The illustrations in the *Musical America* story included a portrait of Challis, but for Wahl, only pictures of his instruments. They resembled the German production harpsichords of the period, appearing to be of heavy case construction and utilizing thick leather plectra. As with Challis's instruments (and indeed nearly all revival instruments produced before 1950), the registers were controlled by pedals. Wahl was reported to have made some instruments with knee levers to operate the stops, but none of this type was illustrated. The article concluded:

> The possession of a fine harpsichord is no longer beyond the reach of anyone who can afford a medium-priced piano. A harpsichord takes up less floor space than a baby grand piano. . . .
> The harpsichord has been employed by Manuel de Falla in a harpsichord concerto and in his El Retablo de Maese Pedro, by Poulenc, Milhaud, Stravinsky, Ravel, Walton, and Piston. Popular musicians have tried modern compositions on it with occasional good effect; Artie Shaw made good use of the instrument in his old Gramercy Five recordings. A small chamber orchestra is incomplete without the rich toning undercoat of resonance provided by the harpsichord in the performance of the older music. The modern American-made instruments are well within the reach of many schools. There is no reason why their use should not continue to expand and

develop, as the qualities of their tone are appreciated and the flexibility of their tonal combinations is explored.

For those who enjoy playing or hearing the keyboard compositions of Bach, Handel, Scarlatti, Purcell, Byrd, and Rameau, there is no substitute. The harpsichord is not merely an old-fashioned piano. It is the medium for which a great and distinctive literature was written, and it deserves the place it has belatedly won among living instruments. John Challis and Julius Wahl are doing a great deal to end the harpsichord's career as a museum piece and to bring it into homes and schools where the most intimate music is made, and where it may regain its high position in musical life.[24]

CLAUDE JEAN CHIASSON

"It may seem strange . . . but although I have been building harpsichords in America longer than almost anyone else, I have never built as a builder. It has been primarily an avocation for me rather than a vocation. . . ."[25] This was a strange viewpoint for one who was working on his thirty-third instrument when he made these comments in 1972. Claude Jean Chiasson (1914–1985) was another New Englander of French descent. Brought up in Cambridge, he studied piano with Jesus Maria Sanroma at the New England Conservatory. But it was the influence of Putnam Aldrich, just returned from his studies with Wanda Landowska, that made the deepest impression. "I studied every phase of music with him—harmony, counterpoint, figured bass, continuo playing at sight—the works! And most of it I didn't pay for. I took it out in tunings, cleaning [his] apartment and things of that nature."[26]

Through a piano teacher friend in Boston, Chiasson met Julius Wahl in Wellesley. When Wahl became curator of the Skinner Collection, Chiasson went to visit it with Aldrich. Playing on these instruments broadened Chiasson's harpsichord experience, especially the "beautiful tone of the Ruckers double" and "the Hass which had the sixteen-foot choir of strings."[27] Another acquaintance was William Lyman Johnson, who still had two Dolmetsch instruments in his possession—a virginal and a small triangular spinet, both in need of repairs. Johnson determined that Chiasson could do this work, and on the strength of this experience, recommended him to the Museum of Fine Arts in Boston as a repairer for their eighteenth-century Kirckman harpsichord.

Chiasson's own first harpsichord was constructed on the general plan of his Kirckman, with an added 16-foot register, à la Pleyel, and a lute stop. The instrument was completed in 1938 and nicknamed "the monster" by its builder.

Chiasson also became acquainted with John Challis. The story of their meeting involves two other figures of note:

Just about the time the "monster" was finished, playable and in my studio in Cambridge near Harvard Square, a young man came to me and introduced himself. He told me that he was at Phillips Andover Academy and owned a Neupert

Claude Jean Chiasson. (Drawing by Jane Johnson.)

clavichord which he became interested in after attending concerts by the Trapp Family Singers. He indicated that he would be at Harvard the following year and wanted to know if I took pupils.

Well, I did take pupils and later on, in September, when he got squared away, he came back and said "I'm here! I want harpsichord lessons." That is how Daniel Pinkham became my pupil.

In the course of time, he bought a small Challis harpsichord. Not only did he receive the instrument, but Challis came out with it to see that it was in good order and also to visit Melville Smith, an old friend of his who, in the meantime, had become director of the Longy School of Music.

. . . John stayed with Melville during this trip. As a matter of interest, the little harpsichord John was delivering was taken to Melville's house and we had a grand party that evening.

The next day, John visited me and "the monster" and John and I became friends and have remained so over these many years. That was my first introduction both to Challis and a Challis instrument.[28]

Two instruments joined Chiasson's "monster" in Boston: one was built for Margaret Mason, a counterpoint teacher at New England Conservatory; the other for a professor of economics. The Museum of Fine Arts administration invited Chiasson to stay on the staff as coordinator of the Sunday afternoon Museum Concerts; he remained in this position for two seasons, until 1942, at which time he entered the Air Force. During the war Chiasson's first harpsichord was placed in the Cambridge home of Melville Smith.

After five years in the Air Force Chiasson returned to civilian life. He was engaged by Community Concerts as a touring pianist, traveling all over the United States during the next four seasons. Tired of this peripatetic existence ("One can net more by staying home where expenses are not so high. I got tired of supporting hotels and restaurants in all parts of the country"), Chiasson settled in New York, where he shared a workshop with a friend. Here he made four identical instruments, adaptations of a Taskin harpsichord, but with a rounded, Germanic tail. He gave solo concerts, played in orchestras, and "had more than enough work. I was very busy as a player."[29] His recordings primarily of French harpsichord music, were made on these instruments.

Chiasson moved to New Jersey to work as an organist-choirmaster. After two years he gave up this position to devote his time to piano and harpsichord teaching, some concerts, and a continuation of his avocation, building harpsichords.

CHAPTER

8

NEW GENERATION, NEW AESTHETIC

Ralph Kirkpatrick

Harpsichordists Out of Tune

The harpsichord went out when the piano came in. Nobody at the time seemed very sorry: the piano was easier to play, its notes carried further, and it had greater range of tone. But the harpsichord has made a startling comeback—thanks largely to one woman. There has probably been more harpsichord-playing in New York in the past year than any time since the days of George Washington. Last week Manhattan harpsichord fans, a serious-minded lot, could hear either the master herself, stately, 67-year-old Wanda Landowska, or her most successful expupil, Ralph Kirkpatrick.

To the unschooled ear, the harpsichord jangles like a regiment of mice scurrying through a pile of coins. But its connoisseurs find in the harpsichord rarefied and rustling harmonies, comparable to a choir of flutes and mandolins. When Landowska began, nobody was writing harpsichord music; it was a dead art. Composers like Francis Poulenc (her student for a year) and the late Manuel De Falla wrote harpsichord music for her. Said she: "It was a battle, you have no idea what a battle it was, to impose the harpsichord upon the musical world. When I started before 1900, the tradition was not."

Most of the topflight harpsichordists are Landowska-trained: Switzerland's Isabel Nef, Italy's Ruggiero Gerlin, London's Lucille Wallace, Los Angeles' Alice Ehlers, Manhattan's Sylvia Marlowe (who sometimes swings it) and Ralph Kirkpatrick.

Collectors & Cranks. Kirkpatrick, who is now 35, was a sophomore at Harvard when he saw his first harpsichord—a museum piece. When he was graduated (he majored in art history) he went to France, studied at Landowska's academy at Saint-Leu-le-Forêt, gave his first public recital in Berlin in 1933. Today he plays about 70 recitals a season, and is glad to see his audiences spreading beyond the earnest, humorless cultists he once played to. Says he: "Audiences used to be largely record collectors and cranks who also liked folk dancing because it was pure and sexless."

Kirkpatrick, a bachelor, lives in a tiny Manhattan apartment crowded with two harpsichords, an 18th-century piano, a clavichord and a thousand books. To keep his instruments in tune he seldom turns on the radiator ("My friends stay away in the winter to keep from catching cold"). He plays Bach and Mozart with a hard, dry purity—and sometimes, say critics, with a little too much banging. He long ago broke with Teacher Landowska, whose playing is more showy and dramatic. Says Kirkpatrick starchily: "Landowska is a great artist. But other artists take different ways. It generally means a break." Wanda Landowska also long ago stopped speaking of Kirkpatrick as her pupil. Says she: "Shall we say, my pupils must be my friends."[1]

Ralph Leonard Kirkpatrick (1911–1984) was his generation's leading exponent of a less-idiosyncratic and flamboyant style of harpsichord playing. He began his progress toward the music page of *Time* with a decision, during his senior year at Harvard, to devote his life "to the performance of harpsichord and clavichord music in a manner as close as possible to what could be ascertained of the intentions of the composers."[2] He had heard a harpsichord for the first time in 1927 during one of Arthur Whiting's "Expositions of Chamber Music." The gift to Harvard in 1929 of a Dolmetsch-Chickering harpsichord provided an instrument on which Kirkpatrick could begin his proposed study. His first public harpsichord recital was presented at Harvard in 1930. A Bach course, requiring musical illustrations, led him to his first complete performance of the *Goldberg Variations* in 1931. This performance, and one of the Bach D-minor *Harpsichord Concerto,* had a "fortunate outcome in the award of a travelling fellowship for study in Europe."[3]

In chapter 4 we have seen some of Kirkpatrick's early assessments of Landowska in his "European Journal." This document, edited shortly before his death for publication as the book *Early Years*, makes fascinating reading.

> In September 1931, my departure for Europe once again continued my reversal of the westward-bound search of my ancestors for the future Promised Land. My Promised Land lay eastward, and in large measure in a past that I was eager to rediscover. My immediate goal was Paris. My principal aims were the recovery of harpsichord and clavichord techniques and of a command of the musical literature and source material relating to the performance of solo and chamber music. My practical goal was harpsichord study with Wanda Landowska, research in the Bibliothèque Nationale, and the filling of many gaps in my basic musicianship through study with Nadia Boulanger.[4]

Through Boulanger Kirkpatrick met Paul Brunold, the musicologist and incumbent organist of Couperin's Church of St. Gervais, who gave him an invaluable window on French harpsichord music and original sources. He was especially impressed with Brunold's eighteenth-century harpsichord, beautifully restored, and possessing a "richness of tone, one of the very best I have ever heard."[5]

Kirkpatrick viewed some aspects of his study with Landowska enthusiastically:

> This afternoon I went out to St. Leu for one of Landowska's classes. She gave me some more exercises, perfectly terrific ones. I think she is probably wasting a good deal of my time, but the residuum of gain, particularly in precision and strength, will

be worthwhile. I rather dread working on interpretation, because in a good many ways I shall never wish to imitate her, and there is no question of discussion with her. One simply swallows everything without question and regurgitates privately. She wants to keep almost complete control over her pupils in almost every field of activity, in a most useless way. This afternoon I asked her if I could read her copy of the rare "L'Art de Toucher le Clavecin" of Couperin and she said, "Yes, we will go over it paragraph by paragraph." I shall read it at the Bibliothèque Nationale.[6]

The Parisian study year continued. Kirkpatrick's "review" of a harpsichord recital expressed his current manner of thinking about the harpsichord:

In the evening I went to the harpsichord concert of Pauline Aubert. . . . It was in an excellent small hall, and the instrument was a Dolmetsch-Gaveau, possibly the best I have ever heard. In the first number, probably because of nervousness, Mme. Aubert gave what I expected, but after that her playing was positively ravishing. She played Couperin with the most subtle restraint and delicacy, and some Rameau, some French sonatas with flute, one of the Kuhnau Bible Sonatas. Her registration was simple but beautifully chosen and most effective. Her phrasing was sensitive and supple, with ornaments played with a superb grace. Her technic occasionally included some false notes and occasionally one felt a slight lack of vigor in her playing, but her interpretations all possessed a restraint and objectivity that made the fullest effect in a piece after it was finished, a very rare quality in any musician, and admirable for most harpsichord music. . . . When I think of the delicious effects and absolute blending that she obtained from that instrument in playing with the flute, my esteem of the Pleyel sinks even lower. All in all, it was a most inspiring concert.[7]

In the spring of 1932 Kirkpatrick met Arnold Dolmetsch at the home of Dorothy Swainson, a Dolmetsch pupil then living in Paris. Kirkpatrick noted, "He played the clavichord with an extraordinary variety and beauty of tone color, although marred by lapse of memory and the assertion that there is only one way to play a piece and he can prove why! I think that there will be opportunity for me to learn a great deal at Haslemere this summer, in spite of the crazy people with whom I shall be working!"[8]

Just before leaving Paris in July, Kirkpatrick had his break with Landowska:

She called me up in her room and went off on a long and embarrassing tirade on the subject of my letter to Mr. Surette [in which Kirkpatrick had expressed his opinions of Landowska and her teaching]. I am sorry I haven't a record of all the extraordinary things she said, but among them was something like this: "How can you expect to comprehend the mystery and complication of that phenomenon which is Wanda Landowska?" At this point the dog came in and committed an indiscretion![9]

Kirkpatrick spent the rest of the summer with the "crazy people" in Haslemere and pursuing his research at the Bibliothèque Nationale in Paris. Making his European debut in Germany, he performed the Bach *Goldberg Variations* again, this time in a concert series under the direction of fellow Landowska-student-colleague Eta Harich-Schneider. The year, 1933; the place, Berlin. During preparations for this event Kirkpatrick played many of the variations on "Bach's own harpsichord" in the Berlin instrument collection;[10] had a lesson with the organist of St. Thomas in Leipzig, Günther Ramin;[11] and heard Erwin Bodky play parts of the same work, "making me feel better about my own performances of them!"[12] As for the concert,

> I was not at all satisfied with my playing, but apparently the evening was a great success. The harpsichord turned out to be a perfect mousetrap of an instrument, and *no* joy to play. . . . The variations, as I played some of them, sounded like a fantastic, nightmarish, Satanic caricature. . . .
> However, I am considerably encouraged by the certainty that I am capable of playing much better than I did, and that in the future I can face the "anstrengend" [exhausting] task of playing forty-five uninterrupted minutes from memory, with more sureness.[13]

After several months in Berlin, where Harich-Schneider continued to aid Kirkpatrick's technical progress and to provide a Neupert harpsichord on which to practice, Ralph traveled through northern Germany, eventually visiting the Gläser harpsichord firm in Jena. Here he learned about a vacant professorship in harpsichord at the summer course in the Salzburg Mozarteum. After an extended trip south through Germany and a revelatory time in Italy (where he played his first paid concert, in the library of Bernard Berenson's villa I Tatti), Kirkpatrick's "formal" teaching career began in Salzburg in the summer of 1933.

Back home in America the following year, Kirkpatrick played for the first time in New York City. *Musical America* reported about the April concerts at the New Music School, "Mr. Kirkpatrick displayed not only a keen understanding of the music itself but also a perfect command of the technique of the instrument. A large crowd was present."[14]

A more subjective description of these debut concerts was written by Paul Rosenfeld, who, noting that the young player resembled "somebody grinding for a Ph.D. in English in the Yale Graduate school," commented on Kirkpatrick's sense of style and his "reverence for [the] music's quality."[15] In two evening recitals of music by J. S. Bach, Kirkpatrick played both clavichord and harpsichord. The programs included six preludes and fugues from *The Well-Tempered Clavier,* *French Suites* in E major and G major, the B-flat major *Partita,* the *Chromatic Fantasy and Fugue,* and a complete performance of the *Goldberg Variations.*

For his first professional American concerts Kirkpatrick was dependent on the availability of a harpsichord, as his only personal instrument was the clavichord he had purchased from Arnold Dolmetsch in September 1932. In the autumn of 1934 a group of friends in Boston made it possible for him to buy Busoni's Dolmetsch-built Chickering harpsichord, then in the possession of Lotta Van Buren. "During these years no one could be found on the entire east coast who was genuinely capable of regulating a harpsichord, and I who had never been a gadgeteer was obliged to become my own harpsichord repair man, often under the most onerous and trying circumstances. Here perhaps may be seen the origin of my profound dislike of the harpsichord."[16]

Further travails of travel contributed to Kirkpatrick's often-underlined dislike of his chosen instrument:

> In the days of the Railway Express it was possible to ship an instrument anywhere in the United States where there was a railway station. I found that an itinerary could be worked out in conjunction with the central office. But nevertheless one was constantly telephoning to find out at which transfer point the instrument had been held up. One was never able to practise. It was during these years that I learned that I must be able to go on stage absolutely cold because the harpsichord would have been in a baggage car or in a hall inaccessible to me except for purposes of tuning, and that any real practising had to be done before leaving home. I acquired such a habit of not warming up before a performance that to this day I never do it.[17]

Kirkpatrick's recording career began in 1936. Bach's *Italian Concerto* was the first release of the newly formed Musicraft Records. Additional albums by Kirkpatrick followed, including a six-record recital of music by Bach and his predecessors. Within a short time Kirkpatrick made his first appearance with the Boston Symphony Orchestra, received a Guggenheim Fellowship, and, most important, was given a continuous performing opportunity—a series of approximately fifty concerts in the Governor's Palace in Williamsburg, Virginia, spanning the years 1938–1946. This was enough early American music for Kirkpatrick, who noted that "since 1946 I can hardly have been guilty of playing James Hewitt's *Battle of Trenton* more than once or twice."[18]

Typical programs from Williamsburg, a set *sans* America, are these from the last season of Kirkpatrick's involvement:

> In the candlelit ballroom of the colonial Governor's palace in Williamsburg, Virginia, the first of six chamber-music concerts, comprising the ninth annual festival of eighteenth-century music, took place. Ralph Kirkpatrick, noted harpsichordist who has directed these festivals since their inception in 1938, was again the organizing spirit. Two identical series, each of three concerts, were heard this week under the sponsorship of the corporation administering the restored city as part of a program to recreate the colonial capital of two centuries ago. Assisting Mr. Kirkpatrick in the performances were Alexander Schneider, violinist, Daniel Saidenberg, 'cellist, Mitchell Miller, oboist [later to figure prominently in the popular-music return of the harpsichord], Viola Morris, soprano, and Victoria Anderson, contralto.
>
> The first pair of concerts, on October 14 and 17 [1946], presented sonatas for violin and harpsichord by Corelli and Mozart, the Partita in E Major for violin by Bach, a triple concerto by Couperin, and an early Trio by Joseph Haydn. On October 15 and 18, Viola Morris and Victoria Anderson, known on the concert stage as the "English Duo," performed duets by Pergolesi, Handel, Alessandro Scarlatti, Purcell,

Ralph Kirkpatrick playing his Dolmetsch-Chickering harpsichord, 1939.
(Ralph Kirkpatrick Archives, Music Library, Yale University.)

and Couperin, while Ralph Kirkpatrick provided variety with an assortment of
harpsichord pieces by Rameau, Domenico Scarlatti, and Couperin. The final pair of
concerts, on October 16 and 19, brought music by Veracini, Handel, Mozart, and
Rameau for various combinations of instruments.[19]

Scholarly activities, balanced alongside his concert career, were a constant in
Kirkpatrick's life. His edition of his signature work, Bach's *Goldberg Variations,*
was published by G. Schirmer in 1938. A twenty-eight-page preface presented a
polemic for a scholarly interpretation of the work on its intended keyboard instrument. Considerable information about ornamentation was included, and suggested
executions of these sometimes-mystifying signs were placed in smaller notes above

the original notation. When the voice-leading might be misconstrued, the editor wrote the right-hand part on two staves and placed them above the original also. Kirkpatrick was adamant in his belief that the harpsichord is the appropriate instrument for the performance of the work:

> Any thorough examination of the character of the harpsichord is enough, it would seem, to show that Bach, with however much approval he might have regarded the modern piano, would have composed for it altogether differently. By this time it should be universally realized that the keyboard music of Bach is not piano music, and that on the piano it must be regarded as transcription.[20]

It is touching and illuminating to read the final paragraph of this erudite introduction, especially in view of the importance of the *Goldberg Variations* in Kirkpatrick's career:

> But for all their lyricism and tragic passion and exuberance, the Aria and the Variations seem of a divine substance entirely refined and purified of anything personal or ignoble, so that in playing them one seems only the unworthy mouthpiece of a higher voice. And even beyond the scope of the emotions that have been aroused, the effect of the whole is one of boundless peace, in which one returns cleansed, renewed, matured to the starting point, which seen a second time seems so transfigured in the light of this traversed spiritual journey. . . .[21]

Kirkpatrick taught at Bennington College for a brief time, then was appointed to the music faculty of Yale University in 1940. A fellow freshman on the faculty was composer Paul Hindemith. That Kirkpatrick's teaching was something special even to non-harpsichordists was elegantly attested to by Willie Ruff, eminent French horn player and jazz musician, writing about his first days at Yale:

> We found ourselves . . . among an international crowd of music students, drawn to the campus to be near another Yale musician, composer Paul Hindemith. It didn't take long to learn, however, that the king of the mountain among the school's performers was Mr. Kirkpatrick. Most notable of all, for me, was that he spent his time being king away from Yale, mostly in Europe. A few of his students—"the harpsichord mafia"—spread rumors that the great man regularly shipped his harpsichord and cutaway off to the continent, then flew over to cover several countries by bicycle while his beloved instrument caught up to him by rail in time for carefully arranged recitals in target cities—cities that had great art on exhibit or, better yet, art for sale. He'd been a much sought-after concertizer, a bike man, and incurable art collector for years already, often trading the proceeds from his recitals for works by Dürer, Delacroix, Daumier, Degas, Cézanne—the best of what appealed to his educated but eclectic eye.
>
> I pressed one of the female members of the clavier mob one day. "Tell me," I pleaded, "what is all this fuss about this harpsichord man? Why are tickets to his concert being snatched up and reserved even before they are printed? What is he, Art

Tatum or somebody?" "My Deaaah!" she said, smiling. "His will be *the* concert of the season. He's playing Bach and several of those mah-velous Scarlatti sonatas he recently uncovered in Europe."

The smile stayed on her face but the amusement vanished. "Take my advice, Dahling, use your student's privilege and pick up your complimentary ticket today!" I took the lady's advice and I thank her still, for that evening was the beginning of a series of lessons I was to learn from Kirkpatrick on the function of time in music.[22]

The war years and those immediately following saw notable continuo performances by Kirkpatrick. Among others were annual performances (1943–45) of Bach's *Saint Matthew Passion* with the New York Philharmonic, Bruno Walter conducting; and many recitals with violinist Alexander Schneider, which led to the recording of most of the repertoire for violin and harpsichord.

Most descriptive of all the contemporary music critics was composer Virgil Thomson, whose comments about a 1940 Bach performance evoke the period in a unique and compelling way:

Bach Goes to Church

Cantata Singers, Arthur Mendel, conductor; complete performance of Bach's *Christmas Oratorio*. The closer the performing conditions for Sebastian Bach's concerted music are approximated to those of early eighteenth-century provincial Germany the more that music sounds like twentieth-century American swing. The exactitude with which a minimum time unit is kept unaltered at all times, the persistence of this unit as one of exactly measured length rather than of pulsation, the omnipresence of the harpsichord's ping, like a brush on a cymbal, the constant employment of wiggly counterpoint and staccato bass, all make it a matter of preference between anachronisms whether one puts it that Bach has gone to town or that some of the more scholarly jitterbugs of the town have wandered into a church.

Last night's performance of the *Christmas Oratorio* was full of swing and gusto. . . . The inexorable rhythm of Mr. Ralph Kirkpatrick's harpsichord continuo sustained the whole with a vigor and a brightness rarely encountered these days. . . .[23]

In 1947, during his first post-war European tour, Kirkpatrick located Domenico Scarlatti's descendants by consulting the Madrid telephone book. His monograph on Scarlatti (published in 1953) occupied him for more than a decade, and as this book neared publication Scarlatti's music figured ever more prominently in his concerts.

Kirkpatrick's Town Hall recitals received these typically favorable reviews:

January 23, 1949: Bach, *Goldberg Variations* and ten Scarlatti sonatas: Kirkpatrick played this set with complete fluency—including an admirable freedom in his left hand—and with perhaps greater variety in registration than he previously has essayed. It was a performance in the best of taste, completely masculine in concept, with none of the finicky approach that looks upon the music as a venerable set of rather dry exercises . . . one of the most satisfactory recitals of the current season.[24]

January 22, 1952: Bach, *Partita in A minor, 12 Little Preludes;* Mozart, *Sonata in B-flat,* K. 570 played on a Challis Mozart piano; six Scarlatti sonatas: This recital by Ralph Kirkpatrick was a superb one, representing a well-nigh perfect synthesis of scholarship, taste, interpretive imagination, and virtuosity.[25]

Kirkpatick made a formidable advocate for Domenico Scarlatti; few authors of major musical biographies are also leading players of their subjects' music. In the same year in which the book appeared, Kirkpatrick issued a selection of sixty Scarlatti sonatas[26] in a clean, urtext edition. He proceeded to perform these same sonatas in concert, on the radio, and on records.

Ralph Kirkpatrick, Harpsichordist, Town Hall, January 20 [1954]

As a natural sequel to the recent publication of his book on Domenico Scarlatti . . . Ralph Kirkpatrick is giving a cycle of three Town Hall concerts—of which this was the first—devoted to that master's keyboard sonatas. In these he is peforming the sixty sonatas he has selected, edited, and renumbered for publication and which have just been made available in a two-volume edition.

The twenty sonatas presented in this opening recital were divided into three groups: Seven early sonatas, five early sonatas, and eight late sonatas. The [K.] numberings are Mr. Kirkpatrick's.

It was a program that revealed beyond the shadow of a doubt Scarlatti's amazing and fertile imagination, his creative inventiveness as harmonist and melodist, his uncanny skill in exploiting the harpsichord's tonal resources to the full, and his full stature as one of the greatest composers of keyboard music who ever lived. His works are as indigenous to the harpsichord as Chopin's are to the piano. The program served to justify, too, Mr. Kirkpatrick's contention that a series of Scarlatti recitals can be as revelatory as the Bach, Mozart, and Chopin cycles we now take for granted.

The sonatas presented were unfamiliar ones, no two of which were alike, yet they all bore the stamp of Scarlatti's unmistakable genius. Nor were the differences between the more mature later sonatas and the earlier ones as apparent to the listening ear as they are to the scanning eye. Nothing like the disparity that exists between the early and later Chopin works was evident in the sonatas played in this recital. One of the seemingly most mature was the early D minor Sonata, K.52, a work of brooding and haunting loveliness and one of the most spellbinding. And if ever a man let the sun shine through his work it was Scarlatti in the bright and cheerful little Sonata in E, K.28, which Mr. Kirkpatrick registered with the brightest four-foot stop at his command, one that had the tinkle of silver bells in it. Whatever the mood, Mr. Kirkpatrick invested each sonata with appropriate colors, some with imitative guitar effects; others, like the solemn G minor Sonata, K.426, were richly suggestive of the organ in the combined use of sixteen-foot, eight-foot, and four-foot stops, and all of them were played with matchless artistry and understanding. Mr. Kirkpatrick is to

Scarlatti what de Pachmann was to Chopin—the interpreter *par excellence,* at one with his instrument and the composer of his choice.[27]

Kirkpatrick knew from his research that Scarlatti's instruments were quite unlike the harpsichords on which he was performing the sonatas. He had discovered that the only instrument on which all of the works could have been performed in Scarlatti's time was a single-manual Iberian instrument with two 8-foot stops. Thus it is with some poignancy that one reads his description of instruments on which he performed most frequently:

> In America I played principally two instruments, the Dolmetsch-Chickering and a Challis. The old Chickering was done in leather with the exception of the upper manual, which was done in quill. . . . Otherwise, the instruments I used during this period were leathered and when John Challis went over my Chickering, leather was substituted in the upper manual [as well].
>
> . . . To keep the 4' from squealing when the keyboard part went into the upper register, I always kept my foot on the 8' and 4' [pedals] (on both the Chickering and the Challis) so as to be able to balance out the 4', doing a kind of temporary voicing when the 4' risked becoming too strong. I did a great deal more than is apparent on the recordings of tapering cadences with my foot. . . . The unconscionable and absurd use of 16' and 4' in my recordings of 60 Scarlatti sonatas for Columbia was forced on me by the absence on the Challis instrument of an 8' with a tolerable sound.[28]

But instruments were coming that would change Kirkpatrick's playing. The innovations of Hubbard and Dowd, which he espoused enthusiastically, were to alter the American harpsichord scene more radically than did any other event in the first half-century of the revival.

His international career, with Kirkpatrick as America's harpsichord ambassador, expanded with his appearances throughout the 1950s in Italy, Ireland, Germany (where he began an extensive series of Bach recordings for Deutsche Grammophon), and the Vienna, Edinburgh, and Ansbach festivals. Ever colorful, Kirkpatrick continued to command attention from the press. No event of his well-chronicled career was more surprising than his actions during a tour of South Africa:

> The deep desire to beat up a music critic has inflamed many artists, but few ever resort to violence. An exception occurred last week in Johannesburg . . . and to the unlikeliest of men. The eminent American harpsichordist Ralph Kirkpatrick is a tranquil artist, known for his scholarly research. But a review from Dora Sowden, 40-year-old music critic of *The Rand Daily Mail,* the only English-language morning daily in the area, was more than even his placid nature could stand. Kirkpatrick's Bach and Scarlatti, she wrote, had a "sameness" of approach.
>
> Kirkpatrick, at 46 a specialist in both those masters of the keyboard, reacted as he never had before. At the start of his concert the next night, he demanded that Mrs. Sowden leave the YMCA concert hall. "I can't play with hostility in the hall," he said. She refused—and he played. Later, at intermission, Mrs. Sowden's husband

Lewis, *The Rand Mail's* drama critic, went backstage and demanded an explanation. Kirkpatrick tried to throw him out of the hall. After ushers had separated them, the harpsichordist finished the concert.

The upshot was that, as might have been expected, Mrs. Sowden had the last word. "Kirkpatrick's show of temper did him good," she wrote. "He was much better in the second half."[29]

CHAPTER

9

TWO "FIRST LADIES OF THE HARPSICHORD"

YELLA PESSL

While Ralph Kirkpatrick represented a less flamboyant, more severe style in harpsichord playing, his was not the only manner of playing to be heard in the United States in the 1930s. A more supple and colorful way of performing, somewhere between that of Kirkpatrick and Landowska, was represented by Yella Pessl. Born in 1906 in Vienna and christened Gabriela Elsa,[1] Pessl grew up in a musical household where some of the leading musicians of the day gathered for weekly chamber music concerts. She was educated at the Academy of Music, where she studied several instruments, including organ and harpsichord. The person who most influenced her musical taste was Alexander Wunderer, who had founded the Wiener Bachgemeinde in 1913.

During her student days Pessl was engaged to play organ continuo for a Bach cantata conducted by Otto Klemperer. After several appearances in Austria and Germany she realized that she preferred the harpsichord to her other instruments. In 1931, when she completed her studies, she made her American harpsichord debut at a concert of the Schola Cantorum. She decided to make her home in the United States and soon found a place in its musical life. For several seasons she was featured in weekly radio broadcasts of "old" music.

In 1936 *Time* once again brought the harpsichord to popular attention:

Harpsichordist

Returning last week to Manhattan from a trip to her native Austria, harpsichordist Yella Pessl had good news for those music lovers who like to hear 17th and 18th Century works on the instruments for which they were written. On its way from Munich was a fine new harpsichord, made by Karl Maendler, famed for his work with archaic instruments, on which she will record some more Bach, Handel, Purcell, [and] old German Christmas songs for Columbia this week. Herr Maendler's aim in constructing from old Viennese cherrywood this super-harpsichord was to

Yella Pessl. (Courtesy of Catherine Dower.)

eliminate the twangling and jangling of the instrument's complicated internal machinery. [A footnote added, "No tinkling music box, the harpsichord has two keyboards, as many as seven stops, can produce more than 100 tonal 'color' combinations."] With this carefully constructed 20th Century edition of the piano's forerunner Miss Pessl hopes to evoke no unwanted vibrations to mar her recording and broadcasting.

Like Chicago's Philip Manuel and Gavin Williamson [and] other skilled musical archeologists in the U.S. and Europe, Miss Pessl is a serious musician, hunts high and low for original scores of classics. To this end she imported last week 235 pounds of old music from Austria to Manhattan. . . . To combine her three interests of mountain climbing, skiing and music, this dark-eyed, energetic young woman carries a portable clavichord on her back on Austrian outings. This summer, benighted at a Tirolean inn, Yella Passl met Karl Maendler. When he heard who Miss Pessl was, Herr Maendler vowed he would build her a famous harpsichord, set to work immediately on his return to Munich. Another summer's adventure occurred when she played at Salzburg for Chancellor Dr. Kurt Schuschnigg who pronounced Miss Pessl's Haydn concerto *entzückend* [delightful, charming]. Last week Yella Pessl announced her present ambition to "shoot" New York's Mayor Fiorello La Guardia with her minicamera.[2]

Pessl was chosen by Toscanini to appear three times with the NBC Symphony, and she was engaged to teach an interpretation course at the Eastman School of Music in Rochester. Her longer-term academic appointments were at Columbia University and Barnard College, where she taught from 1938 until her retirement in 1952.[3]

As a concert artist Pessl played frequently in New York for nearly two decades. A 1941 Town Hall program with Brazilian singer Elsie Houston

was a uniquely interesting event, for singly and together, they re-created the music of four countries, each in a different stage of cultural and social development and each with a different concept of music. They were able to do this because, different as they are, they are both fine executive musicians and musical scholars who have also the rare imaginative insight that can bring to life music that generally only exists by hearsay in musical memoirs.

The first musical era they re-created was France before the influence of Italian operatic styles changed the nature of its vocal music. One song, "L'Amour de Moi," was particularly beautiful in its unforced simplicity, and Miss Pessl's accompaniment was as sensitive and understanding as Miss Houston's singing.

Then Miss Pessl alone brought her listeners forward to the eighteenth century with a *Fantasy in C Major* by Handel and a *Toccata and Fugue in D Major* by Bach. After the intermission, it was Miss Houston's turn to appear alone. The house was completely darkened, and sitting on the floor in the weird light of one yellow spotlight and beating a drum, Miss Houston peopled the stage with Brazilian natives crying out incantations to their primitive gods.

The lights were turned up and Miss Pessl returned to play six Scarlatti sonatas which lifted the audience out of primitive jungles to the serene and light-filled spaces of absolute music. Then together they brought the recital to a close with a group of Spanish folk songs . . . in which the harpsichord was like a guitar. . . .[4]

In a review of a Bach Circle concert in 1942, at which Pessl performed Bach's transcription for harpsichord of a Vivaldi concerto, Olin Downes wrote: "When Miss Pessl played Bach's arrangement she included the ornaments . . . in the Italian style. It was a pleasure to hear the interpretation of an artist not so hide-bound by dubious traditions that she was afraid to indulge in reasonable elasticity of tempo and to singing the phrases on the wiry instrument in a lyrical manner."[5] Later that year Pessl became director of the Bach Circle, succeeding Robert Hufstader, who joined the Army. For the following season the group announced two concerts at Town Hall and three members' concerts to be given at a private residence and at the Metropolitan Museum of Art.

Pessl was not a shy academic. Perhaps by the mid-1940s it was necessary to make memorable comments to keep up with the competition of the always-trenchant Landowska. At any rate the younger import once said to a program annotator for CBS, "I stayed up all night playing Couperin. It was almost as good as making love. *Almost,* I said!"[6]

In 1945 Downes was still reviewing Bach Circle concerts at Town Hall and commenting favorably on Pessl's playing of Couperin:

> The harpsichord pieces played by Miss Pessl were far more persuasive [than a Couperin motet on the same program]. This was as much Couperin's instrument as the piano was Chopin's. . . .
> The four pieces which make the 27th Suite or *Ordre* are each different and each distinguished, in one or another mood. "Les Pavots" has a delicacy of statement and quality of atmosphere fully justifying the program note designating it as "a masterpiece of French impressionism in eighteenth century imagery" and forerunner of Debussy and Ravel.
> Miss Pessl played this music with admirable taste, technical precision, with a treatment of phrases and ornaments which was never academic and always lyrical.[7]

However, Downes noted that the harpsichord in a Bach concerto "slightly overbalanced the few strings." This remark was particularly astonishing, for Pessl's harpsichord was one of the excessivly heavy German instruments built by Maendler-Schramm in Munich, a fact that was proudly stated on her record labels. These harpsichords were built to withstand total war. In fact, a subsequent owner of the firm described the metal frame as a *Panzerplatte* [armor plate].[8] Wolfgang Zuckermann described a nearly hopeless house call to repair Pessl's harpsichord:

> After working for hours on Yella Pessl's instrument, I finally was able to get some sound out of it and proudly played a few chords demonstrating this fact. Miss Pessl, perhaps startled out of her wits to hear the instrument playing, ran in from another room and exclaimed: "Mr. Zuckermann, you are breaking my instrument." I had trouble collecting the $5 fee which was all I thought she would willingly surrender.[9]

In 1946 the *Times* noted that "Miss Pessl's playing has become well and favorably known hereabouts, and it is enough to say that it was quite at its best last night, in the smoothness of its technique, its refinement, its reserve and taste, and its sound musicianship."[10] After February 1947 Pessl is not mentioned again in the New York newspapers. There was a widely circulated story that she had become ill from eating poisonous mushrooms, but the truth was less sensational. She spent the years 1948–1950 doing research on Italian music in the Vatican Library. Upon her return to the United States she settled in Massachusetts, where she pursued a reduced schedule of teaching and playing.

SYLVIA MARLOWE

"If we do not ordinarily think of the harpsichord as an instrument of modern music that is not the fault of Sylvia Marlowe."[11] More than any other member of her generation in the United States, Marlowe (1908–1981) worked to increase the significant contributions of major composers to the literature of her chosen instrument.

Sylvia Sapira (Marlowe's real name) was born in Brooklyn. Family complications forced her to discontinue piano and organ lessons at age sixteen. After two years without formal musical studies, she applied for a scholarship to the Juilliard School, but decided instead to accept an opportunity to spend four years studying piano, organ, and composition with Nadia Boulanger at the École Normale de Musique in Paris. During that time she heard Landowska play in the Salle Pleyel; it was the first time Marlowe ever heard a harpsichord.[12] Back in New York, having won a competition sponsored by the National Federation of Music Clubs, Marlowe presented twenty-two fifteen-minute piano recitals over the CBS radio network between November 1932 and May 1933. In these programs she played both volumes of Bach's *Well-Tempered Clavier*.

In 1936 Marlowe decided to turn her attention to the harpsichord. Initially, having no instrument, she had to rent practice time on a Pleyel for fifty cents an hour.

> I determined . . . that I wanted to own . . . a harpsichord. . . . But the problem then, was where to get [an instrument]. . . . One day I heard of a lady who had a harpsichord for sale. It was a very fancy, very large, white Pleyel. It had gold trimmings and the price was $1,000. Of course this was some time ago when $1,000 was more like $5,000 today. At that time I didn't have $1,000 I could afford to use for a harpsichord, so I borrowed it from Virgil Thomson. I remember Virgil saying, "Well, if you don't pay up, I can always have the harpsichord since I have always wanted a harpsichord anyhow."[13]

As a harpsichordist Marlowe was self-taught, although Landowska's influence was there. "I worked with this Pleyel daily and loved it. I listened to Landowska recordings, read everything I could find and worked, worked, worked."[14]

In May 1939 Marlowe played the Bach "48" again in four concerts at Town Hall, this time on the harpsichord—probably the first American presentation of the complete *Well-Tempered Clavier* on an instrument for which the *Preludes* and *Fugues* had been intended. These concerts also included works by Couperin, Scarlatti, and Handel.

A comment Marlowe made in her studio in Westport, Connecticut, that she considered the harpsichord a "vehicle for modern music, even swing"[15] suggested another career for both artist and instrument:

> I was making a record someplace. It was my first recording for which I got paid nothing. It was called "From Bach to Boogie Woogie." . . . Somebody in the studio called a friend of his who was head of the Rainbow Room, which is a night club on the 65th floor of Rockefeller Center. I had at that time never even been in a night club. He came to the studio to listen to me and offer me a job at an enormous salary. I was terrified! I had never done this before. I played on a revolving stage with glamorous spotlights and the whole bit. I would play a few classical things then some boogie and other popular numbers. I learned a lot from the job.[16]

Marlowe's venture into the world of popular music paid rich dividends. The excellent publicity brought her guest spots on many radio programs, including "The Chamber Music Society of Lower Basin Street," where she appeared with many of the jazz greats. She also played in the series "Lavender and New Lace" and "New Portraits of Old Masters." Eventually she was given her own radio program on the NBC network, a weekly spot that aired for ten years. With an impressive total of more than 1,500 radio concerts, Marlowe's playing brought the sounds of the harpsichord to vast numbers of new listeners.[17]

Marlowe's nightclub experiences served as inspiration for David Keith's mystery *Blue Harpsichord,* a novel dedicated to Marlowe ("Amico Schapiro pro muscipula gratias.") The hero, Terence Kelly, a young Latin professor, meets the Marlowe-like character "on one of the rare evenings he hadn't spent with Madeleine . . . [at] an enjoyable occasion at which a pretty young American harpsichordist named Myra Drysdale played everything from Bach to Basin Street on her tinkly instrument. . . ."[18] All sorts of artistic intrigues are introduced. The book's flavor may be savored in this invented news report:

> The dramatic critic of the *Times* was awfully kind: "The high spot in the revue for this commentator was the playing of a glorified Brazilian samba on an outraged but wonderfully responsive harpsichord, by the invaluable Myra Drysdale. Hitherto praise of Miss Drysdale has been the prerogative, in the columns of this newspaper, of those concerned with the goings-on in night-clubs and concert halls: the present writer wishes to express his thanks to whoever is responsible for at last bringing Miss Drysdale under his jurisdiction. . . . Being so completely entranced by Miss Drysdale's performance, to the point of half-expecting the harpsichord itself to start dancing a samba, so marvellously intense and evocative were the changing rhythms and tempi that Miss Drysdale induced it to utter, we perhaps paid less attention than we ordinarily might have to the young couple . . . who actually did the dancing."[19]

On more traditional turf, Marlowe was given a warm critical reception in 1946:

> Sylvia Marlowe, harpsichordist, gave her first local recital [*sic*] last night in Town Hall. The youthful artist's seriousness of purpose was reflected in her program,

consisting of masterworks of Bach, Handel, Haydn, and Scarlatti. Loving care was expended on the interpretations of these classics in performances especially commendable for their imagination and charm.

Miss Marlowe's work was cleancut and technically secure. The slips in the Bach "Fantasia in C minor" and the Handel "Chaconne in G" could be discounted, being obviously due to nervousness. The Bach, like all else presented, had rhythmic vitality, transparency and a nice sense of proportion. In it Miss Marlowe displayed her unfailing taste by a restrained use of color effects. But in the Handel "Chaconne" full advantage was taken of the opportunities for highly contrasted tinting in the many variations of the theme. . . .[20]

In 1948, the year of her appointment to the faculty of Mannes College, Marlowe's New York recital featured twelve sonatas of Scarlatti and Bach's *Italian Concerto*. Some memory slips created problems for her, especially in the Bach, but the Scarlatti was deemed "excellent," and Bach's *French Suite* in G was "deftly and poetically projected with vivid and meaningful contrasts of registration."[21]

On a tour of the orient in 1956 Marlowe traveled with suitcase; a two-manual Challis harpsichord with plexiglass pinblock, plastic jacks, and aluminum frame; a clavichord; her husband; and a technician. In three months she gave twenty concerts in such exotic locales as Surabaja, Tokyo, Bandung, and Singapore. It was the first harpsichord playing ever heard in most of these places. Marlowe reported that her audiences "really listened to her programs of works by Bach, Scarlatti, Couperin, and contemporary composers Harold Shapero and Vittorio Rieti," especially since they were accustomed to long programs in this part of the world.[22]

Contemporary composition involving the harpsichord was a dominant theme in Marlowe's programs. The formation of the Harpsichord Quartet in 1952 gave her a steady collaboration with Claude Monteux, flutist; Harry Shulman, oboist; and Bernard Greenhouse, cellist. Their collective search for new repertoire resulted in some of the more significant works of the century. The Harpsichord Quartet commissioned Alan Hovhaness' *Quartet,* opus 97 (1951); Elliott Carter's *Sonata for Flute, Oboe, Cello, and Harpsichord* (1952); and Ben Weber's *Serenade,* opus 39, (1953). Carter's work, which won the Walter W. Naumburg Musical Foundation Award in 1956, has emerged as one of the most respected and most performed of his works. Specific registrations for a large Challis harpsichord are provided in the score. The composer wished

to stress as much as possible the vast and wonderful array of tone-colors available on the modern harpsichord. . . . This aim of using the wide variety of the harpsichord involved many tone-colors which can only be produced very softly and therefore conditioned very drastically the type and range of musical expression, all the details of shape, phrasing, rhythm, texture, as well as the large form.[23]

Such awareness of the instrument's capabilities guaranteed the effectiveness of Carter's composition, which exploited all the instruments in challenging but musically rewarding ways. That the use of the harpsichord was congenial to Carter's

The Harpsichord Quartet. (Courtesy of The Harpsichord Music Society, Sylvia Marlowe, founder.)

creative sensibility was proven a few years later by his second use of the instrument in a major score, the *Double Concerto for Harpsichord and Piano with Two Chamber Orchestras,* premièred in 1961 with Ralph Kirkpatrick playing the extremely challenging solo harpsichord part.

Other commissions by Marlowe and The Harpsichord Music Society, which she founded in 1957, included solo and ensemble works by Paul Des Marais, Arthur Berger, Alexei Haieff, John Lessard, Harold Shapero, Henri Sauguet, and Carlos Surinach. *Concerto for Harpsichord and Chamber Orchestra* by John Lessard received a less-than-ecstatic response:

> Any kind of unidiomatic writing and technical problems of any degree of difficulty are perfectly justified if they result in logical forms or satisfying flow or well-wrought sound, but the *Concerto* made Miss Marlowe sound as is she were only a bad pianist instead of a good harpsichordist. . . . The slow movements seemed labored, the fast ones uninspired.[24]

At the same concert an earlier solo work by Harold Shapero fared better:

> The tightly-wrought, logical and highly idiomatic Shapero *Sonata* restored our faith in Miss Marlowe's skill and in the inventiveness of modern composers for her instrument. It . . . was not just a performance to be admired, but an event which took one into a new world.[25]

Sylvia Marlowe with (left to right) composers Carlos Surinach, Virgil
Thomson, and Paul Des Marais. (Courtesy of The Harpsichord Music
Society, Sylvia Marlowe, founder.)

Sylvia Marlowe at her Pleyel harpsichord with (left to right) Arthur
Berger, Vittorio Rieti, and Ben Weber. (Courtesy of The Harpsichord
Music Society, Sylvia Marlowe, founder.)

The works of the expatriate Italian-American composer Vittorio Rieti figured prominently in Marlowe's repertoire. Among her commissions were Rieti's *Partita for Flute, Oboe, String Quartet and Harpsichord Obbligato* (1945), the three-movement solo *Sonata all' antica* (1946), and *Concerto for Harpsichord and Orchestra* (1955).[26] Ned Rorem also responded to a Marlowe commission. His chamber work *Lovers* (1964) was conceived as a "satellite" piece to the opera *Miss Julie*. A narrative in ten scenes with wonderfully suggestive titles—"Bridge of the Arts," "Before," "During," "After"—this lengthy composition for oboe, cello, percussion, and harpsichord featured a bravura movement, "The Bridge of Sighs," for the solo keyboard instrument.

In addition to works composed specifically for harpsichord by past or present composers, Marlowe was not averse to playing other keyboard music on her instrument, such as piano works of Stravinsky, Colin McPhee, Anton Webern, and Virgil Thomson. She recorded Thomson's *Sonata Four* and one of his *Portraits,* "Cantabile: Nicolas de Chatelain," for Decca and frequently played these works in recital. When queried about other compositions for harpsichord, Thomson replied, "I have never written for harpsichord. The *Sonata* that Marlowe has recorded is just a keyboard piece. . . . So are the *Piano Portraits*."[27]

By far the largest concentration of this cross-over repertoire was heard at a 1972 Carnegie Recital Hall program:

Harpsichordists Turn the Tables

Ever since its invention shortly after 1700, the piano has been stealing music originally composed for its smaller voiced ancestors, the harpsichord especially. Now, the tables are turning. Not content with reclaiming their own music, harpsichord players are busily appropriating piano music for their plucked instrument. Who knows where this may end? A Society to Save the Pianoforte may have to be formed to protect the great black beast from the increasingly bold predator.

Nevertheless, until the reversal goes too far, one can enjoy it. At Carnegie Recital Hall . . . Sylvia Marlowe and Kenneth Cooper played a program for one and two harpsichords that stole imaginatively from the piano repertory. Stravinsky's "Eight Easy Pieces" made the biggest hit with the sold-out house, the duo's two-manual instruments providing wonderfully deep resources of wit and sonority. Not at all surprisingly, when "Three Pieces in the Form of a Pear" [Satie] also made sense in a drily humorous two-harpsichord version. And several Bartók selections from "Ten Easy Pieces" and "Mikrokosmos," played with a watchmaker's precision and an ingratiating bounce by Mr. Cooper alone, sounded entirely idiomatic even while producing startling effects that could not be realized on a piano. Miss Marlowe offered a bit of solo Stravinsky, too, in the form of his *Scherzo* (1902), which had the right color and tone though not the rakishly assured performance required for this deceptively simple music.

The borrowings were not only poetically just, but musically apt. There is, after all, a strong streak of rebellion against the piano's romantic character in Stravinsky and Bartók, who often seem to regard the piano as an outsize harpsichord, generally treating it as a percussive, neutral-toned instrument whose latent emotionalism is rather vulgar. . . .[28]

Thomson's friendship with Marlowe spanned her entire career. In 1948, when she announced her forthcoming marriage to the artist Leonid Berman, Thomson said,

> "The harpsichord is a very jealous instrument. I don't see how you are going to manage to have a husband and a harpsichord." Fortunately I have a very nice husband, but the truth is that the harpsichord *is* a very demanding instrument and to pursue a career as a harpsichordist, you must be able to divorce yourself from a great many things in life that you might otherwise find very agreeable. . . .[29]

The circumstances surrounding Marlowe's first performances of the *Goldberg Variations* gave evidence of her priorities:

> Now this is a true story. . . . Last spring I was going to go to Europe with my husband. All of a sudden I decided I wanted to stay home and work on this. In order to learn it, one must have days like empty canvases. One must have peace and quiet. The Goldbergs aren't something you can sandwich in between other things.[30]

Thomson, again, on Marlowe: "[She is] not quite [in] complete control of her own powerful temperament. That temperament is mercurial, and her exhilarating mind forms one with it. When she gets bored by a piece, as she sometimes does right in the middle of it, all her brilliance and surety leaves her; and the execution falls, for all its taste and learning, straight to earth."[31] Marlowe's former student Kenneth Cooper suggested that it was not so much a question of temperament as a life-long problem of acute stage fright. Whatever the cause, reviews tended to be less complimentary and more critical as Marlowe neared the end of her long performing career. Technical standards were higher and critics expected more from players as the harpsichord became less of a rare breed and more of a mainstream instrument. Harold Schonberg remarked about a Rieti birthday concert in January 1973: "The performances . . . were invariably musical and expert. Miss Marlowe may have had a few momentary lapses—she always does—but her knowledge of the style is beyond dispute, and when she got fired up she offered some brilliant playing."[32]

A further deterioration of Marlowe's abilities was noted by John Rockwell, who reviewed her last public performance of the *Goldberg Variations:*

> But at this stage of her career, Miss Marlowe simply can't play the music well enough to give real pleasure. In some of the simpler variations, or even for bars on end in the flashier ones, she would play along smoothly enough. But then a run would go awry or she would break down for a brief but agonizing moment, peer intently at the music and forge on. And one couldn't help but wonder if some of the slowish tempos had been chosen to accommodate her.[33]

Marlowe's legacy, and her finest performances, are largely to be found on her almost five dozen sides of 78-rpm records and her thirty-nine long-playing discs.[34]

The repertoire ranges from Douglas Moore's *The Old Grey Mare* and part of Chopin's *Polonaise* in A-flat on a children's record, *Said the Piano to the Harpsichord*, to major portions of the oeuvres of Couperin, Purcell, and Bach (including two recordings of the *Goldberg Variations*), and, as one would expect, a generous sampling of the new works Marlowe commissioned. Her years of teaching live on through her students who have achieved professional careers, among them Kenneth Cooper and Gerald Ranck of New York, Doris Ornstein of Cleveland, Shirley Matthews of Maine and Baltimore, and Hendrik Broekman, now of Hubbard Harpsichords.

Nearly twenty years before her death Marlowe wrote,

> In short, the harpsichord world, until recently inhabited by a small group of intense scholars, aesthetes, performers and snobs, has now been taken over by the broad music public. Tired of the constant repetition of the nineteenth-century masterworks, this public looks back to early music for the discovery of buried works of genius and forward to the creation of the new repertoire. The harpsichord, no longer considered an archaic ancestor of the piano, has taken its rightful place as a great contemporary instrument beautiful to see and hear, and with the richest literature of them all. The end of the twentieth century may well be remembered as another "Age of the Harpsichord."[35]

Sylvia Marlowe had quite a lot to do with ensuring that the Age of the Harpsichord happened.

CHAPTER
10

A GOLDEN AGE
Landowska Returns

"Landowska's return to the United States was unforgettably signalized by her recital in Town Hall, New York, on 21 February 1942, when she played the Bach *Goldberg Variations* before one of the most distinguished audiences ever assembled there," wrote Robert Sabin in 1959.[1] But Virgil Thomson was the commentator who best captured the significance of this historic return. His extraordinarily perceptive review remains a classic of music criticism:

Rhythmic Grandeurs

Wanda Landowska's return to us after a fourteen-year interval was celebrated yesterday afternoon at the Town Hall in a ceremony both imposing and heart-warming. She played Bach's thirty "Goldberg Variations" to a full house that was virtually a social register of professional musicians; and she received a welcome and a final ovation from the distinguished assembly that were tribute equally to her penetrating musicianship and to her powers of virtuoso execution on that most exacting of all keyboard instruments, the harpsichord.

I am not going to review the "Goldberg Variations," which are one of the monuments of musical art, except to note that, as Madame Landowska played them, there were no dull moments, though the concert lasted little less than two hours. I should like rather to cast an analytic eye on the work of this extraordinary performer, whose execution, no matter what she plays, is one of the richest and grandest experiences available to lovers of the tonal art. That she should play for two hours without striking a false note is admirable, of course; that she should play thirty pieces varying greatly in volume without ever allowing us to hear any thumping down of the keys proves a mastery of the harpsichord that is, to my knowledge, unique. That she should phrase and register the "Goldberg Variations" with such clarity and freedom that they all sound like new pieces is evidence of some quality at work besides mere musicianship, though the musicianship does run high in this case.

A performance so complete, so wholly integrated, so prepared, is rarely to be encountered. Most artists, by the time they have worked out that much detail, are heartily sick of any piece and either walk through it half asleep or ham it up. It is part of the harpsichord's curious power that the more one is meticulous and finicky about detail, the livelier the whole effect becomes.

All musicianly and expert qualities are observable at their highest in Madame Landowska's harpsichord-playing. But so are they in the work of many another virtuoso. Her especial and unique grandeur is her rhythm. It is modern quantitative scansion at its purest. Benny Goodman himself can do no better. And it is Bach's rhythm, as that must have been. Writing constantly for instruments of no tonic accent, like the harpsichord and the organ, all Bach's music is made up out of length values. If you want to realize how difficult it is to express a clear rhythm without the aid of tonic stresses, or down-beats, just try it on an electric buzzer. And if you want to realize what elaborate rhythmic complications the eighteenth-century performers did manage to make clear . . . on accentless instruments, just take a look at Bach's music for organ and that for harpsichord, particularly the "Goldberg Variations."

. . . (Highly dramatic accents can be obtained with no added force . . . by delaying ever so slightly the attack on the note it is desired to accent. Also, expressive liberties of rhythm only take on their full expression as liberties when they are liberties taken upon some previously established rhythmic exactitude.)

Of all these matters Landowska is mistress. The pungency and high relief of her playing are the result of such a mastery's being placed at the service of a penetrating intelligence and a passionate Polish temperament. The final achievement is a musical experience that clarifies the past by revealing it to us through the present, through something we all take for granted nowadays, as Bach's century took it for granted, but that for a hundred and fifty years has been neglected, out of style, forgotten. That is the cultivation of rhythmic complexity by an elimination from musical thought of all dependence on rhythmic beat.[2]

Such command, such security, and such vitality, at such a time! Because of her Jewish ancestry Landowska and her companion Denise Restout had fled the oncoming Nazi invasion of France[3] and sought refuge in the south. At first, having left nearly everything at St. Leu, Landowska did not even have a harpsichord. This sad situation was rectified when "a student from Switzerland [Isabelle Nef] came to see Landowska at Banyuls-sur-Mer and was distressed to see her without an instrument. So she went back home and sold her life insurance to buy the last available Pleyel in Paris."[4] After eighteen months, Landowska and Restout made their way through Spain to Lisbon. They embarked for the United States, reaching New York harbor on 7 December 1941, an arrival somewhat overshadowed by that day's Japanese attack on Pearl Harbor.

We did look rather suspicious arriving in America with practically no luggage and one large harpsichord. That very day the government had rounded up all the Japanese people and had put them in confinement and we were placed on Ellis Island. We didn't know why we were there or why we were being held. At that time I did not speak one word of English. Not one word. Landowska spoke some English but not me. It was very confusing. Finally we were told that our passports were only good for three months. In order to let us in they had to be for more than that. . . .

Some friends of ours knew we were arriving and they finally discovered that we were being held on Ellis Island. The singer Doda Conrad, who was the son of a classmate of Landowska, went to every musician in New York and got letters from them for the authorities telling who Landowska was and why she should be permitted to enter the country. Finally we were released but we had to deposit a bond of $500 for each of us. That was $1,000 and we only had a total of $1300 to our names, so we arrived in the New World with a harpsichord and $300.[5]

Claude Jean Chiasson described his first meeting with the great harpsichordist:

> When Landowska arrived in this country as a refugee, with a harpsichord and a secretary, she arrived on Pearl Harbor Day, 1941. I had my Christmas programs at church [in] Cambridge and couldn't get away until after the programs were out of the way. I took the first train I could, on a Sunday I believe, after my services and went to New York to meet Landowska. She was in a little rundown New York hotel, the Hotel Langwell which was right off Times Square. It was a dismal building with holes in the carpet. We had a long talk about many things. We shared the same friends and loved the same composers. During the course of conversation I asked her if she needed any money. At this her eyes filled with tears and she lowered her head and said "If you only knew the people I considered friends who have not thought to ask that question. No thank you, I do not need money. Victor has taken care of me. Royalties from the recordings."[6]

Royalties came, at this time, only from earlier recordings. A three-year strike in the recording industry kept Landowska from resuming that part of her career until June 1945. The first project was the *Goldberg Variations,* issued on six twelve-inch records. At the conclusion of the extensive notes to this album appears this notice:

> [These records were made] in the New York studios of RCA Victor. Improved techniques for capturing the true tone of the harpsichord dictated the present recording; hence it is not to be confused with an earlier recording of the Goldberg Variations, made in France a number of years ago by Mme. Landowska and issued by "His Master's Voice" in a limited Bach Society edition, available through subscription only.

Anticipating a limited sale for such an "esoteric offering," Victor was caught off guard. Demand skyrocketed to eight times the original pressing. More than 30,000 copies were sold.[7] On 10 March 1947 Landowska attended a dinner at the Hotel Plaza to receive the *Review of Recorded Music* award for the outstanding instrumental recording of serious music issued during 1946.[8]

Meanwhile, in lieu of recordings, Landowska lived on the proceeds from concerts and private lessons. She had sufficient income to rent a summer house in Scarsdale. Back in the city a larger and more suitable apartment at the corner of 65th Street and Central Park West became Landowska's residence in the fall of 1942.

A glimpse into Landowska's teaching has been preserved in detailed notes about a lesson given to Mrs. Bert Thomas of Columbus, Ohio:

1946: 39 years old. After three telephone calls to the secretary a private lesson was set for February 26th at 6 p.m. I had scarcely time to get from the friends in Greenwich Village to Landowska's place, but I stopped by our Hotel to change from the heavy Oxfords which I had just purchased into lighter shoes and to remove the red from my fingernails, for she might have something against that.

. . . [Denise Restout] brought me into the studio, which was disappointing. It appeared as though they had just moved in although they had already been there for years: no curtains at the windows, not much furniture. It was an elegant dwelling from an earlier age: two large rooms made into one. It was an ideal space for the instruments: two Steinway pianos next to one another covered with cloths. The large Pleyel harpsichord stood near by, covered with two linen cloths and a cover. As I waited for ten minutes I became more and more nervous. Denise said, "I will see what is keeping her." A minute later she appeared.

I knew only her profile from photographs, so I was unprepared for this small serene person, not nearly so large as I, with a rather undistinguished face, keen dark eyes, round brown hornrimmed spectacles.

As she came toward me I didn't know what I should do, but she extended her hand in a reserved way. She wore a long dark velvet dress with lapels and cuffs faced in a tan velvet lace which appeared to be handmade. At the top it was open and she would always lap it over, but it would never stay. She could have used a zipper! Her hair was dark with a little white, very odd hair, parted in the middle, pulled severely to both sides, fastened together in the back. I forgot to observe her profile and don't know whether it is similar to the photos or not. She directed me to sit beside her at a long table, considered me for awhile, asked what I had for an instrument. A Challis concert instrument was in her studio for some days on its way to Boston for one of her students. She said that Challis wanted to know what she thought about the instrument. I found it pleasing, for it had a very beautiful sound, but I can't say anything about her instrument.

She questioned: "What brought you to the harpsichord?" "Playing the recorder." She wanted to know what we had played and the editions, but I couldn't tell her. "Did I play the piano also?" "Yes, I practice almost everything at the piano and I wondered if my lesson was to be at the piano." She opened the harpsichord and said that I could play what I liked. Then she said, "Show me your hands." "How can you play with such long fingernails?" They were not really so long. But the whites of her nails were completely gone and I was happy that the red polish was off mine. "Wouldn't you like to get them right? But you will also need to use water. I have two kinds: one for me, and one for my hands. Take your time and go into the bathroom." I went and she asked me if I had scissors. During this time she played Bach on the piano very beautifully. She had a collection of nailfiles on the harpsichord. Then I had to remove my jacket and take off my wristwatch. "Now play something." I played Couperin's first *Prelude* quite well and she said, "You are very musical; very musical; please play something else, but relax; don't be so nervous. You can see that I am a relaxed person. I love my students as if they were my children; so, play." A *Sarabande* of a *French Suite*. She said, "You have a feel for this music, perhaps from the recorder playing, but you know nothing about how it should be played. You can't learn it in a short time as if you were to jump from the street to the tip of the Empire State Building! Play something else." I had not brought anything else with me, but I knew an *English Suite*. Denise was asked to bring the music. It was a totally different edition than that to which I was accustomed. Landowska recommended the Steingräber Edition as the best.

Here she got down to brass tacks. I played and then she played in the usual teacher-student relationship. She advocated especially the importance of writing in fingering and that one must find a way to play a complete legato without gaps. The ends she went to were most extraordinary. I was so taken with her perfect legato that I looked at her score for a moment and she said, "Look at my hands and not at the music." I cannot describe how unusual her hands were. No fatty tissue at all between the joints, and the fingers agile and totally independent with a wide reach. Once she played a note with both thumbs so that one thumb could hold the key while the other played on. I could not grasp this fingering at once until she had played it for me several times.

Then she showed me something that she said was very private: music which she had edited and music which all her students had to play to learn fingering and phrasing with all notes fingered. I asked her why she had not published it. "No time." "You know that my *Goldberg Variations* were sold out in fifteen days and the record company wants me to make a hundred more recordings! It will bring me to my grave!" As she clarified various details of the music she said often "Very few people know that; only my students play so." She said, "Kirkpatrick's edition of the *Goldbergs* is not really good. He is one of my students, as you know."

I had noticed from recordings that her ornamentation was never fast and she said "The ornamentation is always a part of the melody. The appoggiatura is the most important ornament; the trill is an endless appoggiatura; in Bach the dissonance, the impassioned conflict, which is always followed by the glorious resolution." This she explained with many gestures.

I played further and she explained much and always asked, "Do you understand?" especially for every note of the *Sarabande* from the *English Suite*. As I had begun, she questioned, "But tell me, why do you always play sarabandes? Do you like them so much?" I answered her that I found the legato so particularly difficult in them, and she said, "Yes, they are the most difficult to play." At one point she told me that Denise had come with her to be her secretary and I said, "That is very nice for you." "Oh, it's very nice for *her;* she is very happy to be with me."

After finishing the *Sarabande* I asked her about ornamentation in the *Bourrée* and *Gigue* and she explained it to me.

As I prepared to leave Denise came in and Landowska said to her, "She understands; she is talented." [There followed compliments that Mrs. Thomas looked so young and jokes about the atomic work in which her husband was engaged.] She said, "You are serious about this music; everything is learned a little at a time. It requires hard work, but it is wonderful." (She said that several times.) "I often work until 2 a.m." She instructed me a second time to arrange the ending of the *Goldbergs* for recorder. She told me about her student who had written a very good article about ornamentation in the *Harvard Dictionary* [Putnam Aldrich].

Lessons were to be arranged after a preceding letter. But my first letter had never been answered! Landowska headed toward her own room and said twice, "God bless you" and threw me a kiss with a gesture of her head.

Denise told me the story of how the harpsichord had come to the U.S.

The lesson lasted seventy minutes, and some had told me that it would last only thirty. She was an inspiring woman, in contrast to what many had predicted to me.[9]

Teaching, concerts; concerts, critics. During the 1940s, the Indian summer of her long career, Landowska continued to be idolized by both press and public.

> Wanda Landowska's harpsichord recital of last evening at the Town Hall was as stimulating as a needle shower.
> . . . She played everything better than anybody else ever does. One might almost say, were not such a comparison foolish, that she plays the harpsichord better than anybody else ever plays anything. That is to say that the way she makes music is so deeply satisfactory that one has the feeling of a fruition, of a completeness at once intellectual and sensuously auditory beyond which it is difficult to imagine anything further.[10]
> Wanda Landowska's playing of the harpsichord at Town Hall last night reminded one all over again that there is nothing else in the world like it. There does not exist in the world today, nor has there existed in my lifetime, another soloist of this or of any other instrument whose work is so dependable, so authoritative, and so thoroughly satisfactory. From all the points of view—historical knowledge, style, taste, understanding, and spontaneous musicality—her renderings of harpsichord repertory are, for our epoch, definitive. Criticism is unavailing against them, has been so, indeed, for thirty years.[11]

In 1947 Landowska rented the house in Lakeville, Connecticut that was to be her final home and working place. At first it was used as a summer retreat; but after 1950, when she gave up the Central Park West apartment, it became *the* residence. The charm of this situation for Landowska the nature lover lay in the surroundings:

> [The house] was a large wooden structure painted a mustard yellow which appeared to have seen a number of years of weather. To the rear and left side of the house, large trees grew closely together and cast dark shadows over the building. A large porch covered the front of the building and overlooked an opening in the woods. In the center of this opening stood one of the strangest and most hauntingly beautiful oak trees I have ever seen. It looked as if it were several hundred years old and was anchored in the earth so securely it could stand for several more centuries. The massive trunk was black and gnarled with age. At a height of about fifteen feet, the trunk separated into a dozen or more huge limbs, each the size of a telephone pole, which writhed and twisted about in a very tortured manner.[12]

A reunion with her maid of many years further brightened Landowska's personal life:

> Admitted by . . . Miss Denise, the group [of interviewer, researcher, and photographer] was taken to a small bedroom, for Madame was not yet ready.
> At this point they were introduced to Miss Elsa [Schunicke], who was beaming

Wanda Landowska at her Pleyel harpsichord.

and plump. She, it appeared, had been with Mme. Landowska for more than thirty-five years. . . . Miss Elsa, a personal factotum, was ecstatic. The weekend before she had just arrived in this country, having been separated from her mistress for seven long war years.

Suddenly Miss Elsa announced that Madame was ready. She was introduced in the large living room, where stood the harpsichord. . . . She spoke in a soft voice, in clear, French-accented English. A woman of positive opinions, she objected to one picture angle as unflattering, but agreed to it in exchange for one of her own choice. All the while she played vigorously at the harpsichord.

When the pictures were taken, she insisted on literally taking down her hair, to prove, she explained, that it was all hers. Then she ordered benedictine, and when the photographer pleaded that he had to leave to snap a certain well-known multimillionaire, she said: "Tell him of my mission. He should give money to support it."

Asked if she had ever received any bad reviews, Mme. Landowska said she really didn't know, as she never read the critics. There were, however, several copies of *The New York Times*'s review of her new record album prominently placed around the apartment. By now, it was obvious that she was impatient about something and had retreated into some world of her own. When the drinks were brought in, the impatience was explained: she wanted to practice—and she did, placing a large screen between her and her guests.

Over the benedictine in another corner, Miss Denise and Miss Elsa cleared up several points. No, contrary to some stories, Madame does not play in heavy socks. For greater flexibility in handling the seven pedals on her harpsichord, she wears ballet-like soft slippers, which Miss Elsa makes to match her flowing velvet robes.

Yes, Miss Denise said, Madame works constantly, and especially late at night— which is why the country place in Connecticut is good for her. There she can also walk as much as she likes to. No, she is never nervous over a performance, and yes, she is in excellent health, and eats a diet of broiled meat, vegetables, and fruits.

And, yes, everybody in the household can tune harpsichords.[13]

The popular news magazines were paying an unprecedented attention to the harpsichord. Of course the fact that its high priestess, Landowska, was extraordinarily good copy did not hurt at all. Amid the general acclaim it was refreshing to find an occasional dissenting voice. The thoughtful criticisms of writer-composer Robert Evett foreshadowed a coming aesthetic change, a retreat from the impressionistic, color-filled style of playing that Landowska had championed throughout her long career:

The Romantic Bach

Gertrude Stein says that "it is hard to kill a century almost impossible." She saw the Nineteenth Century dying hard ten years ago [1942], but its thinking is still with us; the apparent indestructibility of Romantic thought lends itself to a rather gratifying comparison with the survival of the Baroque, that exotic product of the Seventeenth Century which reached its fullest musical expression only after it had become *passé*.

. . . In the Romantic view, Bach was a Titan, a self-consciously grand figure, concerned with profundities and, unfortunately, hamstrung by an over fussy style. The idea that a great composer could be capable of an almost kittenish levity is incompatible with Romantic sentiments; because of this, the Romantics tended to apologize for Bach's charm, and to exaggerate that seriousness which is certainly to be found here. . . . Tampering with Bach was a respectable occupation in the 1840s, and it has not yet gone into complete disrepute.

Modern intellectuals, who seem to have a need for Baroque order, have become very leery of the padded Bach; they seem to prefer something approximating the original form, but in this regard they have shown a gullibility which is, at the least, startling. They assume that anyone who advertises himself as a purist is just that, and that anyone who plays the harpsichord is offering them Baroque music in its original form.

In the playing of the harpsichord, Mme. Wanda Landowska has accomplished a feat which should have warmed the cockles of P. T. Barnum's black heart. Mme. Landowska has seduced the brighter part of the American public into believing that she offers it an authentic reading of Bach and his predecessors. What this lady actually uses is a modern Pleyel harpsichord, an instrument that she employs as a sort of dispose-all. The great virtue of this contraption is that it can produce a dozen coloristic effects that were unknown in the Baroque era; its special vice—though, actually, the vice is in the player rather than in the instrument—is in a complicated set of pedals by which the pitch can be altered an octave or more at will. There is no reason that Landowska could not play well on this instrument if she wanted to; like the organ, a modern harpsichord is an agent of taste, and an infallible testing ground for taste. Unfortunately, Landowska, like so many of her contemporaries, uses it as an instrument for producing mud pies. After fifteen years of incredulous listening, I am finally convinced that this woman kicks all the pedals in sight when she senses danger ahead. When she sits down to play a Bach fugue, I go through all the torments that a passenger experiences when he is being driven over a treacherous mountain road by an erratic driver, and when she finally finishes the thing it is almost a pleasure to relax into nausea.

Landowska's furious pedalling seems to be directed more and more towards a lever that controls the sixteen-foot stop. This device, which was virtually unknown on ancient harpsichords, produces an almost unintelligible roar, an octave below the written note, so that clarity yields to an ungodly jangle. More than anyone else, Mme. Landowska is responsible for the current view that, to be authentic, old music must sound bad.[14]

Another observer who was not totally submerged by Landowska's mystique was Halina Rodzinski, wife of the conductor Artur Rodzinski:

Mme. Landowska was to play Mozart and Haydn Concertos [with the New York Philharmonic], and, according to Artur's inflexible rule, the two were to have a work session alone before the orchestral rehearsal. The rule was bent slightly, however; the work would be done at Mme. Landowska's apartment on Central Park West. I went along, partly from curiosity, partly as a courtesy. Ultimately, it was for laughs.

Mme. Landowska was a creation. When Artur and I arrived, the door was opened by one of the musician's two live-in assistants. We were led by her into a music room suggestive of a Pleyel showroom or funeral parlor. It was stuffed with the black, coffinlike cases of several harpsichords, and a piano. Soon the other assistant came to greet us, then the two assistants opened the door for "Mamusia" (Little Mother), as they called her, who made an entrance almost as spectacular as Paderewski's so long before at his Swiss residence. Mme. Landowska stood, effectively backlit, in the doorway, transfixed like some gorgeous, huge, wine-red butterfly, its velvet wings lightly shedding dust motes. It was a shock when she actually moved forward to greet us, quite effusively, I should add, and extended a hand for Artur to kiss.

After a short discussion about the Mozart specifics, Mme. Landowska moved toward her piano to play for Artur. Her assistants preceded like acolytes, to open the piano case and keyboard with great ceremony, place her music on the rack, then drape on the floor the folds of her dress. Raising her handsome head, its raven hair parted down the middle to a knot at the nape of her neck, she stared into space. Then her long graceful hands darted out of her cavernous sleeves to play the Mozart. From time to time she abruptly stopped to explain how or why she executed a certain passage, then continued her reading, which, if taped, could have been spliced into consecutive sense, so thoroughly did she pick up a dynamic level or an ictus.

When she moved to a harpsichord for the Haydn Concerto, the same little procession and ritual ensued. I was fascinated by the show of it all, without which she could never have brought the harpsichord and its literature into vogue again. People who entered the Landowska cult for a whimsy came away musically enriched. But her eccentricities were also a large part of the whole thing, though some of them were rather private. . . .

Her appearance on stage was electrifying: she glided on like a classic Roman matron. Her performance was a thing of great exquisiteness, and Artur strove to give her the cleanest, most sympathetic accompaniment he could; but unknown to him, he made a faux pas—awful, but not irreparable. After the orchestral tutti before the first movement cadenza in the Mozart, Artur rested his left hand on the piano case. Landowska rose up in an explosion of velvet and stood back as if bitten or stung. She walked over to Artur, lifted his hand from the lid, then executed the pyrotechnics. Later, Artur said he was so startled he almost forgot to cue the orchestra for the coda. But he accepted her peculiarities as the price of her artistry. And it was art that made her move his hand. "It affects the sound of the piano," she explained.[15]

Another aspect of Landowska's career was her championing of a few contemporary works:

Without trying to imitate the effects or procedure of older composers the king of instruments, resuscitated, will lend an attentive and benevolent ear to the nostalgic searching of modern composers, granting them the unexplored wealth of its sonorous possibilities. It will set ablaze the whole ensemble with its rhythmical flashes; it will pour out the flamboyant rustling of its radiant timbres. With its volatile double keyboards, now a mysterious organ, now a hyperbolic guitar, it will stir by its sharpness and enrapture the somewhat blasé body of the orchestra. Surrounding it with its quivering and scintillating sonorous web, and its slender although firm rays, the harpsichord will allow imagery and that which is whimsical or unexpected to escape from its swishing meshes.[16]

In *Concert Champêtre,* for harpsichord and orchestra, by French composer

Francis Poulenc listening to Wanda Landowska, St. Leu, summer 1928.
(Photograph by Momo Aldrich.)

Francis Poulenc, Landowska had such a twentieth-century work at her disposal. Poulenc had heard Landowska play the première of Falla's *Retablo* at the home of the Princesse de Polignac in Paris in 1923. Upon meeting him, Landowska said, "Write me a concerto." Eventually he did, working on the score from October 1927 until September 1928. Not satisfied with the writing for harpsichord, Landowska went over each note in the score with the young composer. Poulenc recalled, "We did not change a measure or a melodic line, but the keyboard writing and the choice of instruments for the orchestra were the chief aims of our most extensive research. Above all, we clarified the writing, either by condensing chords or by suppressing notes. . . ."[17]

When Landowska performed this elegant and beautiful work for the last times on 17, 19, and 20 November 1949 at Carnegie Hall, Leopold Stokowski, her old friend and champion, conducted the New York Philharmonic. This first American concert presentation of the work with harpsichord has been preserved on records.[18] The performance presents an incredibly youthful-sounding soloist reveling in Poulenc's youthful music. "Will my audience forgive this explosion of dionysiac joy, this flaming torrent. Evidently this is no longer expected of a lady of seventy. But I can't help it," wrote Landowska in her diary.[19]

There are lamentable lapses in the orchestral playing, but the sheer magic of Landowska's performance comes through and makes all subsequent recordings sound stodgy. On receiving a copy of the recording, the composer wrote to Landowska,

How can I tell you my emotion at hearing my goddess play the *Champêtre?* What joy you gave me! I suddenly felt rejuvenated, happy. The cherries from your garden at Saint-Leu were in my mouth. I confess to stealing some in those days, long ago, when I was but a student musician. Now that I wonder every day if my music will live, you have given me the illusion that it will. For this, thank you from the bottom of my heart.[20]

Joy had been a theme of Landowska's concerts in 1949:

During the course of her recital [Town Hall, 23 February] Mme. Landowska told her listeners that she had been working all winter at her Connecticut home "to make you happy." She succeeded, to the extent of her fondest hopes. The capacity audience heard her play Couperin's Passacaille; Handel's Suite in G minor; Haydn's Piano Sonata in E-flat Major, opus 66, the only piano work on the program; and Rameau's Suite in E minor; demanded a generous group of encores; and then recalled her a half dozen times to express its gratitude for a musical revelation of the loftiest kind. A lifetime of devotion, labor and concentration have brought to her a complete control of every aspect of musical interpretation. Le Rappel des Oiseaux, from the Rameau suite, was incredibly deft and fluid; the tone and phrasing of the Haydn piano sonata rivalled the human voice or the violin in their plasticity; and the Handel suite was performed with towering majesty.

Mme. Landowska always plans her programs carefully as to key relationships, changes of mood and variety of style. This one represented a progress from darkness to light, from tragic solemnity to pastoral gaiety. She used appropriately sober registration for the Couperin passacaglia and the Handel suite, achieving a remarkable variety of emphasis in the Couperin work, despite its reiterative theme and design. In the Handel music her matchless comprehension of eighteenth-century style was exemplified in her embellishments. Not only was the music enriched by ornaments, but she added a beautiful variant in the Sarabande, in the manner of the period. Again, in the Haydn sonata, the cadenzas and entrances were improvised with the most exquisite taste. By using a piano technique analogous to harpsichord technique in its meticulous clarity, quantitative rhythm, and finger legato, Mme. Landowska succeeds in making the modern instrument sound like its ancestor of Haydn's day. Those who heard Ralph Kirkpatrick play a reproduction of an eighteenth-century piano at the New York Public Library benefit concert earlier this season must have been struck by the similarity of effect between that instrument and Mme. Landowska's modern grand.

The richest colors of harpsichord registration were employed in the Rameau suite, especially in the Rigaudons, Musette en Rondeau, and La Villageoise. This music actually drugs the senses with its hypnotic rhythmic drone and melodic sweetness. Among the encores were the Purcell Ground in C minor and Mme. Landowska's own Bourrée d'Auvergne.[21]

As summation of a brilliant career, Landowska began her most ambitious recording project slightly before the major Bach anniversary year of 1950. In its inimitable way, *Time* magazine described the goings-on:

Grandma Bachante

Each Saturday and Sunday for the past three months, a little procession has arrived punctually at 6:30 p.m. at RCA Victor's midtown Manhattan recording studios. The routine never varies. The youngest, Mlle. Denise Restout, goes straight to the harpsichord, yanks open her tool kit, and starts tuning. The huskiest, Mlle. Elsa Schunicke, carries the pillows and the hamper, loaded with sandwiches, a vacuum jug of coffee, and a supply of specially blended horehound drops. Then, her hands folded before her, and her craggy features blissfully composed, Mme. Wanda Landowska herself floats in like a tiny wraith, nods her greetings and disappears into the dressing room.

Last week, comfortable in blue knee-length socks, red fur-trimmed bedroom slippers and a loose-fitting smock, the great harpsichordist was finishing up the first sixth of a monumental recording task begun in her seventieth year. In the darkened studio, her eyes closed, she began to play the great *Prelude and Fugue No. 3 in C-Sharp* of Johann Sebastian Bach. Before the weekend was over, she had also played the rippling *No. 6 in D minor* and the fugue of *No. 7 in E-flat* to complete the first eight of the 48 brain- and finger-cracking preludes and fugues—two in each of the 24 keys—that constitute the musician's bible and byword: Bach's great *Wohltemperirtes Clavier (Well-Tempered Clavier)*.

Perfection. To Landowska, "this is my last will and testament. I have to make it perfect." She was taking plenty of time to make it that way—to make sure that exactly the balance and quality she wanted to hear would come off the wax. In her weekly sessions, she had worked 42 hours, making retake after retake, to record 45 minutes of music. At seventy . . . the somewhat mystic, sometimes earthy little Polish-born woman is the acknowledged high priestess of the harpsichord, the sweet-sounding, twangy-bangy instrument she rescued from oblivion fifty years ago. She did not need much preparation before sitting down to record.

She had been playing Bach on the harpsichord in public for forty-six years: the great Hungarian conductor, Arthur Nikisch (1855–1922) had long ago punningly tagged her "The Bachante." And she had performed all of Book I of the *Well-Tempered Clavier* last year in a series of Town Hall recitals to which her worshipful disciples—musicians, students and teachers alike—had flocked, music in hand. Some were occasionally surprised at her interpretations; Bach himself gave a few hints of exactly how fast and how loud his music should be played. But few had failed to be impressed with her magnificent authority—and delighted with her puckish platform informality. (Between numbers, she chats confidentially with her audience: "I have worked so hard to make this pleasure for you.")

Pep. Although she is as spry and sparkling-eyed as ever ("I feel as young as a child"), Landowska has given up touring.

. . . Although she seldom goes out, she keeps up with the music and art worlds, mainly by voluminous reading. Listening to a playback after a recent recording session, Landowska cracked to a studio technician: "Sounds like old Grandma Moses here still has pep."[22]

The scene of Landowska's recording efforts moved to Lakeville shortly after this.

For the past few years she has been living in a large, old house on a hill not far from

Lakeville, Conn. . . . the wood-paneled living room has been transformed into a recording studio, and the library is used as a control room. . . . On this secluded Connecticut hillside Mme. Landowska can play to her heart's content. She has been known to get out of bed at 3 a.m. and play into the dawn while her household slept.

Some years ago, not long after coming permanently to this country, she said, "Everything begins to blossom—pupils, concerts, friends. Life for me is beginning all over in America." Life is moving along serenely for her today, with music, particularly the treasured music of the past she has revivified, at its core.[23]

In 1952 *Time* chronicled the progress of Landowska's *WTC* in a full-page Personality sketch:

> The good citizens of quiet Lakeville, Connecticut, go to bed early—with one exception. But even the rare, late-homecoming villager is no longer surprised at the single globe of light shining from the ungainly green-and-yellow hilltop house which broods over the main street. He knows, along with those of his neighbors who have seen it, homeward bound from a church supper or Saturday-night movie, that Mme. Wanda Landowska is at her devotions: her altar, the harpsichord.
>
> Pint-sized (4 feet 8 inches) Mme. Landowska, 73, is unchallenged high priestess of the plunky, double-keyboard instrument for which Bach wrote, before the piano supplanted it in the eighteenth century. Under her dedicated leadership, the harpsichord is having something of a revival, and her recording of Bach's *Well-Tempered Clavier* is already a modern classic. Next week RCA Victor will release its fifth album, leaving her one album still to do.
>
> . . . [After several hours at the harpsichord] ("I never practice, I always play"), Mme. Landowska takes an hour's walk around the countryside. Neither rain nor snow stops her from venturing outdoors among the Berkshire foothills she has loved since first she came in the summer of 1947.
>
> In cold weather, cocooned in several layers of shawls and scarves, and wrapped in a huge old overcoat, she sallies forth. Her hands nest mandarin-style in the large sleeves. Each day's walk ends the same way—with a visit to her last "sweetheart," an 80-year-old carpenter of Lakeville. "I spend my relaxation ration with him. We understand each other—we are both craftsmen: he loves his carpentry as I love my music. Our conversation is very condensed." With a birdlike flutter of her thin-boned hands, Landowska adds: "But his niece—she is too bourgeoise. She does not understand why I am there every day. She is shocked, even now."[24]

Then, in 1955:

> "Now I have learned the key to the mystery. I must be concentrated about my work. This is why I came here to this house. I have to meditate about each note. Before I put a single sound on a record, I have to think a long, long time. . . .
>
> "All my remaining time must go to my work. If I have the wish to see other people, *they* will come to me."
>
> There is no arguing with this logic. RCA officials shrugged their shoulders and sent a crew of engineers to Lakeville with instructions to turn part of the house into a recording studio. They soundproofed the walls, ripped up flooring and installed

expensive recording equipment. Mme. Landowska, biting her lip fiercely, insisted that all the alterations conform with her decorative scheme; she ordered the engineers about as if they had been a team of moving men.

None of them complained. Though, on occasion, Wanda Landowska enjoys playing the prima donna to the hilt, no one who comes in contact with her can be annoyed with her for long. . . . Once, an engineer, impressed with her talent for comedy, asked her why she didn't go on television. With all the hauteur that her years could muster, she answered: "Television cannot afford me."[25]

But television lured her once, in 1953. For NBC's Wisdom series Landowska gave a filmed interview with her recording engineer, John Pfeiffer.[26] In this unique document she played several of the works with which she was most identified: the second and third movements of the Vivaldi D-major *Concerto* as arranged for harpsichord by J. S. Bach; a dance, she said, much loved by Tolstoy—the *Bransle de Montirande* by Antoine Francisque; and the first movement of the *Italian Concerto* of Bach. She also introduced a vast audience to "my child, the harpsichord," which she described as an organ-like instrument. And she spoke about the great struggle of her life, the effort required to bring the ancient instrument back into the concert life of the twentieth century: "[Today] everywhere you can find a harpsichord-player. . . . They sprout like mushrooms. . . . They didn't even know how hard the struggle was. Now everything is ready, victory is won, the table is laid. They only have to sit down and play—badly, perhaps—but anyway, they play!"[27]

Landowska's highly regarded series of recitals at the Frick Collection in New York, which were broadcast by radio station WNYC, came to an end in 1954. William Buckley, Jr., recounts this anecdote:

A friend was present at the Frick Collection at what proved to be the last public performance of Landowska. She was playing an obscure [work] by Fischer . . . which my friend happened to have been studying. So that he knew it when what was being played suddenly ceased to be Fischer, becoming Landowska, improvising. My friend was concerned. What was she up to? memory lapse? But, the work being largely unknown, the audience did not react, and in due course she was back, playing what Fischer wrote.

Next on the program was the famous "Chromatic Fantasy and Fugue." As was her habit, Landowska bowed her head slightly before beginning, bringing her hands— extended—to her lips, as if in prayer. Then the right hand was raised dramatically, as if to strike a hammer blow. Suddenly she stopped, wheeling thoughtfully about to address her audience in her heavily accented, high-pitched voice.

"Ladies and gentlemen, lahst night I had a visitor. It was Poppa Bach. We spoke, of corrse in Cherrman. He said to me, 'Vanda, haff you ever trried *my* fingerring on the "Chromatic Fantasy"?' 'No,' I said to him, and he said the next time I *must trry,* So tonight, I will use a different fingerring and maybe the result will not be the same azz my *incomparable* recorrding."

Wheel back to the instrument. Hands pressed together, raised to the lips. Right hand up.

Wanda Landowska in 1953. (Photograph by Helen Merrill.)

And then the "Fantasy." Landowska, having experienced the difficulty with Fischer, evidently did not know whether her memory, suddenly insecure, would sustain her through the "Fantasy" which, unlike the [earlier piece], is as familiar to Baroque-minded audiences as "Twinkle, Twinkle Little Star," precluding surreptitious inprovisation.

No dramatist, given a full year's notice, could have written lines more disarming than those she extemporized. And, of course, no one, in her presence, would profess skepticism about her personal familiarity with Poppa Bach.[28]

The completed *Well-Tempered Clavier* appeared in 1954, with RCA Victor issuing the last of the six long-playing discs late in the year. To mark Landowska's seventy-sixth birthday on 5 July 1955, the entire set was made available in a limited edition of 1,000 copies, covered in black moire and signed by the artist in her customary purple ink.[29]

"In addition to intellectual integrity and instrumental mastery, Landowska possesses a magical individuality and expressiveness," wrote pianist and critic Abram Chasins. "Even when an interpretation or a tempo is at drastic variance with one's preconceived ideas, her intentions are so clear, and the force of her personality so overwhelming that one is ready to grant her conception, or more usually, to succumb." But he does not succumb to her written commentaries on the pieces: "However, if Landowska wrote as perfectly as she played, the gods might become jealous and seek to destroy her."[30]

It is difficult to overestimate the importance of these late Landowska recordings; they are the performances by which an entire generation of music lovers discovered the harpsichord. Aided by a craze for buying examples of the new technology, the black vinyl long-playing discs sold by the thousands. The *WTC* was followed by successive recorded triumphs: "Landowska Plays for Paderewski," in which she programmed Polish works to honor the centenary of her great countryman— including such bewitching music as her own compositions *The Hop* and *Bourrée d'Auvergne:* Chopin's *Mazurka*, opus 56, number 2 (a fitting retort to all the years of pianistic Baroque?); and French works in the Polish style by Couperin and Rameau.[31] In an autumnal return to her other love, Landowska played Mozart works on the piano. A Haydn program was divided between piano and harpsichord. Then came "The Art of the Harpsichord," in which she played the Fischer *Passacaglia* in D minor and a variety of works by Bach: *Capriccio on the Departure of His Beloved Brother, Partita* No. 2 in C minor, and the brilliant *Fantasia* in C minor, BWV 906. Her last record, also music by Bach, contained the *Two-Part Inventions* and seven of the three-part *Sinfonias*. On 25 July 1959, the last time she sat at her harpsichord, Landowska was preparing the *Sinfonia* in E major for her next recording session.

This session was not to occur: on 16 August Landowska suffered a stroke and died. Her ashes are buried near St. Leu. In a garden at Taverny, a place associated with François Couperin, who had composed a *Musète de Taverni*, Restout's father "designed the grave [with] a bench where one may rest, meditate, and enjoy the beautiful view."[32]

What of her legacy? Landowska taught a number of students in her later years. Among the most brilliant who carried on the Landowska tradition was Rafael Puyana (born 1931) of Colombia. His first exposure to harpsichord was at New England Conservatory, which he entered in 1949. He had been allowed to look at the Dolmetsch-Chickering instrument at the school, but the first harpsichord which he could actually *touch* was the "bad Kirckman copy" at the home of one of his teachers, Margaret Mason. (She had purchased it from Claude Jean Chiasson.) Puyana studied with Landowska from 1951 until 1957, the year of his Town Hall debut. His American tours, accomplished in style with a large Buick station wagon, driver, and Pleyel instrument, delivered harpsichord music to localities large and small. Played with South American fire and musical brilliance, Puyana's concerts were long remembered by those who attended.[33]

Marie Zorn was already a professor of piano at Indiana University when she went to play Bach for Landowska in 1956. Zorn remained for two years, returning to Indiana to teach on her Pleyels until 1976.[34] Other Landowska students were Irma Rogell, Paul Wolf, and, of course, Denise Restout, the inheritor of Landowska's Lakeville home, who continued to teach there at her Landowska Center.

Other expatriates from Europe helped to spread the gospel of early music played on a suitable keyboard instrument. Ernst Victor Wolff (1889–1960) recorded the Bach *Saint Matthew Passion* with Koussevitzky in Boston; Erwin Bodky (1896–1958) founded the Cambridge Collegium Musicum, now the Cambridge Society for Early Music, which perpetuates his name by sponsoring the prestigious Bodky International Competition for young performers; and Edith Weiss-Mann (1885–1951), from Hamburg, who had been influenced by Landowska in the early years of the century in Berlin, and who played the first complete cycle of the harpsichord concertos of J. S. Bach in New York with conductor Otto Klemperer. These and others left the war-torn continent and found new lives and new careers in the United States. But it was Landowska, the artist who was most gifted, most recorded, most tenacious in her mission, who was able not only to capture the public's interest but, most remarkably, to hold it. What other name immediately evokes an image of the harpsichord?

Twenty years after Landowska's death, Joseph Hansen's mystery *Skinflick* was published. The central character, detective Dave Brandstetter, "pushed the power button. Harpsichord, Bach, Wanda Landowska. . . ."[35] In *Cornbury: The Queen's Governor,* a comedy by William M. Hoffman and Anthony Holland, the stage directions read: "We hear harpsichord music—Couperin—from another room. . . . Enter Africa, massaging her fingers like Wanda Landowska. . . .[36] In a cartoon in *Stereo Review* an audiophile speaks to his butler, "This toccata by Wanda Landowska sounds a wee fit fuzzy, Manchester. Try a little more spit on the stylus."[37] And so it continues. Landowska, as synonym for harpsichord, has triumphed with the general public.

For succeeding generations of players accustomed to instruments more closely patterned on Baroque models than was Landowska's Pleyel, and to interpretations more in keeping with the registrational possibilities inherent in the Baroque harpsichord, Landowska's colorful performances might seem anachronistic—more indicative, in many ways, of the impressionistic, turn-of-the-century aesthetic in which she matured. Despite volumes of polemics for her chosen instrument, neither Landowska herself nor any of her disciple-apologists has been able to equate, convincingly, the heavy, modern Pleyel harpsichord with any instrument known to a Baroque composer. True, a 16-foot register was to be found occasionally in the old instruments; yes, a registrational device such as a pedal or a knee-lever could be found; perhaps the wooden jacks in Landowska's Pleyel might be considered more authentic than the plastic used by some other contemporary builders. On the other hand the early harpsichord never had such a complicated mechanism; never was the sound produced by hard leather considered the normal harpsichord color—such are the arguments against her instrument.

But, apart from the type of harpsichord chosen as her medium, the deep musical instincts of Wanda Landowska rang true to the spirit of the bygone composers. The letter of the law might have been lacking, but the content was overwhelming. Generation after generation of grateful listeners respond to her astounding rhythmic vitality and her love for music. Her playing reaches across the years to stimulate and move, to cause a tapping of feet or a motion of the body as she inflects the infectious rhythm of a dance. The strength of this musical personality, an artist to be emulated not imitated, is with us still.

CHAPTER
11

THE PAST IS FUTURE

FRANK HUBBARD AND WILLIAM DOWD

Ten years before Landowska's death a new direction for the harpsichord revival was set by two young Harvard men—Frank Hubbard (1920–1976) and William Dowd (born 1922). Who could have known then that this short-lived partnership would alter the direction of early keyboard instruments both in the United States and in Europe, or that players and builders alike during the next two decades would be pulled "kicking and screaming, into the eighteenth century"?[1] The two men who accomplished this unprecedented maneuver had been English majors. How they came to set up a shop dedicated to the building of harpsichords in a historic manner and how they founded the first firm in the twentieth century to build classical harpsichords of various historic types is quite a story:

> [Frank Hubbard and I] were boyhood friends and were both in college together. Frank was two years ahead of me and graduated before the war, went into the army, then returned to get his Master's degree. I left, came back four years later and got my AB degree.
>   . . . We decided to make harpsichords when we were still in college. . . .
>   I had been in love with the harpsichord ever since I was a freshman [in 1940] and first saw one . . . in the music department. . . . It was built by Chickering. It was supposed to be in working order but it had fallen into disuse, between Ralph's [Kirkpatrick's] time there and mine. Actually a classmate . . . Daniel Pinkham . . . sprung the thing loose again. In those days, when harpsichords were rare, and no one knew what they were, an instrument could sit locked up in a room for years. Danny applied to the powers that be and brought the instrument back into use.
>   One of my teachers was Irving Fine, a brilliant young composer, and I asked him about it. He took me in and opened up the instrument. When I saw it for the first time it was so beautiful and marvelous it took my breath away. A little while later, I heard it in a concert at The Museum of Fine Arts, played by Claude Jean Chiasson.[2]

Hubbard, the graduate student, had a stall in Widener Library in the section then occupied by music books:

I found myself poring over the beautiful picture books devoted to musical instruments. Once I stumbled across a treasure: Heron-Allen's *Violin-Making, As It Was and Is* (1884). This young Victorian gentleman's curious evocation of the world and technique of violin makers . . . fascinated me, and I spent a whole summer making a violin after his instructions. Alas for romantic scholarship, I found his technical devices often deficient and that his varnish wouldn't dry, but the experience was meaningful for all that. The violin still hangs on its nail in a dark closet, a sort of instrument maker's family skeleton.

About this time [Bill Dowd's] passionate interest . . . in the harpsichord began dimly to indicate a path out of the intellectual maze in which I found myself wandering. Together we examined the books in Four West, attended the concerts of the only practicing harpsichordists in the area, Claude Jean Chiasson and Daniel Pinkham, and gradually concocted the grandiose project of reviving single-handed the whole baroque orchestra. I, it was decided, would deal with strings, Dowd with keyboards, and winds in some unspecified way would take care of themselves.

The only makers of such instruments we had ever heard of . . . were Arnold Dolmetsch in England and his disciple, John Challis, in Detroit. Since my G.I. Bill support was a bit more substantial than that of Dowd, it was decided that I would go to Dolmetsch, Dowd to Challis.[3]

Frank Hubbard was accepted by the Dolmetsch shop as a non-paying, non–paid apprentice. Although "the old man" had died seven years earlier the shop was going strong, making not only keyboard instruments but recorders and stringed instruments as well.

At Dolmetsch's I was permitted to drill identical holes in thousands of small objects, make tea at eleven each morning, and sweep. Occasionally, but not always, my questions were answered. Still by watching, if not doing, I learned something of woodworking and the sort of compulsiveness that makes a craftsman. Of the history of the harpsichord or the glorious examples still extant I learned nothing.[4]

After a year in Haslemere Hubbard parted ways with the Dolmetsch clan. He found a second year's work in London, with Hugh Gough, who "had seen many old instruments and had notebooks full of details I devoured."[5] He also made visits to the important instrument collections at the Victoria and Albert Museum and on the continent (Paris, Brussels, The Hague). Armed with a reader's card at the British Museum Hubbard began his research into period descriptions of harpsichords.

Dowd, in Detroit, "had a very successful year and a half. . . ."[6] His work consisted largely of making cases, some of walnut plywood, some of solid walnut, to surround aluminum frames. He also worked on actions, both new and those in need of repair. The most important of these repair jobs was the releathering for one of Kirkpatrick's Chickering harpsichords, an instrument the concert artist owned in addition to the harpsichord that had belonged to Busoni.[7] Dowd was impressed with Challis's "integrity as a craftsman. [The man] set . . . a standard of professionalism. In other words, the instrument *had* to give good service, it *had* to work well. If it didn't you had to do something about it. You just couldn't build an instrument and run off."[8]

Hubbard continued the saga:

> In November of 1949 Dowd and I rented an unheated loft in a ramshackle building on Tremont Street in Boston's South End. We managed to scrape together enough money to buy a circular saw, band saw, drill press, two benches, and a surplus army coal stove wich devoured endless quantities of fuel without producing any noticeable heat. Cold winter mornings we huddled around that stove until eleven before we could find courage to venture into the corners of the room. Even so, we did manage to lay down four harpsichords which were epoch making in the simple fact that we were attempting to follow old models. Subsequent opportunities to examine the interior construction of old harpsichords have indicated how far we inadvertently departed from ancient practice, but at least we had been the first to set foot on the new path. That our philosophy of harpsichord making filled a need sensed by many musicians is indicated by the fact that all four were sold before they were finished.[9]

Of these first harpsichords based on a 1637 Johannes Ruckers single-manual instrument, the first went to Thomas Dunn, the second to Albert Fuller. The third went, for a short time, to an amateur, Austin Ashley, and then to David Fuller. Number four, a two-manual harpsichord to the same design as the three single-manual instruments, was purchased by Stoddard Lincoln.[10] Between 1949 and 1955 the partners also completed fourteen restorations of antique instruments and built four clavichords, six small Italian harpsichords, and two English double harpsichords. A large German harpsichord with 16-foot register was designed by Hubbard and Dowd, but Dowd did most of the actual construction of this project, while Hubbard went back to Europe for two years to continue his research on historic harpsichords.

During Hubbard's absence Dowd reorganized the business. The workshop was moved to the barn of the Lyman Estate in Waltham, Massachusetts, and Charles Fisher joined the firm as a third partner. An important new design based on the work of Pascal Taskin was initiated, and the first five of these instruments went to a trend-setting crew of younger harpsichordists: Louis Bagger, Thomas Dunn, Albert Fuller, David Fuller, and Ralph Kirkpatrick (next to Landowska the best-known player in the United States at this time). David Fuller's Taskin model, Hubbard and Dowd number fifty-five, was the first of the firm's instruments to have Delrin plastic plectra. The partners had discovered that this synthetic material produced a sound similar to that made by quill in antique instruments.

In 1958 Hubbard bought out Dowd's share of the partnership. The following year Dowd established his own workshop in Cambridge, where he continued to build the Taskin model as well as a newly designed Italian harpsichord. "Frank never liked to do the same thing twice, and I did. I also felt that we had come to a point where we had produced some excellent instruments but we really hadn't done anything with them. We were years behind in orders and were making enemies because we weren't producing anything on time."[11]

Important changes were occurring in the basic concept of the harpsichord. In 1964 Dowd introduced a newly designed harpsichord based on a Blanchet instru-

William Dowd and Frank Hubbard in the early days of their partnership.
(Courtesy of William Dowd.)

ment of 1730. Like the earlier Taskin-style harpsichord, it became extremely popular with professional harpsichordists. In 1965 Dowd rethought the keyboards of his instruments, copying the key size, pinning, and balance point of historic models. In 1966 he dropped the widely used plywood cases in favor of solid softwood cases made of linden or poplar. Step by step he was reinstating the practices of the past.

Professional concepts of what constituted a proper harpsichord were changing radically. As Dowd pointed out, the three great controversies of mid-century were "the sixteen-foot choir, quill versus leather, and pedals." The 16-foot stop was not offered in Dowd harpsichords after the earliest unsuccessful experiments, and it was gone from the instruments of most other builders by 1970. Quill-sounding Delrin was the plectra material, the only exception being an occasional instrument with a soft buffalo leather *peau de buffle* stop added. Dowd was willing, through the late 1960s, to build pedals if one insisted on them, but he used his considerable skills to talk his customers out of the idea.[12]

Hubbard was pursuing a similar path, building a reputation for exciting instruments made with consummate craft, a reputation only slightly marred by the haphazard organization of his shop, which cast doubt on predictions of delivery dates. Both makers attracted hordes of young apprentices, many of whom went on to establish their own shops, making the "Boston School of Harpsichord Makers" more nearly a university. Even a partial list of alumni is impressive: Jeremy Adams, Christopher Bannister, Walter Burr, Carl Fudge, Willard Martin, John Nargesian, William Post Ross, Thomas and Barbara Wolf, and fortepiano makers Philip Belt and Robert E. Smith. The third of the most established Boston builders, Eric Herz (born 1919), spent two years with Hubbard and Dowd, then started his own shop in Harvard, Massachusetts, in 1954. He settled in Cambridge in 1963. Herz's well-regarded and widely played harpsichords owed more to John Challis's spirit of innovation than to the Boston School's search for historic truth. The use of fiberglass lamination for the soundboards and a generally heavier construction of the instruments' cases were quite far removed from the norm for the Boston builders.

In a move that expanded both his business and his influence, Hubbard surprised many by producing do-it-yourself instruments in kit form. When asked "What led you to the kit idea?" he responded, laughing, "Money!" The great success of this venture was evident in the number sold: more than 1,000 kits or partially assembled harpsichords by the time of Hubbard's death in 1976.

> There are really several things. To begin with I was hounded by amateurs who wanted to make their own harpsichords and came around for advice and I found myself repeating the same things over and over again. Then too, my natural bent in harpsichord making is somewhat experimental and fussy in nature and I am not very well psychologically equipped for mass production. I got married and was starving to death so it seemed to me that this kit might turn out to be a meal ticket which would subsidize making harpsichords and that's exactly what it is.
>
> In addition I found the problem interesting. The problem of designing an instrument and methods of making it which an amateur could build without too much experience and training. I enjoyed working that out.[13]

An enduring legacy of Frank Hubbard's scholarship was his pioneering book, *Three Centuries of Harpsichord Making*, published by Harvard University Press in 1965. Nearly twenty years later Gustav Leonhardt wrote,

> Whatever refinements have been made and will be made in the knowledge of early harpsichord making, his monumental book will last, as it laid the foundation for the structure of knowledge as well as creating the structure itself. Only those now fifty years of age can comprehend how large a step Frank Hubbard took. He could hardly

Frank Hubbard at work in his shop. (Archives of the Museum of Fine Arts, Boston.)

take for granted the accuracy and completeness of earlier researches and found that many widely held beliefs even proved to be erroneous.[14]

Dowd, too, made an enduring impression on the European harpsichord scene when, in 1972, he reversed centuries-old cultural patterns and established a second

William Dowd, 1979. (Smithsonian Institution, photograph
by Dane Penland.)

location for harpsichord construction in Paris. With the operation directed by
Reinhard von Nagel, the shop made William Dowd harpsichords for Europe. The
Paris atelier had produced 235 instruments by May 1983—a mighty nudge in the
direction of an effective classical revival on the Continent.[15]

KIRKPATRICK JOINS THE SURGE TO THE PAST

The effect of the Hubbard and Dowd instruments on harpsichord playing was
nowhere more evident than in the work of the foremost concert player in America,
Ralph Kirkpatrick. Looking back at the end of his distinguished career, he wrote:

With the arrival on the scene of Hubbard and Dowd and their imitators there began what for me was a joyful period; but it began far too late. I now discovered new resources of playing and I enjoyed the privilege of bringing out the beauties of an instrument rather than being obliged to conceal its defects. I was not only enabled to get rid of all those fancy registrations, but I was able as the action improved to cultivate a vocabulary of articulation that far exceeded anything I had before possessed.

. . . Thanks to these instruments I was able during the years of the late 1950s and 60s to make enormous progress in my playing. For the first time I played a harpsichord by Martin Skowroneck [born 1926], one of the few European instrument makers at that time who was working along the same general lines as Hubbard and Dowd. I discovered that thanks to its action I had no trouble in balancing the eight-foot of the upper manual against the tutti of the lower manual while literally following Bach's indications of *piano* and *forte* in the Italian Concerto. At last I was able to play this piece without tinkering with the registration, as I had been obliged to do on all my existing recordings of it. My report to Bill Dowd of this experience may have had something to do with that alteration in the action of his keyboards that made it possible to balance one register against another by means of touch. . . .[16]

Kirkpatrick, playing the responsive new harpsichords, toured widely in the United States. A typical news account of his activites in 1960 appeared in the *Cleveland Plain Dealer:*

There is going to be more harpsichord playing in the United States by both professional and amateur musicians, Ralph Kirkpatrick, harpsichordist, predicted yesterday after rehearsal with the Cleveland Orchestra at Severance Hall.

Kirkpatrick will be the first harpsichordist to appear as assisting artist in the regular series of the orchestra in its 42 years. He will play in three concertos for harpsichord and orchestra, Robert Shaw conducting. . . .

He believes that a harpsichord type of instrument is destined to play a household role comparable to that of the old upright piano of the American parlor at the turn of the century, and that it will become common for American children to take harpsichord lessons.

He said such a trend was already well established in Europe, especially in Germany, where there is now mass production of harpsichords. He said that at Steinway's in Hamburg he saw three times as many of these as pianos.

Kirkpatrick is in the process of recording all the keyboard music of Bach (except that for organ) on the harpsichord and clavichord for a German recording company.

He attributed the revival of interest in these instruments, popular in the seventeenth and eighteenth centuries, in part to a change of musical taste and to increased appreciation and respect for composers of those times.

But he said that such instruments (whose strings are plucked) are also suitable for expressing the musical ideas of modern composers. He will soon give an entire program of modern music for an audience in California.

One concerto he will play here is a modern work in one movement by Quincy Porter [1897–1966], who is Joseph Battell Professor of Music at Yale University. . . .

Ralph Kirkpatrick and Quincy Porter discussing the latter's *Concerto,* Cleveland, 1960. (*Cleveland Plain Dealer* photograph by David Vormelker, collection of the Cleveland Public Library.)

The harpsichord Kirkpatrick will play is a new one marked "William Dowd Boston 1960," which the musician termed "magnificent." It was borrowed for the concerts from the First Unitarian Church . . . Shaker Heights, where Robert Shaw is minister of music.

Kirkpatrick said there is no doubt that the best harpsichords in the world are made in the United States.

Kirkpatrick is credited with being an important influence in the revival of popularity of keyboard music for plucked strings. . . . Through hundreds of personal performances and recordings over many years he has familiarized people with this instrument and the music made for it.[17]

The other works with solo harpsichord on this program were Bach's *Concerto* in A major, BWV 1055, and Manuel de Falla's *Concerto for Harpsichord and Chamber Ensemble.*

Kirkpatrick's interest in new music for the harpsichord was genuine and ongoing. In 1939 he gave a program of twentieth-century works at Carnegie Chamber Music Hall, with compositions by Ernst Lévy, Otto Luening, Robert Oboussier, H. A. Seaver, John Barrows, Robert McBride, and Florent Schmitt. In a Town Hall concert with violinst Alexander Schneider on 30 November 1945, Kirkpatrick premièred one of the most distinguished American works with harpsichord, *Sonatina for Violin and Harpsichord* by Walter Piston (1894–1976). Subsequently this work was recorded for Columbia Records as part of the Modern American Music Series.[18] The concert of modern music mentioned in the Cleveland interview was given at the University of California at Berkeley on 26 January 1961. Kirkpatrick wrote in his program notes:

> This is my first complete program of modern harpsichord music in over twenty years. While it represents only a small segment of the music that has been composed for the harpsichord in our time, and while it does not even pretend to present a balanced sampling of styles and schools, it contains a number of works I have long intended to play, and one at least, especially written for this program. It is my intention henceforth frequently to perform contemporary harpsichord music and to encourage those experiments with the harpsichord in which nearly every composer of my acquaintance has expressed an interest. . . .
>
> I have always been more interested in what can be suggested through the harpsichord than in the mere harpsichord itself. . . . Therefore, while I see the practical future of modern harpsichord music substantially oriented toward exploitation of its most striking peculiarities . . . I welcome with interest and hope any attempt . . . at liberating the instrument from its confining specialties and making for it a place, no matter how modest, in the main stream of musical expression.

The concert began with the première of *Set of Four* by Henry Cowell (1897–1965), which seems tailor-made for Kirkpatrick:

> I never asked Henry if he so intended it, but the passages with the tone clusters [in the opening movement, Rondo] always reminded me of a hymn tune played on a wheezy old harmonium. Somewhere in the piece [at the very end of the fourth movement, Fugue and Resumé] there is a trill in octaves for the left hand which Henry put in at my special request. Along with other corresponding features I have abnormally large hands whose extensions were further increased by stretching exercises given me by a piano teacher when I was eleven or twelve years old. The result has been that I have always been able to trill in octaves with either hand but found little use in classical keyboard literature for this slightly monstrous capacity. However when I was still playing continuo I occasionally noticed the page turner looking with horrified astonishment at my left hand creeping over a bass doubled in legato octaves.[19]

Also on this program were works by Lou Harrison (*Six Sonatas*[20]), Frederick Delius, Ernst Lévy, Peter Mieg, Halsey Stevens, Douglas Allanbrook, Daniel Pinkham, Mel Powell, Vincent Persichetti (first movement of *Sonata for Harpsichord,* opus 52), and David Kraehenbuehl (*Toccate per Cembalo,* 1955).

Kirkpatrick was recognized as a man of stature outside the world of music: In 1963 he was elected a Fellow of the American Academy of Arts and Sciences, and in 1964 a member of the American Philosophical Society. In 1965, after twenty-five years at Yale, Kirkpatrick was promoted to full professor. "High time," he is reported to have snorted when a colleague congratulated him.

An aging master in 1973, Kirkpatrick returned to earlier repertoire when he played the *Goldberg Variations* again:

> Ralph Kirkpatrick played . . . in Houston's Rothko Chapel on February 10 and 11. Indeed, so great was the demand for tickets that he played Bach's superb work three times in less than twenty-four hours. One might have feared, having tickets for the third presentation, that such an effort would leave the artist in less than full command of his technical resources, but such was not the case. Kirkpatrick played magnificently with a prodigious technical command of the work as well as with spacious feeling for the overall architecture of Bach's most lengthy set of variations.
>
> Mr. Kirkpatrick's playing has mellowed through the years. A sense of nuance, not always present in the past, is now most gratifyingly there. He played the *Goldbergs* complete, with all repeats, on his William Dowd instrument of 1966, a harpsichord with handstops. There were very few changes of registration: all double keyboard variations were played with the two eight-foot stops, left hand on the upper manual and right hand on the lower. With the richness of sound provided by these two stops, however, all was sufficient. Bach himself provides all necessary changes of color in his masterful creation.[21]

The very next year Kirkpatrick underwent a successful, but serious, heart operation. Soon thereafter the eye problems that had plagued him for thirty-five years became irreversible and he went totally blind.

To watch Ralph Kirkpatrick make his way onto the stage of New England Conservatory's Jordan Hall was a moving experience. His recital on 29 May 1981, was a special event of the first Boston Early Music Festival. Refusing, as always, to be assisted to the harpsichord, Kirkpatrick had affixed a string from the tail of the instrument to the far stage doorway. Touching this thread lightly, he made his way slowly to the instrument. He seated himself, oriented his hands on the keyboards, and began to play works from the greatest of Baroque masters: Couperin (the 18th *Ordre*), Rameau, and his signature composer, Scarlatti (six sonatas). It had been fifty-one event-filled years since his first recital across the river at Harvard's Paine Hall.

Just before this concert, the Boston critic Richard Dyer wrote of the elderly musician:

> Today Ralph Kirkpatrick is still full of energy and vitality. He continues to play concerts as often as he feels like it; he is writing his memoirs[22] and preparing various musicological studies and a "catechism" for performers for publication;[23] he plays the great Romantic literature of the piano for his personal pleasure; he continues to restudy his own repertoire (about thirty full recital programs, from memory); he is putting poetry in several languages into Braille; and he has decisive opinions about everything, which he sets forth with charm, verve and edge.
>
> "If you concern yourself exclusively with the keyboard, you will asphyxiate yourself." "Boston is full of memories for me, but you must not forget that it is the land of the bean, the cod, and the tin ear." "I don't teach master classes. You cannot

paint a house that has not been built." . . . "My best recorded playing is in the second book of the 'Well-Tempered Clavier,' particularly in the clavichord version." "Students found me disturbing because I asked questions rather than answering them."[24]

Looking back at a rich life devoted to music and a career that extended from the pioneering days of the early-music movement to the post-classical harpsichord revival, Kirkpatrick wrote:

> With so many people in the [early music] game, it is natural that there are the mediocre who are attracted by mediocrity. They often attach themselves to composers who ought to have been buried as soon as possible after their exhumation, many of them keyboard composers. But nevertheless there are all sorts of admirable and beautiful things to be found in this over-populated world of early music. Let us hope that once more sanity will return, that music will once more dominate over concern with instruments. . . .[25]

With concerted opinions the two primary revivers of the historic harpsichord expressed a similar view. To the question "Have you any philosophies pertaining to your life as a builder that you would like to share with us?" Frank Hubbard responded:

> I would say that I see myself faced with a body of music that, of course, is part of the period in which it was composed. . . . [A] composer from the past had a talent greater than anything I will ever have. He used the means at his disposal in an imaginative way that staggers my imagination. Therefore, the only word I can apply is arrogance to the people who feel they can devise a harpsichord more suitable to his music than the instrument he had, because he wrote his music for that harpsichord. That's why I feel so strongly that one should attempt to return to the original instruments. . . .[26]

And William Dowd made this summation:

> The classical revival is more than thirty years old and has long since prevailed over the modern school. The vast majority of harpsichords made today in the United States and Europe are to classical designs, and the least distinguished among them sounds better to us than the best of those made before 1950. To be musical, however, far more is required of a harpsichord than beauty of sound. A good harpsichord not only sings, but it "speaks" articulately. That is to say, its tone quality is such that minute differences of detaché can be perceived making it possible to mold and phrase a musical line. The player can create an illusion of crescendo, decrescendo, or even sforzando. Each stop should have its own characteristic quality, while not being unnaturally different from the others, and the ensemble should grow from its parts. . . .
>
> I would like to think that these instruments, if presented to the great harpsichordists of the seventeenth and eighteenth centuries, would not only be accepted as normal to their use, but would please them.[27]

CHAPTER
12

MARATHON MAN
Fernando Valenti

Students of Ralph Kirkpatrick shared the spotlight with Landowska's progeny as the next generation of harpsichordists began to make its impression on the concert-going public. And on others:

Midnights in Manhattan

One day last spring a young (28) Manhattan musician named Fernando Valenti found himself stuck in a customs office in Peru. That big instrument he had with him, said the officials, was undeniably a piano, and therefore subject to import duty. It was not a piano, insisted Valenti; it was a harpsichord. Then and there, the oldtime mechanism of strings and quills was uncrated, and Valenti sat down to play while some 150 people listened. After an hour of music, officialdom was satisfied, and Valenti proceeded on his concert tour. "I have never refused to do anything unusual," he says, "so long as it is within the bounds of respectability."

Last week he was nestled in the respectable but unusual surroundings of Manhattan's Little Club, a dim East Side spot with some Broadway overtones, for a series of Sunday-midnight concerts. Looking a little like a pudgy, scholarly Satan, Harpsichordist Valenti threaded his way among the tables, mounted the platform and affectionately patted the maple-colored instrument. Then he launched into pieces by such 18th century composers as Rameau, Domenico Scarlatti and Bach. The music was brief, gracefully decorated with trills and curlicues, and its precise pinpoints of sound and muffled thunder filled the small room better than they do a larger concert hall. Customers found the music relaxing and, after the strangeness of the first few notes had worn off, a good blend with bourbon or Scotch.

As a direct musical descendant of modern harpsichord greats (he is a pupil of Ralph Kirkpatrick, who is a pupil of Wanda Landowska), Fernando Valenti thinks harpsichordists must play for wider and wider audiences if interest in the instrument is not to die out. He is building a reputation as one of the most imaginative harpsichordists in the U.S., giving some 20 solo recitals a year and lecturing about the music he plays. Valenti has begun a musical marathon: recording all 555 of Scarlatti's gemlike *Sonatas* (for Westminster). In the past three years he has completed 72, but half seriously, wonders whether he will ever be able to finish the lot.[1]

Valenti was born in New York in 1926 of Spanish parents. Piano studies with José and Amparo Iturbi, who were friends of his parents, prepared him for a debut at age nine. Valenti went to Yale University as a history major, but his contact with Ralph Kirkpatrick led him to the harpsichord. "I discovered that I liked to play Bach and Scarlatti better than Liszt. And so I played Bach and Scarlatti," said Valenti.[2] Just how far the harpsichord revival had progressed might be inferred from the fact that there was no question but that Bach and Scarlatti would now be played on the harpsichord.

A concert tour of South America during Valenti's undergraduate years was so successful that it was repeated by popular demand. Shortly after his graduation Valenti was invited to play in Pablo Casals's historic first Bach Festival in Prades during the Bach celebratory year of 1950. His New York debut in Town Hall, soon followed. The *Times* reported that Valenti "played with assurance, with technical expertness and often—as in a group of Scarlatti sonatas—with a romantic ardor that belied the reputation of the harpsichord as a whispering collection of wires and bones."[3] A movie soundtrack, a television appearance, and Poulenc's incidental music for the run of Jean Giraudoux's play *The Enchanted* at New York's Lyceum Theatre kept Valenti in the public eye (and ears) during the season. In the academic year 1951–52 he became the first harpsichordist to join the faculty of the Juilliard School.

New music for the harpsichord figured in Valenti's recitals and appearances at this time. Vincent Persichetti's *Sonata for Harpsichord,* opus 52, was premièred on 10 January 1952. The three-movement work proved to be wonderfully idiomatic for the instrument, a splendid prelude to the flowering of harpsichord sonatas later composed by Persichetti. Several commentators suggested dubbing him "Domenico," since no other twentieth-century composer had written so many major works for the instrument.[4] The *Recitative and Toccata Percossa* by Mel Powell was another new work composed for Valenti. Its first hearing was at one of the four midnight concerts in New York's Little Club, a not unusual venue for Powell, who had made quite a name for himself as a jazz keyboard artist.

Valenti's claim to marathon status began with the project of recording all the Scarlatti keyboard sonatas for Westminster. The history of this undertaking is best told by the artist himself, a witty and entertaining writer.[5]

> I became involved in this amiable lunacy about two years ago [1952] while in full possession of the knowledge that the "old boy" wrote well in excess of 550 works of this species. My eyes were wide open. I was as sober as any musical masochist ever is, and there was full consent of the will. If since the outset I have occasionally felt like a man who is going on an exclusive diet of Chinese mustard for five years, my friends at Westminster Records have skillfully prevented my temperamentalities from unfavorably affecting the outcome of the project. All through the recently completed recording of more than 100 of these Sonatas they seem to have known unfailingly when to scold, cajole, sooth and refresh me, and when to "give me my head!"[6]

At the outset there was no thought of recording the complete Scarlatti *opera,* but the favorable reception and excellent sales of the first releases moved Westminster's vice president to ask:

"Can you give me a dozen more by the end of the month?"

That does it, I thought! Spanish fire came sizzling through the telephone, right in the face of the innocent recording vice-president. What did he think I was, anyway, a small-town super-market with double-keyboards where you could order Scarlatti Sonatas by the dozen as if they were Grade-A eggs? Or by the pound, like jelly-beans at Easter time? I was an artist, a musician, not a musical artesian well! "Well," he said, in the tone of a man who was wearied of word-mincing, "you can take all the time you want about it, but you might as well get used to the idea that we are going to cover this Scarlatti boy just like a tent. So hang up, stop being such a gas-bag, and start practicing." I did.[7]

Critical reaction to Valenti's Scarlatti was glowing:

Those who think of the harpsichord as a frail instrument, to be stroked by the pale, thin fingers of antiquarians will learn a salutary lesson from Mr. Valenti's virile, exuberant, and richly sonorous performances. He plays the Sonata in F minor, Longo 475, with intoxicating power. Mr. Valenti emulates Wanda Landowska in thinking of the harpsichord as an heroic as well as a lyric instrument. His registrations are sometimes too rich, and he pounds occasionally, but the fire and intensity of his playing more than compensate for these indiscretions. Every one of these twelve sonatas is a masterpiece, and one can listen to them scores of times without ever tiring of them.[8]

Even more distinguished approval came from an unimpeachable source:

Shortly after it was tacitly understood between me and Westminster that I would be wallowing in Scarlatti for years to come . . . I had occasion to interview a prospective pupil. His musical credentials were good, his playing excellent and his enthusiasm unbounded, so I decided to accept him. I arrived at this decision in spite of his having confided to me that he was a "spiritist" and benefitted from frequent communications with the "other world." He assured me that he was on a "first-name" basis with the majority of the Ptolemies and had shared many a chuckle with President Martin Van Buren. After six months of instruction he requested permission to bring a portable tape-recorder to one of our lessons. I tried to be adamant about this but his entreaties were heart-breaking and I am, at best, not very adamant at all. The result was that he brought this little toy to our next meeting, turned it on, and I went through two of the most inhibited and tutorially unsatisfactory hours I have ever experienced in my life.

When the session ended I made the mistake of asking him what he was planning to do with the tapes. He said he was going to play them for his friends. Deeming this a strangely tasteless bit of procedure, I inquired as to the identity of these "friends." He

Fernando Valenti. (Courtesy of Fernando Valenti.)

then explained to me, in a tone as casual as if he were asking to borrow my lawn-mower, that he intended to play the tapes for his good friend Brahms, who, he was sure, would put him in touch with Domenico Scarlatti, who would then pass judgment on my approach to his keyboard music and make manifest either his approval or its opposite. When the student left I thought it might be a good idea to take a cold shower.

A day or so later the pupil telephoned to say (my telephone answering-service is a witness to this in case the reader does not believe the story) that Scarlatti was very pleased indeed with my handling of his Sonatas and would be very much in favor of my going ahead with making recordings of all of them. Thinking this was rather a funny story ("funny" having both meanings here), I told it to some Westminster people at lunch one day. The idea enchanted them. The Scarlatti project became half-music, half-necromancy. There could be no quitting now![9]

Matters supernatural (or even infernal) have long been associated with Fernando Valenti: "It has been said that you play with such brilliance and fire that you must be possessed by the Devil. What is your comment to that statement?" asked an interviewer. "The statement is flattering and I accept it as graciously as I can. But with it, I also accept the sometimes intimated criticism that my playing should be more controlled. There is a force that I feel which carries me with it. It comes from the music. And I guess my Spanish blood starts going . . . you know . . . the bull fights and all that."[10]

Even the harpsichordist's Spanish fire could not keep the Westminster project alive to its completion. In 1960, after nearly 300 of the sonatas had been recorded, Westminster ran into financial difficulties. Not only was the recording effort curtailed, but all except three of Valenti's records were dropped from the catalog. Valenti's (and Westminster's) very subjective approach to the project—twelve randomly selected sonatas per disc, without the now-accepted Kirkpatrick pairings (which were only announced at the publication of the Scarlatti biography in 1953, after the recordings had commenced)—made for some adventurous presentations, but this attitude was scarcely designed to create an enduring research document for libraries or scholars. The use of inappropriate instruments—Valenti's Challis in the United States and whatever German production instruments happened to be available for those discs recorded in Vienna—also lessened the value of the project. But for a non-specialist's sheer musical enjoyment, the brilliance, fire, and the Spanish blood infusing Fernando Valenti's playing could not be faulted.

Valenti's identification with the Scarlatti repertoire continued throughout his career. He enjoyed opportunities to perform consecutive evenings of sonatas, as, for instance, the week of 26–30 November 1973, when he presented twenty sonatas each evening for five nights at New York's Carnegie Hall. Utilizing a Zuckermann harpsichord built by David Way, Valenti did not indicate in his program nor did he announce from the stage which works would be included. He just played.

One hundred sonatas in five nights may have been a bit much, even for Valenti. The next year he limited the marathon to three evenings. At this round he announced that he would play some of the *Essercizi,* a set of thirty pieces published during Scarlatti's lifetime, for as he noted ruefully, "I've got to record them soon and I'd just as soon leave the wrong notes here. There seems to be an abundance of them this evening." Allen Hughes of the *Times* noted that there weren't really that many errors:

> Mr. Valenti's playing has a kind of humanity that begins by attracting listeners' attention and ends by winning their affection. The interpretations grow out of scholarship but they are not smothered by it. When a passage comes up that he finds particularly appealing, he just leans on it a little to be sure you get the point. One

thing he does not do is tell you in advance, or ever, what Scarlatti sonatas he is playing.[11]

The man who "has probably played more Scarlatti than anyone since Queen Maria Barbara's teacher"[12] had many amusing experiences throughout his active concert career. One of his favorite stories concerns an American woman who telephoned Valenti shortly before a concert to ask if he would play her favorite sonata. She was unable to quote its number, and her efforts to hum it were not very helpful, so Valenti queried, "What key?" "Oh," she responded, "since you've been so helpful and kind, play it in any key you like."

Of course other harpsichordists of Valenti's generation were playing concerts and making recordings, among them several other students of Ralph Kirkpatrick: Albert Fuller (born 1926) succeeded Valenti as harpsichord professor at the Julliard School in 1964 and subsequently added harpsichord teaching at Yale (1976–79) to his load. Eiji Hashimoto (born 1931), from Tokyo, is especially noted for his continuation of the Kirkpatrick tradition of providing reliable playing editions of Scarlatti sonatas. He became professor of harpsichord at the Cincinnati College-Conservatory of Music in 1968. Robert Conant (born 1928), professor of harpsichord at Roosevelt University in Chicago, has double interests—in authentic early instruments (he was curator of the Yale Collection, 1961–66) and in contemporary works for the harpsichord (he was harpsichordist for the first recording of Lester Trimble's evocative chamber work *Four Fragments from the Canterbury Tales* for Columbia Records)—that represented the path many harpsichordists would pursue in their careers.

Another familiar name to record buyers was that of Joseph Payne (born 1938), who had studied, as a very young fellow, with Landowska and later with Valenti. Payne made many converts to harpsichord music with his blockbuster sets of recordings for Vox and Turnabout Records in the 1960s.

Daniel Pinkham (born 1923), a gifted composer, also concertized as harpsichord-ist, especially in a violin-harpsichord duo with Robert Brink. His early work with Claude Jean Chiasson and study with Putnam Aldrich and Wanda Landowska[13] prepared him well for such a career. For the concerts with Brink several works were commissioned, among them another of Henry Cowell's "Sets," *Set of Two* [movements] *for Violin and Harpsichord* (1955); and the haiku-like *Duet for Violin and Harpsichord*, opus 122, by Alan Hovhaness—three short movements lasting three minutes. This work was commissioned on 16 May 1954, composed on 17 May, and premièred two weeks later in Frankfurt, Germany. Pinkham's own works for harpsichord show a decided neo-classical bent that suits the instrument well. *Epitaph* "in memoriam Janet Fairbank" (1948) is a retrograde canon (according to the composer, "Immediately apparent to Walter Piston!"). *Partita*, composed as background music for a documentary film, consists of typical Baroque forms, each movement dedicated to a notable figure in the harpsichord world: "Toccata, Andante, and Fugue" for Melville Smith, "Three Inventions" for Sylvia Kind, "Interlude and Rondo" for Albert Fuller, "Fantasia" for Sylvia Marlow, "Scherzo and

Trio" for David Fuller, and "Envoi" for Chiasson. The useful *Lessons for Harpsichord,* Pinkham's emulation of Couperin's *L'art de toucher* preludes, concentrate on particular technical aspects of harpsichord playing.[14]

Of all these players, however, Valenti and Sylvia Marlowe remained at the forefront. In 1980, on the occasion of his thirtieth anniversary as a concert harpsichordist, Valenti reminisced: "You know, when I remember 'way back then, we sort of established people in the field had very much as one of our ambitions to bring the harpsichord back into the mainstream of musical activity. And now I think 'We did it.'"[15]

CHAPTER
13

KITS, RECORDS, AND
ALL THAT JAZZ

Come-On-A Stan's House, He Give You Harpsichord

New York—"Better get down to the studio a little early," said Mitch Miller to Stan Freeman. "We're going to use a harpsichord."

So Stan Freeman went to the Columbia studios and cut *Come On-A My House* with Rosemary Clooney, barely aware that this was the greatest musical event since Little Satchmo, playing in the streets of New Orleans, fired the Shot Heard 'Round the World. . . .

"Fernando Valenti, a fine harpsichordist who'd loaned his instrument for the session, helped me figure out the seven pedals and two keyboards. You know how he got the harpsichord? He once wrote a tune that Freddy Martin recorded, and had it built to order with the $5,000 royalties he earned from the record.

. . . "I still don't think I take full advantage of all its uses," [Freeman] added. He hasn't taken full advantage of all the publicity, either. To make a guest radio or TV appearance he would have to lay out a $200 harpsichord rental fee.

Local 802 [American Federation of Musicians] lists exactly seven harpsichordists, one of whom lives in Beverly Hills. Of the other six, only Valenti, to Stan's knowledge, owns his own instrument and is willing to rent it out—"and even he guards it with his life while you're using it."

. . . Stan is just about the only competent classical pianist who can run the whole gamut of music. . . . So you see, he has no intention of staying in, or monopolizing, the harpsichord field. And therefore, if you feel an urge to emulate him, all you need to have is $5,000 and talent. Maybe you'll make some of those guest shots before Stan gets around to them.[1]

The obvious association of Baroque continuo playing, with its improvised keyboard realizations above a figured bass line, and the improvised licks of the jazz musician using a lead sheet has been pointed out by many writers on the twentieth-century Baroque music revival. Perhaps the first to draw solid correlations was Roger Pryor Dodge. Writing in 1934, he argued that jazz performance was related to the customs of old, especially regarding spontaneity of invention, but he did not go so far as to suggest the introduction of the harpsichord into the contemporary jazz instrumental ensemble.[2]

In 1940 Artie Shaw and his Gramercy Five cut several jazz records for Victor. At the harpsichord was the swing pianist Johnny Guarnieri (born 1917). Titles included "Special Delivery Stomp," "Smoke Gets in Your Eyes," "Cross Your Heart," and "Summit Ridge Drive."[3] Soon after this innovative foray into the jazz world, Mitchell Miller, an oboist familiar with the harpsichord through joint classical recitals with Yella Pessl, was asked by Alec Wilder to think of a new instrumental combination for recordings. The resulting group was the Wilder Octet, with Miller as oboist and Walter Gross at the harpsichord, joined by flute, clarinet, bass clarinet, bassoon, double bass, and drums. This group made about thirty record sides for Columbia.

The greatest popular surge for the harpsichord came in 1951, however, when Miller, now head of the popular records division at Columbia, engaged Stan Freeman (born 1920) to play the harpsichord in Rosemary Clooney's blockbuster hit "Come On-A My House" (a song in Armenian dialect by William Saroyan and his cousin Ross Bagdasarian). Inspired by the phenomenal sales of this recording, Freeman made a voiceless version of the same hit, "Come On-A Stan's House," scored for harpsichord, guitar, bass, and drums. Other Freeman sides with harpsichord include the Scarlatti-like "My Blue Heaven," "St. Louis Blues," and four pieces by Wilder in boogie-woogie style for Mitch Miller, horns, and harpsichord: "Horn Belt Boogie," "Singing Horns," "Serenade for Horns," and "Horns O'Plenty."[4] Freeman was also at the harpsichord when Clooney and Marlene Dietrich recorded "Dot's Nice—Donna Fight! " "Good For Nothin'," "It's the Same," and the hilarous "Too Old to Cut the Mustard" for Columbia in 1952.

Two of America's finest black musicians used harpsichord in significant works: Erroll Garner (1921–1977), following his 1957 European tour, played harpsichord in a recording *Paris Impressions* for Columbia. It was Mitch Miller who urged him to add the antique instrument to his tonal palette. On 27 March 1958 and again a month later Garner recorded "Don't Look for Me" and "Côte d'Azur," accompanied by his regular collaborators Edward Calhoun, bass, and Kelly Martin, percussion.[5] In 1965, Edward Kennedy "Duke" Ellington (1899–1974), "for decades a leading figure in big-band jazz [who] remains the most significant composer of the genre,"[6] was added to an extrardinary group of composers commissioned to write for the harpsichord by the Swiss patron Antoinette Vischer (1909–1973). His contribution, *A Single Petal of a Rose*, is actually from his 1957 composition *Queen's Suite*, dedicated to Queen Elizabeth II of Great Britain.

The connection between the Swiss harpsichordist and the American musician was effected by Newport Jazz Festival promoter Charles McWorther:

> Madame Vischer is an outstanding harpsichord artist and is greatly interested in reviving the harpsichord as a modern musical instrument. She has commissioned special compositions by a great many of the best modern composers such as Stockhausen, Martinů, Berio, Messiaen[7] and Lieberman. These pieces, usually of

Stan Freeman at the harpsichord. (Courtesy of Stan Freeman.)

two or three minutes in length, have been performed and recorded by Madame Vischer. Madame Vischer also happens to be interested in jazz and is an admirer of Duke Ellington. She would like him to write a piece in his own style for the harpsichord. Ellington would be free to write anything he wishes. He would merely dedicate the composition to Madame Vischer and give her the right to the first performance and recording. He would retain all ownership rights in the composition. . . .[8]

In the notes to her Wergo recording of *A Single Petal of a Rose*[9] Vischer described her reaction upon receiving the score: "At Christmas 1965 I received the usual volume of New Year's greetings, among which was a large envelope from New York. . . . [There followed] a shriek of excitement—it was a piece from Duke Ellington. . . ."[10] There is some question as to the actual dedication to Vischer; the three-page manuscript bears the autograph "To Antoinette Vischer—Thanx for a good performance. Good Wishes, Duke Ellington." Extremely pianistic in its arpeggiations and sustaining-pedal effects, the work must be "realized" for any sort of adequate performance.[11]

All this attention to a "grand old lady" of an instrument from the spunky youth-oriented jazz musicians did not seem strange to some classical players. Sylvia Marlowe, herself adept at swing, expressed her approval at the instrument's use in all styles of music, including boogie-woogie. Marlowe claimed that

> one of her chosen instrument's most attractive features is the opportunity it offers the player to improvise within the scope of the written music. So many combinations of stops and registers are available to the harpsichordist that two musicians will play the same work note for note and make it sound like two different compositions. Jazz enthusiasts who have always criticized the restrictive nature of classical music will be interested in this flexibility, which offers the musician an opportunity to add his personal touch to the touch of the composer.
>
> Miss Marlowe feels that the harpsichord's plucking action makes it perfectly suited to the needs of modern composers. . . . The prospect of a harpsichord on the stage of New York's Paramount Theatre taking a few hot licks with a dance band does not seem at all ludicrous to her.[12]

Not only harpsichords with pedals were heard in the popular repertoire. A William Dowd instrument of classic design was the choice for Donald Angle's wide-ranging records *Don Angle, Harpsichord; New Angle on Harpsichord;* and *Another Angle on Harpsichord,* on which such favorites as *Limehouse Blues,* Gershwin's *Summertime* and the Beatles' hit *A Hard Day's Night* were heard.[13]

Pedals of another variety were the feature of several albums by America's leading recording artist of the classical organ, E. Power Biggs (1906–1977). Enamored of his John Challis pedal harpsichord, Biggs recorded some of his favorite Bach pieces on this instrument. His second offering was a hilarious romp through the most unlikely of literatures:

> The harpsichord is a classic instrument, but the music I have recorded here is largely Romantic and partly modern. Yet, all seems to go together, and some "improbable" pieces by Beethoven, Brahms, Falla, et al, appear perfectly suited to the joyful nature of the harpsichord. . . .
>
> Turn about is fair play, and, for an organist turned slightly harpsichordist, to conduct a raid into such music is mere justice, considering that for a century, from Liszt and Busoni on, pianists—as well as orchestral conductors—have raided the organ literature for some of its ripest plums. . . .

E. Power Biggs at his Challis pedal harpsichord. (Courtesy of Margaret Biggs.)

So—here's Holiday for Harpsichord, or Harpsichord Heresy, call it what you will! I hope you'll enjoy it every bit as much as I enjoyed recording it.[14]

Biggs retreated (re-treaded?) to Bach, recording the *Six Trio Sonatas* at the pedal harpsichord in 1967, but it was back to the lighter side for two albums of ragtime by Scott Joplin, issued in 1973 and 1975:

Ragtime—baroque sounds. Music of the saloon, on the instrument of the salon. Music from the high era of classic American ragtime, performed on the oldest and most courtly of keyboard instruments. Somehow—it all goes together, in a suitably elegant and somewhat irreverent manner!

. . . In this . . . music, romantic or ragtime, with its ranging bass and constant zigzag motion of the left hand, one gives the bass to the pedals, playing in detached or sustained manner as the music requires, while the left hand does its usual duty with the off-beat chords. Used in this non-contrapuntal way, the pedals become the equivalent of the sustaining pedal of the piano, and the absence of a sustaining pedal on the harpsichord—on all harpsichords—is overcome.[15]

Biggs was not the first to record Scott Joplin's music on harpsichord. Two discs had already been cut in California by the Los Angeles artist William Neil Roberts, a student of Alice Ehlers. Roberts managed this music using only the manuals of the harpsichord.[16] Others had preceded Biggs with recordings at the pedal harpsichord. Bruce Prince-Joseph (born 1925) made a splendid record of Bach, Vivaldi-Bach, and Mozart on a huge Neupert pedal harpsichord in the 1950s.[17] And he was the first to play harpsichord at a national convention of the American Guild of Organists, in San Francisco, on 3 July 1952. On his program (which also included organ works) he performed *Sonata* in D major of Haydn, *Fantasia* in C minor of Bach, and compositions by Byrd, Handel, Lully, and Mozart.

The harpsichord continued to be heard at AGO conventions: Egbert Ennulat played ensemble and solo works in Atlanta in 1966; Isolde Ahlgrimm gave highly successful recitals at the Denver Convention of 1968; Larry Palmer played Bach's *Chromatic Fantasy and Fugue* and chamber works by Trimble and Rieti in Dallas in 1972[18] and gave a program with orchestra in Minneapolis for the 1980 gathering;[19] and Gustav Leonhardt was a featured artist at the Cleveland Convention in 1974.

DO IT YOURSELF: THE UBIQUITOUS KIT

For an instrument we used to think had been killed off in the eighteenth century by the modern piano, the harpsichord is showing startling signs of life. It is not only back with a resounding tinkle, it is all over the place. . . .

. . . Some 3,000 harpsichords were imported from Europe last year [1967], and our few domestic craftsmen are swamped. *Saturday Review* regularly carries harpsichords-for-sale advertisements. And, believe it or not, Build-It-Yourself Harpsichord Kits sell briskly for $150 and up.[20]

The shape of things to come had been presaged by the publication in 1954 of a forty-two-page book, *How to Build a Baroque Concert Harpsichord.*[21] Following some words of thanks to builders Hubbard and Dowd, twenty drawings showed a general layout for an instrument, a keyboard side elevation, the layout of the keyboard, and other design features.

The prime mover of the "do-it-yourself" phenomenon in harpsichord-building was not one of the established front-runners of the craft, but an ex-piano technician from Berlin, Wolfgang Joachim Zuckermann (born 1922), better known as "Wally." Zuckermann built his first instrument in 1954 after looking at an antique Italian harpsichord and a modern instrument by Dolmetsch. For simplicity's sake Zuckermann eliminated the curve in the bentside of his instrument, resulting in a "straight bentside," an oddity that remained the most obvious design feature of Zuckermann harpsichords for some years.

A second harpsichord, a two-line classified advertisement in the *New York Times*, five orders, and a visit from Sylvia Marlowe occurred in rapid succession. After a disastrous fire destroyed his shop in 1958, Zuckermann went into a new workshop, which reached full production in 1960. Having made about seventy instruments by this time, he calculated the number of service calls that might be necessary in the next few years and tried to devise ways of avoiding this potential service commitment. He "realized that most people approach a harpsichord with caution, the way they do a vicious dog, [and] decided that the only way they might lose their fear of harpsichord maintenance was to go through the process of building the instrument for themselves."[22]

A collection of pre-cut parts and directions for assembling cost $150, rather than $800 for a finished instrument from the Zuckermann shop. The price was maintained for quite some time as mass production and design simplification offset the escalating cost of materials.

> The kit harpsichord is the very same instrument which we have been making here in the shop for the last seven years. We have built instruments for the Philadelphia Orchestra, Metropolitan Opera, Columbia University, New York University, the New York City Center, Columbia Records, numerous churches and performing groups, and countless individuals, both professionals and amateurs. They have been used in innumerable concerts, recitals and recordings in the New York area. Individuals who have made their own harpsichords using this kit include college professors, doctors, students, ministers, artists, advertising men, and professional musicians. Some of them have already used their own harpsichords in concerts and recordings.
>
> The instrument itself is simple, though versatile, and the design is essentially classical. Modern materials such as plywood are used, but were adopted only after the most careful experimentation. The instrument has one keyboard ranging from A to F (4 ¾ octaves) and one set of strings. There are two stops, one enabling the player to go from loud to soft and vice versa, and one which produces a harp or lute effect. With the two stops four combinations of sound can be achieved.
>
> The volume of this harpsichord is surprisingly good. It can be heard in large halls, and it cuts through even a large ensemble of other instruments. It is ideal as a practice instrument for the student, a "continuo" instrument for the accompaniment of baroque ensembles, and an all around delight for the musical amateur or professional.[23]

The time required to build this intrument was estimated at four to twelve weeks of spare time work, or 100–150 hours.

The popularity of this offering led to a production of 1,600 kits a year. By 1969, the year of publication for Zuckermann's book *The Modern Harpsichord,* some 10,000 of his kits had been sold. Of course, not everything turned out right:

> If anyone had been around when Claude Jean Chiasson recently sat down to play the harpsichord, they probably wouldn't have laughed. They would have howled.
>
> "I touched the keys," Mr. Chiasson recalls, "and the tail fell right on the floor."
>
> For the great majority of Americans who know nothing whatsoever about harpsichord nomenclature, an explanation is in order. To wit: a harpsichord's tail is the short wooden piece of the instrument's rim that is at the opposite end from the keyboard. And, more importantly, if a harpsichord is at all well built, the tail doesn't clatter to the floor when the keys are touched.
>
> But all harpsichords aren't well built these days. The reason is that there's a sort of mild mania taking place in certain circles, musical and otherwise, involving do-it-yourself harpsichord kits. For example, and for those who like statistics to document trends, consider the fact that Zuckermann Harpsichords Inc. of New York City, acknowledged to be the largest harpsichord-kit maker in the world, last year [1973] sold 2,500 kits in the U.S. and 1,500 abroad, compared with 2,000 kits in the U.S. and only a handful abroad in 1972.
>
> One might also consider the fact that the aforementioned Claude Jean Chiasson, who builds harpsichords from scratch (rather than from kits)—and builds them well—says he has recently spent time *re*building three do-it-yourself harpsichords brought to him by three disillusioned kit purchasers. One of the three had the unfortunate falling tail. "You need a certain cabinet making talent to satisfactorily complete a kit," says Mr. Chiasson, who lives in Fairfield, N.J. and whose talents also include teaching and playing both the harpsichord and the piano.[24]

Frank Hubbard offered a more sophisticated kit, available in either single or double-manual versions. By 1974 his kit sales had reached about 200 a year, measured against 5,000 inquiries generated by advertisements in such popular journals as *Saturday Review, The New Republic, Scientific American, The New York Times Sunday Magazine,* the recently founded *Early Music,* and *The Harpsichord.* Hubbard's prices ranged from $600 to about $2,700, depending on the amount of finishing already accomplished, but the average expenditure ran about $1,500. Hubbard's directions amounted to 103 pages plus a fourteen-page preface, a seven-page glossary, and twenty-four diagrams—not a document to be taken lightly.[25] A third source for harpsichord kits was the William Herbert Burton firm of Lincoln, Nebraska.

Was this phenomenon similar to the growth of the Arts and Crafts movement in England at the end of the nineteenth century? Did the do-it-yourself explosion foster a new generation of Dolmetsches? The number of new professional harpsichord makers whose early (and often, subsequent) instruments were built from kits has been legion. So, in that sense, the question must be answered in the affirmative.

The constant expansion of recorded harpsichord music, both in an increasingly esoteric survey of the repertoire from its own period and in newer popular combinations with a greater mass appeal, certainly consolidated the instrument's place.

But the sheer numbers of the kit instruments to be found throughout the land—in symphony halls, colleges and universities, churches, schools, and, most of all, in homes—made it official that the harpsichord was a heavyweight contender in the musical arena. "People felt they had been missing something in music," Ralph Kirkpatrick observed. "We appreciate our thick tonal carpets, like Wagner, but we don't want to walk on them all the time."[26] The leaner, tonally more-diet-conscious "queen of instruments" had entered the mass market in a way that none of the harpsichord pioneers could ever have envisioned.

EPILOG

THE HARPSICHORD LIVES

The Plectra Pluckers

The harpsichord boom is concentrated in college towns and big cities. Los Angeles had two 20 years ago (one of them was Sigmund Romberg's), now there are more than 30. Jose Ferrer and Edie Adams each have one as the newest thing in Hollywood chic. Pamona's retired English Professor Harlan Smedley, 53, who plays a harpsichord as "a countermeasure to all the tensions and noisiness of the day," thinks that "you can't be a pest on a harpsichord." Most harpsichord buffs are piano players who discovered baroque music on LP's; once accustomed to the sweet, incisive, brilliant tone of the harpsichord . . . they find its sound mystically satisfying. West Coast Psychologist Bob Johnson, 39, heard his first harpsichord on a recording by Yella Pessl, found, while living in Portland, that he felt "sad and in limbo because there was no harpsichord in 1,000 miles." He bought two, now holds frequent meetings for fellow harpsichordists at evening sessions in his home.

Professional people are especially harpsichord-prone. Doctors, psychiatrists, teachers and ministers are among the most active amateurs in the New York area. In New Orleans, Attorney Thomas B. Lemann finds himself hard put to explain his own harpsichordia ("Why do you prefer bourbon to Scotch?"), but admits that "there is a simplicity about it" that appeals strongly to his children, who are being raised without any knowledge of the upstart piano. Most harpsichord buffs have a strong proprietary sense. When a New Orleans amateur, Charles Hazlett, lent his harpsichord to touring virtuoso Fernando Valenti, the visitor was amazed. Said Valenti: "It's almost like lending somebody your wife."[1]

The widening scope of harpsichord mania was suggested in this 1960 *Time* article, and newer stars on the harpsichord horizon were publicized by the magazine as well: "Prince Igor" Kipnis (born 1930) was hailed as the most successful player of his generation at the time of a New York Philharmonic debut in 1975.[2] And Anthony Newman (born 1941) was dubbed "Hip Harpsichordist" as he played a Bach program to a sold-out Philharmonic Hall in New York. The audience was "mostly young [and] blue-jeaned," and Newman had them, "after nearly three hours, cheering for more!"[3]

Perhaps what the cheering crowd needed was a repeat performance of the longest harpsichord-celebratory event of the century. *HPSCHD*, pronounced *harpsichord*, John Cage's and Lejaren Hiller's multi-media event created for Antoinette Vischer, was first experienced on 16 May 1969 at the Assembly Hall, University of Illinois at Champaign-Urbana, from 7:30 P.M. until midnight. The music consisted of twenty-minute solos for one to seven harpsichords and tapes for one to fifty-two amplified monaural machines, these materials to be used in whole or in part in any combination, with or without interruptions. The players and their instruments made a varied group: David Tudor played an electronic instrument, the Baldwin solid body harpsichord; Antoinette Vischer and Philip Corner played Neupert double-manual instruments; William Brooks, a Challis single; Ronald Peters, a Brueggeman double; Yuji Takahashi, a Dowd double; and Neely Bruce, a double by Hubbard. "In addition to playing his own solo, each harpsichordist is free to play any of the others," read a note in the program. Some idea of the effect was captured in *Time:*

Of Dice and Din

John Cage was in his element—chaos. The audience of 7,000 wandered to and fro. . . . Wandering happily right along with them, Cage drank in the beeps, doinks and sputterings coming from loudspeakers spaced along the walls. He gazed serenely at the color-crazy patterns sprayed by rotating slide projectors on the walls and the temporary translucent ceiling. He stared at the NASA space film and the clips from the silent era that flickered on the movie screens.

A student stepped up, handed Cage a book and asked him to autograph it: "In view of what's going on here tonight, I thought it would be an appropriate place for your signature." It was a Donald Duck comic book.

. . . Cage patterned six of the harpsichord solos after a 200-year-old romp known as Dice Music. Attributed to Mozart . . . [it] consists of a waltz theme and a set of variations that are determined in a Cage-like manner, by rolling dice.

. . . Meanwhile, some 52 loudspeakers spouted sounds from as many different tape tracks, each confined to a different slice of the octave, each containing from five to fifty-six microtones, each following a pattern programmed by Cage's collaborator, Composer Lejaren Hiller—and then fed to a computer. "The theme is diversity, abundance and Mozart, as opposed to unity, fixity and Bach," Cage explained obscurely. "The idea is to fill the hall with sound."[4]

For the slightly more traditional ambience of the opera house two prominent composers of the century included harpsichord in major works: Benjamin Britten, in *A Midsummer Night's Dream* (1960),[5] and Igor Stravinsky, in the masterpiece of his neo-classic period, *The Rake's Progress* (1951). In the latter, the harpsichord functions both in its wonted role as recitative accompanist and as sinister accomplice to the chilling card scene in which Nick Shadow loses his competition for Tom Rakewell's soul.[6]

Many other composers specified harpsichord in dramatic works, and once in a while the instrument invaded the score of one who did not. In one such reversal, "a harpsichord replaced the piano during the armchair episode [of Ravel's *L'Enfant et les Sortilèges]* to underscore the chair's vintage" in a recording of the work conducted by André Previn.[7] Other appearances of the harpsichord occurred in motion pictures after its film debut in *Wuthering Heights,* where it suddenly appeared even though an earlier scene had featured a piano. The harpsichord showed up in Frank Capra's *Arsenic and Old Lace* (filmed in 1941 but not released until 1944). In the 1960s series of Agatha Christie–Miss Marple mystery romps starring Margaret Rutherford—*Murder She Said, Murder at the Galop, Murder Most Foul,* and *Murder Ahoy*—the harpsichord provides the jaunty signature tune. Tony Richardson's highly honored *Tom Jones* (1963) also helped in the subliminal acceptance of plucked-keyboard sounds. Commercials, too, did their part; radio and television spots with a harpsichord background have been heard and seen frequently. In a mass-media exposure a 1985 Dewar's Profile showed a formal tail-coated image of thirty-nine-year-old harpsichord builder Thomas B. Stevens with instrument, on the back covers of magazines such as *The New Yorker.*

An expanded interest in the harpsichord resulted in some cases from the post-war European study for young professionals made possible by the American Fulbright Exchange Program. Subsequently academic instruction in harpsichord playing was introduced to many American schools. Oberlin Conservatory's Fenner Douglass, returned from organ and harpsichord study in Frankfurt, added harpsichord to his teaching. Christopher Bannister, later a professional harpsichord maker, was the school's first graduate in harpsichord (in 1959). The popularity of harpsichordist Isolde Ahlgrimm's teaching of Oberlin's junior class of music students, all of whom, beginning in 1958, were sent abroad for a year at the Salzburg Mozarteum, led to Ahlgrimm's appointment as guest professor of harpsichord at the Ohio school for the spring semester of 1961. Oberlin's first fulltime professor of harpsichord was Lisa Goode Crawford, a student of the Dutch harpsichordist Gustav Leonhardt. She was appointed to the position in 1973.

Southern Methodist University in Dallas appointed Leonhardt student James Tallis to begin its graduate program in harpsichord in 1968. After Tallis's death in 1969 Larry Palmer, a student of both Ahlgrimm and Leonhardt, was hired to continue the program. Between 1970, when the first master's degree was conferred, and 1986 nearly thirty graduate degrees in harpsichord were granted by the University's Meadows School of the Arts. SMU confirmed its perception of the impact of the harpsichord revival when it conferred an honorary doctorate on Leonhardt in 1983. The Eastman School of Music entered the field later than many other schools, but the distinguished player Arthur Haas was appointed to its faculty in 1983. Among others who have taught harpsichordists in significant numbers are Northwestern's Dorothy Lane, Stanford's Margaret Fabrizio, the University of Washington's Carole Terry, Arizona's John Metz, and Michigan's Edward Parmentier.

Books about the harpsichord and its music seem to be largely an American contribution. The important pioneering studies, Donald Boalch's *Makers of the Harpsichord and Clavichord 1440–1840* (1956) and Raymond Russell's *The Harpsichord and Clavichord* (1959) were, to be sure, by British authors; but the second edition (1973) of Russell's study was revised by the American Howard Schott, who also wrote *Playing the Harpsichord* (1971), one of the most successful instruction books for the instrument. Ruth Nurmi's *A Plain and Easy Introduction to the Harpsichord* was published in 1974, the same year that saw Frances Bedford and Robert Conant's extensive listing of this century's production of harpsichord music, *Twentieth-Century Harpsichord Music: A Classified Catalog.* The importance of

Frank Hubbard's 1965 study, *Three Centuries of Harpsichord Making,* has already been noted. The only survey of harpsichord making in the twentieth century has been Wolfgang Zuckermann's *The Modern Harpsichord* (1969).

The Diapason, an organists' journal, has included harpsichord news and features in its monthly publication since 1967, when a harpsichord column was initiated under the direction of Phillip Treggor. Since 1969, when Larry Palmer became harpsichord editor, the offerings have been varied, culminating in the July 1979 issue, devoted entirely to the harpsichord in celebration of the centenary of Wanda Landowska's birth. *The American Organist* (formerly *Music*), the offical monthly journal of the American Guild of Organists, has pursued a vigorous publishing schedule of harpsichord features under the direction of Miami's Frank Cooper, a noted player and collector of instruments.

Harpsichordists have formed regional societies, (e.g., Southeastern Historical Keyboard Society, Midwestern Historical Keyboard Society) that sponsor conferences, conventions, and competitions for young players and composers for the instrument. A biennial Magnum Opus playing competition in Grand Rapids, Michigan, celebrates both the large instrument constructed by Keith Hill and the exuberant playing of emerging keyboard artists.

The harpsichord in America presents a thriving panorama because of the people who build it and who play it: people such as Gertrud Roberts in Honolulu, who performed her own compositions on brightly decorated John Challis or Rutkowski and Robinette harpsichords for schoolchildren throughout the islands; Fred Hyde in Tuscaloosa, Alabama, who owns Dowd Harpsichord number one; Betty Louise Lumby, whose growing collection of superlative instruments graces Montevallo, Alabama; Willard Martin, the supremely gifted harpsichord maker who builds his exciting instruments in a former Greek Orthodox Church in Bethlehem, Pennsylvania; George Lucktenberg in Spartanburg, South Carolina, traveling with his "Harpsicart" to play concerts in many locations; or David J. Way, who, after publishing Zuckermann's book and building his own kit harpsichord, decided to buy the firm, turn it toward the production of instruments of a more historic design, and continue the business of providing ever-improved do-it-yourself instruments for eager consumers. The list goes on. History does not consist only of neat compartmentalized information.

In 1970 John Challis responded to the publication of Zuckermann's book with these wise words:

> If you had told me forty years ago when beginning my career that there would be so many harpsichord builders in this country and in the world, or that there would be such an interest in seventeeth- and eighteenth-century music, I would never have believed it. It was then like lighting a candle in the darkness. How things have changed in forty years!
>
> . . . Little did I know forty years ago what kind of harpsichord I would now be building! Nor do any of these later builders—if they survive—know what they will be building forty years from now! Changing circumstances and new materials have

their effect. Each artist must produce in accordance with his talents and ideals—just as each person must live according to his talents and ideals.

There has never been a time in the four centuries of harpsichord making when instruments of such wide variety and consummate skill have been made. There has never been a time when so many harpsichord makers have given their art such complete devotion to their individual ideal. I can understand and admire all of them without ever losing my own ideals, which have not yet and probably never will be completely fulfilled.

Fortunately we live in a country where individualism is allowed and still encouraged. Let us never lose it![8]

Notes

PROLOG

1. An inventory of confiscated instruments drawn up by Antonio Bartolomeo Bruni (1759–1823) listed 346 harpsichords and spinets. In a fascinating bit of supplementary information Bruni noted that only thirty-two of the raided houses did not also contain a piano. See Albert G. Hess, "The Transition from Harpsichord to Piano," *Galpin Society Journal* VI (1953): 83–87.

2. Raymond Russell, *The Harpsichord and Clavichord: An Introductory Study*, 2d ed., revised by Howard Schott (New York: Norton, 1973), p.119.

3. Donald H. Boalch, *Makers of the Harpsichord and Clavichord 1440–1840*, 2d ed. (Oxford: Oxford University Press, 1974), p.86.

4. Raymond Russell. "The Harpsichord Since 1800," *Proceedings of the Royal Musical Association* 82 (1955/56): 62 (reprint, Nendeln/Lichtenstein: Kraus, 1968).

5. Ibid. The instrument is described and pictured in Stefano Vittadini, *Catalogo del Museo Teatrale alla Scala* (Milan, 1940), pp.182–183.

6. Russell "1800," p.62.

7. Now in the Steinert Collection of Yale University.

8. Built by Pet Forsman, a maker not listed in Boalch's catalog. See P. Sween, "The Nineteenth Century View of the Old Harpsichord," *The English Harpsichord Magazine* II:7 (April 1979): 92.

9. Alfred J. Hipkins, *A Description and History of the Pianoforte and of the Older Keyboard Stringed Instruments*, 3d ed., 1929 (reprint, Detroit: Detroit Reprints in Music, 1975), p.64.

10. Sween, p.92. "In London, several clavichords have been seen which were made in Finsbury Park, and from their appearance they were made in the 1880–1900 period. . . . Another late nineteenth-century maker was Mr Dove, who made spinets so like those of Baker Harris, that there is doubt as to whether they were rebuilds of old spinets or new creations. Mr Dove is reputed to have made a beautiful copy of a harpsichord which survived the blitz in a house in London, but was destroyed, according to an eye witness, by firemen when they came to demolish the house and refused to carry it out."

11. The first editions of these Liszt works may be seen in the British Library, London; all three bear only the designation "Pro Clavicembalo."

12. "We knocked. A loud, rough voice bid us come in. We found the old giant in a thick cloud of smoke, his long pipe in his mouth, sitting at his old two-manual harpsichord. The quill pen he used in writing was in his hand, a sheet of music paper before him . . ." (Arthur Mendel and Hans T. David, *The Bach Reader*, rev. ed. [New York: Norton, 1966], p.381).

13. Letter to Cav. Luigi Ferrucci, Librarian of the Mediceo-Laurenziana of Florence, dated Passy, 18 October 1868; see chapter 1, p. 12, below. In conversation with Richard Wagner, Rossini is quoted as saying, "On the evening of the première of *Il Barbiere*, when, as was customary then in Italy for opera buffa, I played the clavicembalo in the orchestra to accompany the recitatives . . ." (Edmond Michotte, *Richard Wagner's Visit to Rossini*, translated from the French by Herbert Weinstock [Paris, 1860; Chicago: University of Chicago Press, 1968], p.32). *The Barber of Seville* was first performed on 20 February 1816.

14. Boalch, p.111. There is no positive documentation that Chopin did use a harpsichord but he was passionately fond of the music of J. S. Bach and, more surprisingly for his century, that of Domenico Scarlatti. See Larry Palmer, "In Search of Scarlatti," *The Diapason*, December 1985, p.13.

15. Robert Browning, *Men and Women and Other Poems*, edited by J. W. Harper (London: Dent, 1975), p.23.

16. Rev. Francis Kilvert, *Selections from the Diary,* edited by William Plomer (London: J. Cape, 1938–40), p.255.

17. Charlotte Moscheles, *Life of Moscheles,* adapted from the original German by A. D. Coleridge (London: Hurst and Blackett, 1873), pp.236–237.

18. Harold C. Schonberg, *The Great Pianists* (New York: Simon and Schuster, 1963), p.118.

19. Russell, *The Harpsichord and Clavichord,* pp.121–122. For a listing of Engel's instruments now in the museum, see Howard Schott, *Victoria and Albert Museum: Catalogue of Musical Instruments* (London, 1985), pp.9–10.

20. *The Musical Times,* 1 November 1885, p.649.

21. Hipkins, Introduction by Edwin M. Ripin, p.xi; and Russell, "1800," p.63.

22. Hipkins, p.91. Hipkins's comment raises some questions, however, since English double harpsichords of the period were always equipped with a dogleg arrangement so that the upper-manual 8-foot register was available on the lower manual. See Frank Hubbard, *Three Centuries of Harpsichord Making* (Cambridge: Harvard University Press, 1965), pp.153–160. Did Hipkins, perhaps, play a non-English-style instrument for the *Goldberg Variations?* See note 29 below.

23. Hipkins, p.64.

24. *Zeitschrift für Instrumentenbau,* 1 March 1888; quoted in Eta Harich-Schneider, *Die Kunst des Cembalospiels,* 3d ed. (Kassel: Barenreiter, 1970), p.14.

25. Both comments were quoted in Schonberg, p.269.

26. *The World* (London), 24 May 1893.

27. The instrument is now in the Russell Collection of the University of Edinburgh.

28. This instrument is now in the Musical Instrument Museum, Berlin (Staatliches Institut für Musikforschung, Preussischer Kulturbesitz), no. 17 in the catalog of the collection: cembalo of Pleyel, Wolff, Lyon & Cie. Another early example of Pleyel's work is in the collection of the Smithsonian Institution in Washington, D.C.

29. Information based on Howard Schott, "The Harpsichord Revival," *Early Music* II:2 (April 1974):85–95; and Staatliches Institut für Musikforschung, Preussischer Kulturbesitz, *Das Musikinstrumenten-Museum Berlin—Eine Einführung in Wort und Bild* (Berlin, 1968). Concerning the sound of these instruments, George Bernard Shaw's description of the Pleyel harpsichord used in a concert by Alfred Hipkins early in 1893 is a classic: "Is there the smallest reason to suppose that if we took to making harpsichords we would make good ones? Alas! the question is already answered. . . . Mr. Hipkins [played] . . . on a new harpsichord manufactured by a very eminent Parisian firm of pianoforte makers; and not only did it prove itself a snarling abomination, with vices of tone that even a harmonium would have been ashamed of, but it had evidently been deliberately made so in order to meet the ordinary customer's notion of a powerful and brilliant instrument" (*The World,* 11 January 1893; quoted in G. B. Shaw, *Music in London 1890–94* [London: Constable, 1932], vol. II, p.225).

30. Program by the Société des Instrumens Anciens given in the Salle Érard, Paris, 1 April 1893; collection of the author.

31. Schonberg, pp.269–270. Diémer's student Alfredo Casella played harpsichord professionally beginning in 1906 as a member of Henri Casadesus's ensemble of ancient instruments. "This was a new type of activity for me, and I received some good advice from Diémer, who played the instrument very well" (Alfredo Casella, *Music in My Time,* translated by Spencer Norton [Florence, 1941; Norman: University of Oklahoma Press, 1955], p.72).

32. Angel Record S-36095 (1976). The work was published by Henri Lemoine, Brussels; no. 9598.H.P.690.

33. Isidor Philipp, "Charles-Marie Widor: A Portrait," *The Musical Quarterly* 30 (April 1944): 130–131.

34. See Michael de Cossart, *The Food of Love. Princesse Edmond de Polignac (1865–1943) and her Salon* (London: Hamish Hamilton, 1978), pp.51–52.

35. The composition is the second of the *Épigrammes de Clement Marot,* published by Max Eschig (Paris), no. E-571.D.

36. Information about this première is found in Arbie Orenstein, *Ravel, Man and Musician* (New York: Columbia University Press, 1975), p.21. The discography (p. 249), lists a recording of the work by Paule de Lestang, soprano, in which she accompanies herself at the harpsichord: electrical disc, 25 cm. Gramophone [France] K5338; 1927.

37. The harpsichord had already been used in the opera orchestra in Vienna, under Gustav Mahler; and at London's Covent Garden, where the conductor Hans Richter led several Mozart perforances using the instrument to accompany the recitatives.

38. James Harding, *Massenet* (New York: St. Martin's Press, 1970), p.170. An example of the music for harpsichord is given. In describing the musical and dramatic qualities of the opera Harding writes, "The most effective stroke of all is the harpsichord passage noted earlier" (p. 172).

39. From notes to a recording of *Thérèse,* London AOSA 1165, conducted by Richard Bonynge.

1.

A PASSION FOR COLLECTING

1. Morris Steinert, *Reminiscences,* compiled by Jane Marlin (New York: Putnam's, 1900), pp.195–196.

2. Ibid., p.196.

3. Ibid., p.210.

4. Ibid., pp.210–211.

5. Steinert probably owned the only harpsichords in playing condition in Boston, and possibly in all of the United States! In 1885, when Mr. B. J. Lang organized a celebration of J. S. Bach's 200th birthday, he needed a harpsichord for a performance of the *Coffee Cantata,* so he borrowed one from the Steinert Collection. It was almost certainly the first time in sixty years or more that a harpsichord had been heard in public concert in Boston (William Lyman Johnson, "Musical Life in Boston," *Bulletin of the Library of the Harvard Musical Association,* April 1946).

6. Steinert, p.221.

7. The 1710 date on the Hass harpsichord is very doubtful. A checklist of the *Yale Collection of Early Instruments* (1968) notes that "the third digit has been altered" and gives the date ca. 1770. The Ruckers mother-and-child virginal (a regular 8-foot instrument in the same case with an octave-sounding 4-foot instrument) is dated ca. 1590 in the same checklist.

8. Reprinted from *The New Haven Register* in *Musical Courier* 26:24 (14 June 1893): 32. The instrument is pictured in Eva J. O'Meara, "Historic Instruments in the Steinart Collection," *Yale Alumni Weekly,* 29 March 1929, p.795.

9. Belle Skinner of Holyoke, Massachusetts, discovered a Ruckers double-manual harpsichord rebuilt by Blanchet (1756) during an early trip to Europe. The purchase of this instrument whetted her appetite for more. Her collection eventually included an additional five harpsichords (among them the large Hass that Steinert had found in Vienna), two clavichords, three virginals, and four spinets (including an ottavina by Taskin). In 1960 this collection, too, was presented to Yale University. More of the Steinert instruments have been added to the original gift, including the long-term loan of the Albert Steinert Collection from the Rhode Island School of Design.

10. *Musical Courier* 19:25 (18 December 1889): 520. The instrument did not remain in Milwaukee forever. It was presented to the Groton School, Groton, Massachusetts, in 1939 by Mrs. Fanny Reed Hammond. The history and full description of the instrument are given in M. Sue Ladr's notes to Titanic Records, Ti-49 (1979), a recording of works by Handel and Scarlatti, played by Mark Kroll.

11. Eloise Lownsberry, "Nelly Custis' Harpsichord," *The Etude* 59 (February 1941):92.

12. *The Music Trade Review* 38:17 (1904): 26.

13. Emanuel Winternitz, *Keyboard Instruments in the Metropolitan Museum of Art* (New York, 1961), p.6. *The Catalogue of Keyboard Musical Instruments in the Crosby Brown Collection* (New York, 1903) is a profusely illustrated volume of more than 300 pages. The scholarly introduction on the history of keyboard instruments was written by A. J. Hipkins.

14. See Cynthia Hoover, "Music at the Smithsonian," *The Smithsonian Journal of History* II:1 (Spring 1967):55–56.

15. Albert A. Stanley, *Catalogue of the Stearns Collection of Musical Instruments* (Ann Arbor: University of Michigan, 1921), p.11.

16. Important instruments from the collection were sold at auction during the 1970s.

17. Raymond Russell, *The Harpsichord and Clavichord: An Introductory Study* 2d ed., revised by Howard Schott (New York: Norton, 1973), p.124.

18. Raymond Russell, "The Harpsichord Since 1800," *Proceedings of the Royal Musical Association* 82 (1955/56): 62 (reprint, Nendeln/Lichtenstein: Kraus, 1968.)

2.
AN EXPLORER ARRIVES

1. The life story of Arnold Dolmetsch is an absorbing one; fortunately there is a well-researched biography by Margaret Campbell, *Arnold Dolmetsch: the Man and his Work* (London: Hamish Hamilton, 1975), from which these and other details unascribed to other sources have been taken.

2. Mabel Dolmetsch, *Personal Recollections of Arnold Dolmetsch* (London: Routledge and Kegan Paul, 1957), p.8.

3. Gevaert's obituary in *Musical Courier* 57:27 (30 December 1908):37 includes a portrait of the old gentleman seated at a two-manual harpsichord.

4. Campbell, pp.15–23.

5. Ibid., pp.29–30.

6. "Dolmetsch and His Instruments," brochure from Arnold Dolmetsch, Ltd. (Haslemere, Surrey, 1929), p.3.

7. George Bernard Shaw, in *The World,* 4 July 1894, quoted in Campbell, p.83.

8. "Dolmetsch and His Instruments," p.3.

9. At number 6 Queen Square one may now see Dolmetsch's name inscribed with those of his fellow members in the Art Workers' Guild (founded by his friend Morris), who took over the spot when Dolmetsch vacated it; fittingly a conference on Early Music in Britain was held here in 1979, chaired by Dolmetsch's student Robert Donington.

10. John Runciman, *Saturday Review,* 11 May 1895; quoted in Campbell, pp.87–88.

11. A description of this instrument, with pictures of the decoration, appeared in *International Studio* 10 (New York):187–194. This opus one, which Russell compares to an Italianate instrument, had but one 8-foot stop, with a compass of GG–f3. The decorative painting was done in tempera. It must have been the haste of finishing the instrument for the exhibition that precluded a second register, as there seems to be room for one in the instrument. The three pedals include one for a harp stop and one for shifting the pitch of the instrument up or down a half-step. The harpsichord had to be sold during Dolmetsch's bankruptcy proceedings in 1901; it was returned to him thirty years later through the generosity of a friend, Gerald Cooper. The harpsichord is now in the portion of the Dolmetsch Collection owned by the Horniman Museum, Forest Hill, London, on display at the Ranger's House, Blackheath, London (Howard Schott, "The Harpsichord Revival," *Early Music* II:2 [April 1974]: 87).

12. Campbell, pp.117–118.

13. George Moore, *Evelyn Innes* (1898), pp.1–2. For comments on this work, see

Elizabeth Roche, "George Moore's *Evelyn Innes:* a Victorian 'early music' novel," *Early Music*, XI:1 (January 1983):71–73.

14. Mabel Dolmetsch, p.31.

15. Campbell, pp.137–141.

16. A program for this event is in the collection of the Library of Congress, Washington, D.C.

17. Richard Aldrich, *Concert Life in New York 1902–1923* (New York: G. P. Putnam's Sons, 1941), p.18.

18. The Boston Public Library has a collection of clippings dealing with Arnold Dolmetsch's American years: ML46, B6D55, Brown Collection, compiled by the Music Department, Boston Public Library, 1946.

19. "From the Makers of Music," *The Music Trades,* 24 January 1903; p.7.

20. Campbell, p.148.

21. The libretto of *Ariadne auf Naxos* presents the comic scenario of an *opera buffa* and an *opera seria* being performed together with scenes intermingled rather than as two separate musical works.

22. Campbell, pp.161–162.

23. Ibid., pp.163, 165

24. "Dolmetsch and His Instruments," p.3.

25. C. M. Ayars, *Contributions to the Art of Music in America* (New York: H. W. Wilson, 1937), pp.113–116.

26. Margaret Campbell, "Dolmetsch's American Years," *Bulletin of the Dolmetsch Foundation* 19 (August 1972):4.

27. Jo-Shipley Watson, in *The Musician* (Boston) 17 (January 1912):11.

28. "As auxiliary harpsichordist for our chamber concerts we had a young Californian (one-time infant prodigy) named Charles Adams, employed by Chickering to demonstrate pianos. He took to the harpsichord with immense enthusiasm and acquired a nice easy touch. Thus we were able once more to complete our ensemble which had suffered a loss through the return to England of Kathleen Salmon" (Mabel Dolmetsch, p.69).

29. "President Roosevelt Greatly Interested in Clavichord," *The Music Trades,* 26 December 1908, p.9.

30. Mabel Dolmetsch, pp.69–70.

31. "A Small Plaster House—Luquer and Godfrey, Architects," *The House Beautiful and American Shrubs,* April 1912, pp.135–136.

32. Campbell, "Dolmetsch's American Years," p.3.

33. William Lyman Johnson, "Musical Life in Boston," *Library of the Harvard Musical Association, Bulletin No. 14* (April 1946): n.p.; in Dolmetsch Scrapbook, Boston Public Library.

34. Dolmetsch Scrapbook, Boston Public Library Collection, n.p.

35. Mabel Dolmetsch, pp.77–78. The description of the harpsichord includes the phrase "the first to be equipped with a sixteen-foot register." This appears to be an error, as will be pointed out below; I have, thus, omitted this phrase at the ellipsis marks.

36. Ferruccio Busoni, *Letters to his Wife,* translated by Rosamond Ley (London: E. Arnold, 1938), p.172. A picture of Busoni at his harpsichord was published in *Early Music* XI:1 (January 1983):32.

37. Mabel Dolmetsch, p.78.

38. Translated in Campbell, *Arnold Dolmetsch,* p.177. The original French text of this letter appears on p.176.

39. Breitkopf & Härtel Nr. 4836.

40. See Anthony Beaumont, *Busoni the Composer* (Bloomington: Indiana University Press, 1985), p.215 and Plate 15.

41. See Larry Palmer, "Harpsichord Repertoire in the 20th Century: the Busoni Sonati-

na," *The Diapason,* September 1973, pp.10–11, for a full discussion of this work. The first recording on the harpsichord was made by the author for The Musical Heritage Society on MHS 3222, *The Harpsichord Now and Then.*

42. Mabel Dolmetsch, pp.81–82.

43. This should put to rest, once and for all, the controversy concerning the date of Dolmetsch's introduction of the 16-foot register into his harpsichords. Busoni's instrument, number sixty of the Chickering production, was eventually repurchased by the firm from Busoni's widow. It was sold first to the American harpsichordist Lotta Van Buren and then to Ralph Kirkpatrick, who used it for his early concerts and recordings. This instrument does not contain a 16-foot register. It should be noted that Dolmetsch's 16-foot evidently predated the first such register in the Pleyel harpsichords. Their Landowska model, so-endowed, was introduced in 1912. German builders had included the 16-foot stop even earlier. The Gemeentemuseum in The Hague owns a Wilhelm Hirl harpsichord of 1899 modeled on the spurious "Bach harpsichord." Hirl's instrument was built for the Dutch musical amateur Daniel Scheurleer.

44. Johnson, Boston Public Library Collection.

45. Mabel Dolmetsch, pp.88–89.

46. Johnson, n.p.

47. Campbell, *Arnold Dolmetsch,* pp.181–182.

3.
DOLMETSCH'S AMERICAN LEGACY

1. Quote from the *New York American* printed in a Namara advertisement, *Musical Courier,* 17 January 1918, p.23. A portrait of Namara and friends with pianist-accompanist Rudolph Ganz seated at the two-manual harpsichord appeared on p. 24.

2. John Ardoin, "Namara: A Remembrance," *The Opera Quarterly* I:4 (Winter 1983):76. Namara, who had toured with Caruso and McCormack, danced with Isadora Duncan and starred in a silent film with Rudolph Valentino. She sang into her eighties (she died in Spain in 1974). She recorded Falla's *Nana* accompanying herself at her spinet.

3. Richard Aldrich, *Concert Life in New York 1902–1923* (New York: G. P. Putnam's Sons, 1941), pp. 528–529.

4. From a brochure in the Koussevitzsky Bequest, the Library of Congress, *Le Célèbre Société des Instruments Anciens* (Paris, printed by M. Surugue).

5. *New York Times,* 17 January 1926. Mason was a member of a distinguished American musical family and professor of music at Columbia University beginning in 1909. For a fascinating picture of musical life in the United States in the early years of the twentieth century, see his *Music in My Time and Other Reminiscences* (New York, 1938). The full text of Landowska's letter is given in chapter 4 below.

6. Sigmund Spaeth, "Musical Uplift for the Collegian," *Opera Magazine* 1 (April 1914):32.

7. *New York Times,* 12 December 1907.

8. Arthur Whiting, *The Lesson of the Clavichord,* [n.d.], pp.5–6. From the collection of The Library of Congress, Washington, D.C.

9. Mabel Dolmetsch, *Personal Recollections of Arnold Dolmetsch* (London: Routledge and Kegan Paul, 1957), pp.75–76.

10. Whiting, p.6.

11. Ibid., p.8.

12. Ibid., p.9.

13. Mabel Dolmetsch, p.82.

14. Spaeth, pp.31–32.

15. *Baker's Biographical Dictionary of Music*, 6th ed., edited by Nicholas Slonimsky, p.1304.

16. *Musical Courier*, 22 April 1914, p.37.

17. *The Musical Monitor*, May 1918, p.425.

18. *New York Times*, 7 March 1926, sec. VIII, p.6.

19. Ibid., 22 March 1918, p.11.

20. Ibid., 6 January 1937, p.19.

21. "Deep River Antiques," *Time*, 19 August 1935, p.32.

22. Biographical information is taken from a typescript sketch for a biography made by Lotta Van Buren's husband, Henry Bizallion (Van Buren Papers, Harold B. Lee Library, Brigham Young University, Provo, Utah).

23. *Musical Courier*, 12 June 1912.

24. Ibid., 26 January 1922.

25. *Musical America*, 9 August 1924.

26. *Musical Courier*, 11 March 1926, p.47.

27. *Musical Observer*, October 1923.

28. Script for radio program "So You Haven't the Time?" by Alice Pentlange, Station WQXR, New York 26 May 1937 (Van Buren Papers).

29. Eva J. O'Meara, "Historic Instruments in the Steinert Collection," *The Yale Alumni Weekly*, 29 March 1929, pp.795–796. O'Meara was the librarian of the School of Music.

30. *Fortune*, August 1934, p.10.

31. A Recital Upon Old Instruments, 2 April 1940, Palmer Auditorium, Connecticut College, New London, Connecticut (Van Buren Papers).

4.

THE INCOMPARABLE WANDA LANDOWSKA

1. Pitts Sanborn, "Wanda Landowska," *The Nation* 118:3066 (9 April 1924).

2. Harriette Brower, *Modern Masters of the Keyboard* (New York: Frederick A. Stokes, 1926), p.85.

3. Denise Restout and Robert Hawkins, eds., *Landowska on Music* (New York: Stein and Day, 1964), p.19.

4. *The Etude* 23 (November 1905):444; translated from the French by Edward Burlingame Hill.

5. *Musical Courier*, 29 November 1923, p.20.

6. Ibid., 3 January 1924, p.14.

7. Ibid., 24 January 1924, pp.24–25.

8. Ibid., 28 February 1924, p.32.

9. Charles E. Watt, *Musical News*, 21 March 1924, p.6.

10. *Musical Courier*, 20 March 1924, p.60.

11. See Restout and Hawkins, Discography, pp.411–422. See also Julian Morton Moses, *Collector's Guide to American Recording, 1895–1925* (New York, 1949), where these selections are listed as Victor Records 973 and 1038, recorded in 1924.

12. Arthur Shattuck, *The Memoirs of Arthur Shattuck*, edited by S. F. Shattuck (Neenah, WI: privately printed, 1961), pp.106–108. Shattuck (1881–1951), a touring artist of some reputation, had an enduring interest in older music. In 1928 he acquired a Beethoven piano that had been restored by Lotta Van Buren and presented it to the Beethoven Association. A large Pleyel harpsichord acquired in 1929 was inaugurated in his Paris apartment by Landowska's pupil Ruggiero Gerlin. The same instrument eventually was brought to Shattuck's New York apartment, from which it was borrowed on at least one occasion by Landowska. The harpsichord was bequeathed to the Lawrence Conservatory of Music in autumn 1952 (*Memoirs*, pp.224–225).

13. George Painter, *Marcel Proust: A Biography* (Boston: Little, Brown & Co., 1959–1965), "An Indian Summer," vol. 2, pp.334–335. I am grateful to Momo Aldrich for pointing out this citation to me. She also mentioned that according to Landowska, her husband, Henri Lew, was something of a sadist, and that he insisted that Wanda try every experience possible—a necessity, in his opinion for an artistic personality.

14. Brower, p.83. Brower interviewed Landowska in "her artistic studios, high up in one of New York's residential hotels, situated in the heart of the city. . . ."

15. *Musical Courier,* 20 November 1924, p.34.

16. *Time,* 27 October 1924, p.12.

17. Pitts Sanborn, "The 1925–26 Season," *Modern Music* 3:4 (May–June 1926):3–9.

18. *New York Times,* 3 January 1926.

19. *Musical Courier,* 4 February 1926, p.20.

20. *Time,* 15 March 1926, p.18.

21. Olin Downes, *New York Times,* 7 January 1927.

22. The Boston program was the eleventh of the orchestra's forty-sixth season, given on Friday, 31 December 1926 and Saturday, 1 January 1927 (information from Boston Symphony program books). See also Larry Palmer, "The Concertos of Falla and Poulenc," *The Diapason,* July 1979, pp.9–11. The statement in Ronald Crichton, *Manuel de Falla: Descriptive Catalogue of his Works* (London: Chester Music, 1976), p.45, that Landowska "never played the work again [after the Barcelona première]" is in error in view of existing programs and published critiques.

23. *Musical Courier,* 3 February 1927, p.45.

24. Conversation with Momo Aldrich, Honolulu, 29 December 1979.

25. *Musical Courier,* 22 December 1927, pp.22, 24. This is the only notice found of any Landowska appearances during this mysterious visit; the next press note details her sailing.

26. Ibid., 26 January 1928, p.10.

27. Momo Aldrich, "Reminiscences of St. Leu," *The Diapason,* July 1979, pp.3, 8.

28. *Musical Courier,* 10 February 1927, p.44.

29. Ibid., 3 March 1927, p.41; a report by Edouarde Combe from the *Tribune,* Geneva, Switzerland.

30. Eta Harich-Schneider, *Charaktere und Katastrophen* (Berlin: Ullstein, 1978), pp.81–83; freely translated by the author.

31. Ralph Kirkpatrick, *Early Years* (New York: Peter Lang, 1985), p.68.

32. Ibid., p.69.

33. Ibid.

34. Lucille Wallace (1898–1977) was born in Chicago. In 1931 she became the wife of the noted British pianist Clifford Curzon, also an interpretation student of Landowska's.

5.

LEWIS RICHARDS, AMERICAN HARPSICHORDIST

1. Landowska's debut with the Philadelphia Orchestra took place twelve days later.

2. *Musical Courier,* 31 January 1924.

3. From Lewis Richards program of 2 March 1932, Peoples Church, East Lansing, Michigan; courtesy of Elsa Richards.

4. Quoted in *Musical Courier,* 31 January 1924, p.19.

5. Ibid.

6. Muskegon-Brunswick 3205A/B and Brunswick 2930A/B.

7. *Musical Courier,* 11 February 1926, p.46.

8. Damrosch was no stranger to the harpsichord; he had purchased an instrument from Arnold Dolmetsch.

9. *Musical Courier,* 9 December 1926, p.33.

10. Ibid., 2 December 1926, p.20.
11. Ibid., 30 December 1926, p.25.
12. *New York Times,* 13 October 1929; *Musical Courier,* 9 November 1929, p.39.
13. *Musical Courier,* 5 November 1925, p.26.
14. Ibid., 4 October 1930, p.5.

6.

LANDOWSKA'S AMERICAN CIRCLE

1. Momo Aldrich, "Reminiscences of St. Leu," *The Diapason,* July 1979, p.8.
2. Ibid., p.3.
3. According to Momo Aldrich, this was Putnam's view in the 1930s. But when Landowska returned to the United States in the 1940s, his judgment was that she was "considerably mellowed."
4. Paul Emerson, "Stanford's Aldrich . . . to retire," *Palo Alto Times,* 30 May 1969.
5. Nicolas Slonimsky, *Perfect Pitch* (Oxford and New York: Oxford University Press, 1988), p. 142.
6. Letter from Momo Aldrich to the author, dated 29 April 1988.
7. Elizabeth Borton, "Talking it Over With Unusual Bostonians: Putnam Aldrich," *Boston Herald,* 25 June 1933, p. B7.
8. For the full text of Aldrich's complimentary review, see pp. 79–80.
9. Emerson, *Palo Alto Times.* Actually, Aldrich had been a visiting lecturer at Princeton University in 1939 and, from 1939 to 1942, both lecturer and performer at the Berkshire Music Center in Tanglewood.
10. Putnam Aldrich, "Classics of Music Literature: Wanda Landowska's Musique Ancienne," *Music Library Notes* 27:3 (March 1971):466.
11. Conversation with Arthur Lawrence, 21 September 1979.
12. Information on Aldrich's performing career, when not otherwise credited, comes from a "Putnam Aldrich Bibliography" compiled by Edward Colby, head music librarian of Stanford University and Elizabeth Hays, a Ph.D. student and harpsichordist. This eleven-page listing of publications and performances with dates was provided by Momo Aldrich.
13. Emerson, *Palo Alto Times.*
14. *Time,* 30 October 1939, p.36.
15. *Musical Courier,* 5 January 1928, p.16. The article is signed "C." and was apparently written by Jeannette Cox, who is listed as the journal's correspondent from Chicago. During a conversation with Gavin Williamson in Chicago on 22 September 1979 the author was assured that the story was true.
16. *Music News* (Chicago), 12 January 1923, p.18.
17. *Musical Courier,* 25 October 1928, p.10.
18. Conversation with Gavin Williamson.
19. Bjarne Dahl, "Pleyel," *The Harpsichord* VI:2 (1973): 3.
20. "Le Printemps rejeunit la terre,/Et les semences qu'elle enserre/ Se respandent en mille fleurs:/ Ainsi ceste douce harmonie/ Nous changes,/ Et rejeunit la vie,/ Par ses traitz de mille couleurs." (Spring rejuvenates the earth,/ And the seed which she nurtures/ Blossoms into a thousand flowers./ Thus doth sweet harmony/ That changes us and rejuvenates life/ With its many-toned colors.—Translated by Allegra Aldrich Tarentino.)
21. *Musical Courier,* 14 January 1933, p.22.
22. Lois Watt North, *Musical News* (Chicago), 13 July 1939, p.18. Also on the program was the Chicago première of *Job* by Vaughan Williams, conducted by Adrian Boult. The Bach had been directed from the harpsichords by the soloists.
23. Conversation with Gavin Williamson.
24. *Musical Courier,* 22 March 1928, p.41.

25. *The Manuel and Williamson Harpsichord Ensemble,* circular from Louise Spoor, Chicago; quoted in Sr. Stephen Marie Lyons, "Reawakening Interest in the Harpsichord," M.A. thesis, St. Joseph College, 1966, p.84.

26. Conversation with Gavin Williamson.

27. Letter from Samuel P. Puner to the author dated 13 June 1983.

28. Hal Haney, "Interview with Alice Ehlers," *The Harpsichord* VI:1 (1973):5.

29. Oral History Transcript, UCLA Library 300/57, p.24.

30. Ibid., p.15.

31. Ibid., p.21.

32. Ibid.

33. Alice Ehlers, *Vom Cembalo* (Wolfenbüttel-Berlin: G. Kallmeyer Verlag, 1933), p.6.

34. Oral History, p.171.

35. Ibid., p.59.

36. Ibid., pp.32, 38, 62. Hindemith (1895–1963) professed a strong dislike for the harpsichord as an instrument (could it have had anything to do with too much Daquin?). Sadly, he never wrote a solo work for the instrument, although his musical aesthetic would have seemed perfectly suited to the medium. He did, however, introduce the harpsichord into the score of his opera *The Long Christmas Dinner* (Mainz: Schott's Söhne, 1986).

37. *Boston Herald,* 19 February 1936.

38. Reviews quoted in David Ewen, *Living Musicians* (New York: H. W. Wilson, 1940), p.109. Ewen misstates that this New York concert was Ehlers's "American" debut.

39. Oral History, p.50.

40. Ibid., p.47.

41. Ibid., pp.47–48.

42. Ibid., p.204.

43. Ibid., p.193.

44. Dahl, p.3.

45. Oral History, p.21.

7.

MADE IN AMERICA: HARPSICHORDS?

1. Una L. Allen, "A Dolmetsch of the Middle-West," *The Musician,* November 1932, pp.5–6.

2. Hal Haney, "Portrait of a Builder: John Challis," *The Harpsichord* II:3 (1969): 16.

3. William Dowd, lecture, "The 20th-Century Harpsichord Revival," Smithsonian Institution, Washington, D.C., 24 April 1980.

4. Conversation with Dowd's former apprentice Willard Martin; Dallas, 30 June 1987.

5. Haney, p.16.

6. *Time,* 24 January 1944, pp.92–93.

7. "Many have been interested in the beautiful woods I use in the instruments. The outside casework is of American walnut, beautifully figured, and finished with linseed oil, which brings out the natural beauty of the wood. This, a very old method of finishing, is not used today because of the length of time needed; it requires that the wood be of beautiful grain—which is too expensive for modern manufacturers. The sharps are made of boxwood—a very hard, golden colored wood—and the naturals of ebony. This reversed coloring of the keys was the old custom. While I like the following of custom, this is not the real reason for holding to it. Keys made entirely of wood are much more pleasant to play, and they harmonize with the rest of the instrument which is also of wood" (John Challis, "The Harpsichord's Revival," *The American Organist* 18 [October 1935]: 382).

8. Wolfgang Zuckermann, *The Modern Harpsichord* (New York: October House, 1969), p.93.

9. Information from Haney, p.17, and from Dowd lecture.

10. Zuckermann surmised that the metal was actually anodized aluminum, less than $\frac{1}{16}$ inch thick (p.94).

11. Haney, pp.20–21.

12. Zuckermann, p.97.

13. Brochure, *Instruments Made by John Challis,* pp.4–5

14. Dowd lecture.

15. *Time,* 15 August 1960, p. 56.

16. The author, by fortuitous chance, happened to be present for Biggs's first encounter with this instrument.

17. The author was seated in an adjacent row at this concert. It was pleasant to renew acquaintance with John Challis and to receive an invitation to visit his new quarters, the shop on lower lower Fifth Avenue.

18. *The Diapason,* January 1975, p.14.

19. Bernard Asbell, "After Hours: The Harpsichord with the Forward Look," *Harper's* 216 (June 1958): 80.

20. John Caffrey, "John Challis and Julius Wahl: Harpsichords for Americans," *Musical America,* February 1950, p.131. Zuckermann, p.194, relies exclusively on these facts from *Musical America.*

21. Letter to the author from Max E. Wahl, Julius Wahl's son, dated 5 August 1988.

22. Caffrey, p.131.

23. Ibid.

24. Ibid., p.248.

25. Hal Haney. "Conversation with Builder-Harpsichordist Claude Jean Chiasson," *The Harpsichord* V:3 (1972):9.

26. Ibid., p.6.

27. Ibid., p.7.

28. Ibid., pp.7–8.

29. Ibid., p.9.

8.

NEW GENERATION, NEW AESTHETIC

1. *Time,* 3 February 1947, p.46.

2. Ralph Kirkpatrick, "Fifty Years of Harpsichord Playing," *Early Music* XI:1 (January 1983): 31.

3. Ibid., p.33.

4. Ralph Kirkpatrick, *Early Years* (New York: Peter Lang, 1985), p.65.

5. Ibid., p.77.

6. Ibid., p.71; dated Tuesday, 20 October 1931.

7. Ibid., p.80.

8. Ibid., p.86.

9. Ibid., pp.92–93.

10. Kirkpatrick later gave a concise overview of this spurious "Bach harpsichord" and its effect on registration in Bach's harpsichord music: "Although it never did belong to the Bach family, it came to be regarded as a typical Bach instrument. It now has eight- and four-foot on the upper manual and eight- and sixteen-foot on the lower. . . . Until recent years at least ninety percent of modern harpsichord building in Germany was influenced by this 'Bach instrument.' Friedrich Ernst has proved not only that the four-foot was originally on the lower manual but that the sixteen-foot was actually a later addition to the instrument" *(Interpreting Bach's Well-Tempered Clavier* [New Haven and London: Yale University Press, 1984], p.10).

11. "I took two hours with Ramin, during which I played the rest of the Goldberg Variations and we went over the Fifth Brandenburg Concerto and a Handel Chaconne. Ramin played a certain amount, with a great deal of vitality and a certain grand and very exciting style, along with many false notes and general indifference to detail. His playing is certainly that of a man of great talent, but distinctly personal, romantic and often rather restless" (Kirkpatrick, *Early Years,* p. 100).

12. Ibid., p.99.

13. Ibid., pp.102–103.

14. *Musical America,* 25 April 1934, p.33.

15. Paul Rosenfeld, "J. S. Bach: Three Glimpses. I. Bach the Colorist," in *Discoveries of a Music Critic,* (New York: Harcourt, Brace, and Company, 1936; reprint 1972), pp. 28–30. See also the description of Kirkpatrick's clavichord program in Ralph Kirkpatrick, "On Playing the Clavichord," *Early Music* IX:3 (July 1981):301, where he quotes the review from the *New York Times* of 11 April 1934: "Mr. Kirkpatrick's technique, the precision and delicacy of his touch, are almost faultless. But the remarkable thing about his playing, after one accustoms one's ears to the Lilliputian dynamics of the clavichord, is the illusion of great range in volume he establishes through the complete identification of himself with his subject and the variations of tone color and tonal power, hence emotional vividness, that his sublety achieves, from the tiny, exquisite vibrato of a saraband's slow melody to the brilliant friskiness of a gigue.

"So complete was one's transportation into another and more delicate realm of sound that one left the recital feeling that the most whispered utterance of a piano must henceforth sound gross."

16. Kirkpatrick, "Fifty Years," p.35.

17. Ibid., p.35.

18. Ibid., p.34.

19. Julius Bloom, ed., *The Year in American Music, 1946–1947* (New York: Allen, Towne, and Heath, 1947), pp.57–58.

20. J. S. Bach, *Goldberg Variations,* edited for the harpsichord or piano by Ralph Kirkpatrick (New York: G. Schirmer, 1938), p.ix.

21. Ibid., p.xxviii.

22. Willie Ruff, "A Musician's Legacy: Ralph Kirkpatrick Remembered," *Yale Alumni Magazine,* April 1985, p.20.

23. Virgil Thomson, *The Musical Scene* (New York: Knopf, 1947), pp.62–63.

24. *Musical Courier* 139 (15 February 1949):37–38 signed "R.K." [Rafael Kammerer].

25. *Musical America* 72 (February 1952):212; signed "A.H."

26. Published by G. Schirmer as volumes 1774 and 1775 in Schirmer's Library of Musical Classics.

27. *Musical America,* 1 February 1954, p.24; signed "R.K." [Rafael Kammerer].

28. Kirkpatrick, "Fifty Years," pp.37–38.

29. *Newsweek,* 7 October 1957, p.80.

9.

TWO "FIRST LADIES OF THE HARPSICHORD"

1. Nicolas Slonimsky, ed., *Baker's Biographical Dictionary of Musicians,* 5th ed. (New York: G. Schirmer, 1958), p.1232.

2. *Time,* 12 October 1936, p.50. The article was illustrated with a Bernard Hoffman photograph of Pessl at the harpsichord.

3. Biographical information from *The International Who Is Who in Music,* 5th ed. (Chicago, 1951), p.328; and David Ewen, *Living Musicians* (New York: H. W. Wilson, 1940), p.274. See also Catherine A. Dower, *Yella Pessl: A Life of Fire and Conviction*

(Westfield, MA: Westfield State College, 1986), p.34, concerning the date of Pessl's retirement from Columbia University.

4. *New York Times,* 2 February 1941; signed "R.P."

5. *New York Times,* 3 February 1942.

6. Conversation with Ben Hyams, Honolulu, Hawaii, 12 January 1983.

7. *New York Times,* 27 March 1945.

8. As a novice harpsichord student at the Salzburg Mozarteum in 1958 the author occasionally practiced on that institution's Maendler-Schramm "Bach-model" harpsichord. It was common talk among the students that if the instrument were moved the outside wall against which it was placed would probably collapse. For all its heavy construction the instrument was of that variety known as a "whisperchord." Hearing it at all was a triumph.

9. Wolfgang Zuckermann, *The Modern Harpsichord* (New York: October House, 1969), p.143.

10. *New York Times* 29 December 1946; signed "R.L."

11. Ibid., 4 March 1958; signed "E.D."

12. Information from *Press Book: Sylvia Marlowe, Harpsichordist,* p.5. Mimeographed manuscript from The Harpsichord Music Society, courtesy of Kenneth Cooper.

13. Hal Haney, "Interview with Sylvia Marlowe," *The Harpsichord* IV:3 (1971):6–7. It might be with a bit of a vested interest that Virgil Thomson wrote of Marlowe and her harpsichord in 1947: "One cannot be too grateful to Miss Marlowe and the Boston group for giving us great music from the past on instruments closely resembling those for which it was conceived. I say closely resembling because Miss Marlowe plays a modern harpsichord—a Pleyel, the finest in town, I should think . . ." (*The Art of Judging Music* [New York: Knopf, 1948], p.64).

14. Haney, p.7.

15. *Newsweek,* 8 May 1939, pp.36–37.

16. Haney, p.7.

17. "Musicians mostly don't hold, either, with the popular practice of swinging the classics, though they constantly do it to amuse one another at social gatherings. And yet every age has forced the music of previous ages to obey the rhythmic customs of its own. . . . And I have found charming entertainment in an evening radio hour during which Miss Sylvia Marlowe at the harpsichord and some excellent jazz musicians improvise in the American rhythmic style on melodies from Haydn and Rameau" (Virgil Thomson, "Transcriptions," in *The Music Scene* [New York: Knopf, 1947], p.276.

18. David Keith [pseudonym for Francis Steegmuller], *Blue Harpsichord* (New York: Dodd, Mead and Co., 1949), p.18.

19. Ibid., pp.178–179.

20. Noel Straus, "Sylvia Marlowe in Classic Works," *New York Times,* 17 January 1946.

21. *New York Times,* 29 November 1948; signed "N.S."

22. Harold C. Schonberg, "American in Orient," *New York Times,* 22 April 1956.

23. Else Stone and Kurt Stone, eds., *The Writings of Elliott Carter* (Bloomington: Indiana University Press, 1977), p.272.

24. *Musical Courier* 159 (March 1959):19; signed "J.L.B."

25. Ibid.

26. An additional composition by Rieti, *Concertino for Five Instruments,* was scored for harpsichord, flute, viola, cello, and harp.

27. Letter to the author, 29 September 1970.

28. Donal Henahan, *New York Times,* 14 January 1972. In the Preface to *Mikrokosmos* Bartók suggested the use of the harpsichord for some of the pieces. A recording, "Two Harpsichords Live," with works of Stravinsky, Bartók, Satie, and Thomson from this recital and from Marlowe's last public concert appearance (30 March 1976) was issued by The Harpsichord Music Society Archive as HMS 901 in 1988.

29. Haney, p.20.

30. *Newsweek,* 2 April 1962, p.50.
31. Written in 1948, quoted in Kenneth Cooper, "Sylvia Marlowe: Wit, Warmth, and Wisdom," *High Fidelity,* June 1982, p.55.
32. *New York Times,* 19 January 1973.
33. Ibid., 15 October 1975.
34. Cooper, discography, p.56.
35. *Music Journal* 20:1 (January 1962):71.

10.

A GOLDEN AGE

1. Obituary, *Musical America,* September 1959, p.12.
2. Virgil Thomson, *The Musical Scene* (New York: Knopf, 1947), pp.201–202.
3. For a first-hand account of these harrowing days, see Hal Haney, "Conversation with Harpsichordist Denise Restout," *The Harpsichord* VII:1 (1974): 11, 14–15.
4. Ibid., pp.15–16.
5. Ibid., p.16.
6. Hal Haney, "Conversation with Claude Jean Chiasson," *The Harpsichord* V:3 (1972):12.
7. *Newsweek,* 23 February 1948, p.84.
8. Julius Bloom, ed., *The Year in American Music, 1946–1947* (New York: Allen, Towne, and Heath, 1947), pp.230–231.
9. This account, originally in English, was transcribed into German by Isolde Ahlgrimm who was a teacher of Mrs. Thomas. The retranslation into English, made in 1979 by the present author, has been checked for accuracy by Ahlgrimm. The Thomases, listed previously as purchasers of a Challis harpsichord, were residents of Ohio for many years. They retired to California.
10. Thomson, "A Shower of Gold," 22 October 1942, in *The Musical Scene,* p.203.
11. Virgil Thomson, "Definitive Renderings," 20 November 1944 in *The Art of Judging Music* (New York: Knopf, 1948), p.61.
12. Haney, "Conversation with Denise Restout," p.7.
13. *Newsweek,* 23 February 1948, p.84.
14. *New Republic,* 28 July 1952, pp.22–23.
15. Halina Rodzinski, *Our Two Lives* (New York: Scribner's, 1976), pp.262–263. Further details are offered: "The night of her first Philharmonic appearance, I looked in on her dressing room which adjoined Artur's. She and her assistants had recreated the Landowska environs, yellow roses in a vase atop a piano, clothes, mostly velours, spilling from open suitcases, and, of all things, a chamber pot. Wanda scorned public facilities, perhaps for sanitary considerations, but undoubtedly through a sense of her worth. In either case, it was among the duties of the two assistants to minister to her thunder mug, and even this they did with grace and smiles, so loyal and dedicated a pair they were" (ibid.).
16. Wanda Landowska, "Modern Music at the Harpsichord," quoted by Denise Restout in notes to Poulenc, *Concert Champêtre,* International Piano Library Limited Editions recordings, IPL-107, p.9.
17. Poulenc to Lucien Chevallier in 1929; quoted in Restout, pp.9–10.
18. See note 16. Poulenc had played the work at the piano (the alternative version) with Mitroupoulos in New York in November 1948. Two previous performances with harpsichord had been radio broadcasts: the first movement only, with Yella Pessl as soloist, in 1946; and a complete performance with Sylvia Marlowe in May 1948.
19. Restout, p.13.
20. Ibid., p.11. Before the performances, Poulenc wrote Landowska on 17 October 1949, "That summer in 1928 when I worked with you at St.-Leu remains for me certainly a blessed

time. I can still remember our long hours of work in your hall—our recesses, filled with jokes—our laughter around your famous dinner table, covered with delicious dishes—and the cherries we stole in the garden from the birds who really deserved them. How far away it seems—and yet so near to my heart. But you are a magician and the wrinkles on my old Concert Champêtre will disappear under your fingers. . . . Your child musician (as you christened me at St.-Leu), Francis" (Robert Sabin, "Poulenc: 'The Essence Is Simplicity,'" *Musical America* [15 November 1949], p.27).

21. *Musical America,* March 1949, pp.20, 22; signed "R.S."

22. *Time,* 20 June 1949, pp.41–42.

23. Howard Taubman, "Priestess of the Harpsichord," *New York Times Magazine,* 11 February 1951, p.16.

24. *Time,* 1 December 1952, p.31.

25. Harold Cantor, "High Priestess of Happiness," *The American Mercury,* July 1955, pp.82–83.

26. An editorial extolling the success of this program appeared in *Musical America* for 15 November 1953: "It appeared on NBC on a Sunday afternoon a few weeks ago."

27. The audio portion of this interview was issued on record as side 2 of Veritas, VM 104, issued by the International Piano Library.

28. William F. Buckley, Jr., "Queen of All Instruments: An Amateur Player Recounts His Long Love Affair with the Harpsichord," *New York Times Magazine,* 2 January 1983, pp.34–35.

29. "For the Ages: Record of WTC," *Newsweek,* 11 July 1955, p.71. The price for the six-record set was $49.95.

30. Abram Chasins, "Bach's Will, Landowska's Testament," *Saturday Review,* 27 November 1954, pp.56–57.

31. Vis-à-vis Landowska's Couperin, Ben Hyams, a program annotator for CBS in New York, relates a story told to him by the conductor Bernard Herrmann: "Landowska described a certain place in a Couperin piece, 'And here is the spot where he puts his hand in her blouse' " (conversation with Ben Hyams, Honolulu, Hawaii, 12 January 1983).

32. Haney, "Conversation with Denise Restout," p.23.

33. See David Stevens, "A Harpsichordist Who Dares to Buck the Tide," *New York Times,* 6 October 1985.

34. Interview with Marie Zorn reported in a letter to the author from Lewis Baratz, 14 May 1987.

35. Joseph Hansen, *Skinflick* (New York: Holt, Rinehart and Winston, 1979), p.108.

36. William M. Hoffman, ed., *Gay Plays* (New York: Avon Books, 1979), pp.420–421.

37. *Stereo Review,* December 1984, p.39.

11.

THE PAST IS FUTURE

1. William Dowd, lecture at the Smithsonian Institution, Washington, D.C., 25 April 1980.

2. Hal Haney, "Portrait of a Builder: William Dowd," *The Harpsichord* IV:1 (1971):10, 12. Concerning the actual chronology of these events, William Dowd commented, "Chiasson played his own 'monster' named 'Penthesilea' Queen of the Amazon[s]. I met another freshman and classmate, Dan Pinkham, there and he invited me to see his new Challis 'portable.' The first time I heard the Chickering in concert, Dan played it in one of the Harvard Houses" (letter to the author, 15 October 1987).

3. Frank Hubbard, "Reconstructing the Harpsichord," in *The Historical Harpsichord,* I, edited by Howard Schott (New York: Pendragon Press, 1984), p.6.

4. Ibid., pp.7–8.

5. Ibid., p.9.

6. Haney, p.12.

7. Dowd letter, 15 October 1987.

8. Haney, p.9.

9. Hubbard, p.10.

10. Dowd letter, 15 October 1987.

11. Haney, p.18.

12. From personal experience the author is able to report that his Dowd French double after Blanchet, completed in 1968, was built with pedals. After placing the order it took a trip to Cambridge to convince William Dowd that the pedals would be used in the twentieth-century literature and that they would not be misused in the standard repertoire. Dowd agreed to supply the instrument as ordered. When this harpsichord (his number 167) was returned in 1977 for the removal of its original brass jack slides (replaced with the now standard wooden, leather-covered ones), lightening of the key action, and requilling, Dowd was given the option of removing the pedal mechanism and replacing it with hand stops. His reply was characteristic: "I built the best pedals in the business, so let's just leave them! "

13. Hal Haney, "Interview with Frank Hubbard," *The Harpsichord* VI:1 (1972):14.

14. Gustav Leonhardt, "Preface," *The Historical Harpsichord* I, p.vii.

15. The Dowd-von Nagel partnership ended in the summer of 1983.

16. Ralph Kirkpatrick, "Fifty Years of Harpsichord Playing," *Early Music* XI:1 (January 1983):38.

17. Josephine Robertson, "Harpsichord Popularity Is Seen Growing," *Cleveland Plain Dealer,* 15 December 1960. The harpsichord used at the concerts was described as "in a case of American walnut; it is patterned after one by the 18th-century French harpsichord maker Pascal Taskin. It has two manuals, three sets of strings, and five pedals: an eight-foot stop for the upper manual, an eight-foot and a four-foot for the lower, plus coupler and lute stop. Its full range is more than six octaves. The tone of the instrument is unusually reverberant and 'long-lived,' which fits it well for concert performance in a large hall" (Cleveland Orchestra program book [15 and 17 December 1960], p.352).

18. The work is published by Boosey and Hawkes, B&H 16239; and the recording is Columbia Records, ML 4495.

19. Oliver Daniel, quoting a letter from Kirkpatrick, in Foreword to Henry Cowell, *Set of Four,* (New York: Associated Music Publishers, 1976 [AMP-7436]).

20. *Six Sonatas* by Lou Harrison are lovely two-voice works. "I wrote them individually or in groups of two at several times, thus, the first one actually dates from the mid-30s, but the whole set was not completed until the early '40s. The original impulse came from two sources as the Sonatas themselves have probably already made clear to you. The first of these was my intense admiration for Manuel de Falla and especially for his use of the harpsichord in several instances including the famous Concerto. This was, in my own feelings, perhaps erroneously embedded in a matrix of feeling which concerned California. The 'Mission Period' style of life, artifacts, and feelings intrigued me very much. You will, of course, remember that this was the WPA period and that the dominant impulse was 'Regionalism.' Thus, the Cembalo Sonatas reflect 'Nights in the Gardens of Spain,' 'Flamenco,' as well as 'Indian Dances' and 'Provincial Baroquery' in the West . . ." (letter to the author from Lou Harrison, dated 11 September 1979).

21. Larry Palmer, "Ralph Kirkpatrick and Bach's 'Goldberg Variations,' " *The Diapason,* May 1973, p.7.

22. Ralph Kirkpatrick, *Early Years* (New York: Peter Lang, 1985).

23. Ralph Kirkpatrick, *Interpreting Bach's Well-Tempered Clavier, A Performer's Discourse of Method* (New Haven: Yale University Press, 1984).

24. Richard Dyer, "A Master Returns to the Stage," *The Boston Globe,* 24 May 1981.

25. Kirkpatrick, "Fifty Years of Harpsichord Playing," p.40.

26. Haney, "Interview with Frank Hubbard," pp.16–17.

27. William Dowd Harpsichords brochure, 1983.

12.
MARATHON MAN

1. *Time*, 24 May 1954, pp.48, 50.
2. Hal Haney, "Interview with Fernando Valenti," *The Harpsichord* II:1(1969): 5.
3. *New York Times*, 16 October 1950.
4. See Larry Palmer, "Vincent Persichetti: A Love for the Harpsichord. Some Words to Mark His Seventieth Birthday," *The Diapason*, June 1985, p.8.
5. Typical of Valenti's style is the brief statement at the beginning of his *The Harpsichord: A Dialogue for Beginners* (Hackensack: Jerona Music, 1982): "Many years ago I promised myself that I would never put in print anything that even vaguely resembled a 'method' for harpsichord playing and this is it."
6. Fernando Valenti, "Scarlatti Forever! " *High Fidelity*, November 1954, p.37.
7. Ibid.
8. Scarlatti: *Sonatas for Harpsichord* Longo 463, 321, 209, 386, 388, 136, 418, 103, 205, 381, 475, 323. Reviewed in *Musical America*, July 1953, p.17. Signed "R.S."
9. "Scarlatti Forever! " pp.108, 112.
10. Haney, p.5.
11. *New York Times*, 7 December 1974. At a recital on 28 September 1973 in London's Purcell Room, Valenti played twenty sonatas, which were identified by Virginia Pleasants as follows: Group I—Kk. 419–239, 84–105, 421–54. Group II—Kk. 27–87, 394–395, 314–146. Group III—after an intermission—Kk. 132–133, 460–461, 426–427, 274–535. This gives a window into Valenti's free-ranging programming of these works.
12. John Duarte, "Plucked Strings," *Music and Musicians* 26:12 (August 1978):38. This is a witty way of referring to Scarlatti himself, "Queen Maria Barbara's teacher."
13. According to Ned Rorem, Landowska's "First words to D.P. had been: 'You look so sympathique, young man! Are you a pederast?' 'Oui, Madame.' 'Good. Now let's talk about music! " (*The Paris Diary* [New York: George Braziller, 1966], p.17.
14. *Partita* appeared as Peters Edition 6519; *Lessons*, as Peters Edition 66425.
15. Owen Goldsmith, "Fernando Valenti, Grand Master of the Keyboard," *Contemporary Keyboard*, April 1980, p.31.

13.
KITS, RECORDS, AND ALL THAT JAZZ

1. *Down Beat* 18 (16 November 1951):3; signed "len."
2. Roger Pryor Dodge, "Harpsichords and Jazz Trumpets," *Hound and Horn*, July 1934, pp.587–608.
3. "Special Delivery Stomp reflected a style thought to be lyrically witty and pungent. . . . It presented a distinctive sound for the group . . . derived of course, from the use of the harpsichord" (Vladimir Simosko, "Artie Shaw and his Gramercy Fives," *Journal of Jazz Studies* 1 [1973]:39).
4. Richard Williams, "The Syncopated Harpsichord," *House Beautiful* 95 (January 1953):10. This issue of the magazine includes a picture of an antique spinet, with commentary (p.83). See also Arthur Loesser, "Return of the Harpsichord," *House Beautiful* 98 (January 1956): 82ff.
5. Columbia LP, CL 1212; notes by Martha Glaser.
6. *New Grove Dictionary of American Music*, 1986, vol. 2, p.37.
7. Actually Messiaen did not compose for Vischer.
8. Charles McWorther to Joe Morgan, 8 June 1965; quoted in Ule Troxler, *Antoinette Vischer: Dokumente zu einem Leben für das Cembalo* (Basel: Birkhäuser, 1976), p.98.
9. *Das moderne Cembalo der Antoinette Vischer*, Wergo WER 60028.
10. Troxler, *Dokumente*.

11. Igor Kipnis made a solo arrangement in 1985 for his own use as a concert encore.

12. Howard Goodkind, "The Return of the Harpsichord," *American Mercury,* March 1949, p.350.

13. AFKA Records 276, 274, 278. Don Angle has worked as a voicer in the Dowd Shop since 1962.

14. Notes to Columbia MS 6878 by E. Power Biggs. The repertoire included Schubert's *Marche Militaire,* Chopin's *Military Polonaise,* Saint-Saëns's *The Swan,* Grieg's *In the Hall of the Mountain King,* and Falla's *Ritual Fire Dance.*

15. Notes by E. Power Biggs to Columbia M 32495. Volume II bears the number M 33205.

16. *Great Scott! Ragtime on the Harpsichord,* Klavier Records, KS 510; and *Scott Joplin Ragtime Harpsichord,* vol. 2, KS 516.

17. Cook Records LP 113. The instrument had 16-foot, 8-foot, and 4-foot on the lower keyboard; 8-foot, 8-foot lute (a buff stop), and 4-foot on the upper; a separate pedal instrument had 16-foot and 8-foot stops.

18. Lester Trimble, *Four Fragments from the Canterbury Tales* for soprano, flute, clarinet, and harpsichord; Vittorio Rieti *Concertino* for flute, viola, cello, harp, and harpsichord.

19. Two major twentieth-century works, both dedicated to Larry Palmer, were included on this program: Rudy Shackelford's *Le Tombeau de Stravinsky,* for solo harpsichord; and Gerald Near's *Concerto for Harpsichord and String Orchestra,* which received its première with the composer conducting.

20. Herbert Russcol, "Boom Goes the Harpsichord," *House and Garden,* October 1968, p.74.

21. Richard Allen Schulze, *How to Build a Baroque Concert Harpsichord* (New York: Pageant Press, 1954). The book was not considered a serious contender for the do-it-yourself market.

22. Wolfgang Zuckermann, *The Modern Harpsichord* (New York: October House, 1969), pp.200, 201.

23. Zuckermann Harpsichords brochure.

24. Stanley H. Slom, "A Sort of Mild Mania For Doing It Yourself Hits the Music World," *Wall Street Journal,* 25 January 1974.

25. Ibid., also Bernard Rosenberg and Deena Rosenberg, "Frank Hubbard, Harpsichord Maker," in *The Music Makers* (New York: Columbia University Press, 1979), p.151.

26. Quoted in Russcol, p.76.

EPILOG

1. *Time,* 15 August 1960, p.56.

2. Ibid., 13 January 1975, p.53.

3. Ibid., 28 August 1972, p.37.

4. Ibid., 30 May 1969, pp.85–86. A shorter version of HPSCHD recorded for Nonesuch (H-71224) was sold with an individual computer printout for volume control adjustments throughout the playing, thus assuring the involvement of the listener. "You have all heard of desert-island recordings. Well, this is the one that I *wouldn't* take along. . . . It lasts twenty-one minutes; I had a headache after the first five. . . . At first noisy, this 'experience' ultimately becomes one of tedium and almost unrelieved boredom. What a waste of three harpsichords, which you can hardly hear through the din! Personally, I find the New York subway offers as much sonic anarchy, and at least there you are getting from one place to another" (Igor Kipnis, *Stereo Review,* May 1970, p.121.) Some of the subsequent performances of HPSCHD were given in Buffalo, in Berlin, and at North Texas State University, Denton.

5. "The fairies are characterized by harps, harpsichord, celesta and percussion" (Eric

Walter White, *Benjamin Britten: His Life and Operas,* 2d ed. [Berkeley and Los Angeles: University of California Press, 1983], p.224).

6. At the world première in Venice on 11 September 1951 the specified harpsichord was replaced by a piano, as it was in the first Metropolitan Opera production in 1953. Sylvia Marlowe had been asked to play harpsichord at the Met, but before the production opened it was decided to substitute a piano because of the size of the house. Since these early substitutions, however, the opera, with harpsichord, has taken its rightful place as a repertoire staple in such outstanding companies as the Santa Fe Opera, the Opera Company of St. Louis, and the New York City Opera.

7. John W. Freeman, review of Angel DS-37869, *Opera News,* 4 December 1982, p.52.

8. Letter to Wolfgang Zuckermann, published in *The Harpsichord* III:2 (1970):18.

Bibliography

Aldrich, Momo. "Reminiscences of St. Leu," *The Diapason,* July 1979, pp.3, 8.

Aldrich, Putnam. "Classics of Music Literature: Wanda Landowska's Musique Ancienne," *Music Library Notes* 27:3 (March 1971):461–468.

Aldrich, Richard. *Concert Life in New York 1902–1923.* New York: G. P. Putnam's Sons, c. 1941.

Allen, Una L. "A Dolmetsch of the Middle West," *The Musician,* November 1932, pp.5–6.

Ardoin, John. "Namara: A Remembrance," *The Opera Quarterly* I:4 (Winter 1983):74–81.

Asbell, Bernard, "After Hours: the Harpsichord with the Forward Look," *Harper's* 216 (June 1958):80.

Ayars, C. M. *Contributions to the Art of Music in America.* New York: H. W. Wilson, 1937.

Beaumont, Anthony. *Busoni the Composer.* Bloomington: Indiana University Press, 1985.

Bedford, Frances, and Robert Conant. *Twentieth-Century Harpsichord Music: A Classified Catalog.* Hackensack: Joseph Boonin, 1974.

"The Belle Skinner Collection of Old Musical Instruments, Holyoke, Massachusetts. A Descriptive Catalogue compiled under the direction of William Skinner." Mt. Holyoke, 1933.

Biggs, E. Power. "John Challis," *The Diapason,* January 1975, p.14.

———. Notes to *E. Power Biggs plays Scott Joplin on the Pedal Harpsichord.* Columbia Records M 32495, 1973. Volume two, Columbia Records M 33205, 1974.

———. Notes to *Holiday for Harpsichord, Fun-Filled Favorites from E. Power Biggs and his Pedal Harpsichord.* Columbia Records ML 6278, 1966.

Bloom, Julius, ed. *The Year in American Music 1946–1947.* New York: Allen, Towne, and Heath, 1947.

Boalch, Donald H. *Makers of the Harpsichord and Clavichord 1440–1840.* 2d ed. Oxford: Oxford University Press, 1974.

Boston Public Library. Scrapbook of Arnold Dolmetsch's American Years. Brown Collection, BPL, 1946.

Brower, Harriette. *Modern Masters of the Keyboard.* New York: Frederick A. Stokes, 1926.

Brussel, Robert. "Madame Wanda Landowska." Translated from the French by Edward Burlingame Hill. *The Etude* 23 (November 1905):444.

Buckley, William F. Jr. "Queen of All Instruments: An Amateur Player Recounts His Long Love Affair With the Harpsichord," *New York Times Magazine,* 2 January 1983, pp.18–19, 33–35.

Busoni, Ferruccio. *Letters to his Wife.* Translated by Rosamond Ley. London: E. Arnold, 1938.

Caffrey, John. "John Challis and Julius Wahl: Harpsichords for Americans," *Musical America,* February 1950, pp.131, 224, 248.

Campbell, Margaret. *Arnold Dolmetsch: the Man and his Work.* London: Hamish Hamilton, 1975.

———. "Dolmetsch's American Years," *Bulletin of the Dolmetsch Foundation* XIX (August 1972):4.

Cantor, Harold. "High Priestess of Happiness," *The American Mercury,* July 1955, pp.82–83.

Casella, Alfredo. *Music in My Time.* Translated and edited by Spencer Norton. Norman: University of Oklahoma Press, 1955.

Catalogue of Keyboard Musical Instruments in the Crosby Brown Collection. New York: Metropolitan Museum of Art, 1903.

Challis, John. "The Harpsichord's Revival," *The American Organist* 18 (October 1935):382.

Chasins, Abram. "Bach's Will, Landowska's Testament," *Saturday Review*, 27 November 1954, pp.56–57.

Cohen, Joel, and Herb Snitzer. *Reprise: The Extraordinary Revival of Early Music*. Boston: Little, Brown and Company, 1985.

Colby, Edward, and Elizabeth Hayes. Putnam Aldrich Bibliography. Stanford University Library MSS, n.d.

"Come On-A Stan's House," *DownBeat 18* (16 November 1951):3.

Cooper, Kenneth. "Sylvia Marlowe: Wit, Warmth and Wisdom," *High Fidelity*, June 1982, pp.55–57.

Cossart, Michael de. *The Food of Love. Princesse Edmond de Polignac (1865–1943) and her Salon*. London: Hamish Hamilton, 1978.

Crichton, Ronald. *Manuel de Falla: Descriptive Catalogue of his Works*. London: Chester Music, 1976.

Dahl, Bjarne. "The Ehlers Pleyel," *The Harpsichord* VI:2 (1973):3.

Dodge, Roger Pryor. "Harpsichords and Jazz Trumpets," *Hound and Horn*, July 1934, pp.587–608.

Dolmetsch and His Instruments. Brochure from Arnold Dolmetsch, Ltd, Haslemere, Surrey, 1929.

Dolmetsch, Mabel. *Personal Recollections of Arnold Dolmetsch*. London: Routledge and Kegan Paul, 1957.

Dower, Catherine. *Yella Pessl: A Life of Fire and Conviction*. Westfield: Westfield State College, 1986.

Dyer, Richard. "A Master Returns to the Stage," *The Boston Globe*, 24 May 1981, pp.A1, A12.

Elson, Arthur. "Arnold Dolmetsch and his Instruments," *The Musician* XIII:4 (April 1908):157–159.

Emerson, Paul. "Stanford's Aldrich to Retire," *Palo Alto Times*, 30 May 1969, p.14.

Evett, Robert. "The Romantic Bach," *New Republic*, 28 July 1952, pp.22–23.

Ewen, David. *Living Musicians*. New York: H. W. Wilson, 1940.

Gavoty, Bernard. *Great Concert Artists: Wanda Landowska*. Translated from the French by F. E. Richardson, with portraits by Roger Hauert. Geneva: René Kister, 1957.

Goldsmith, Owen. "Fernando Valenti, Grand Master of the Keyboard," *Contemporary Keyboard*, April 1980, pp.24–32.

Goodkind, Howard. "The Return of the Harpsichord," *American Mercury*, March 1949, pp.345–350.

Grainger, Percy. "Arnold Dolmetsch: Musical Confucius," *Musical Quarterly* 19 (1933):187–198.

Haney, Hal. "Conversation with Builder-Harpsichordist Claude Jean Chiasson," The *Harpsichord* V:3 (1972):5–9, 12, 20.

———. "Conversation with Harpsichordist Mme. Alice Ehlers," *The Harpsichord* VI:1 (1973):4–9, 17.

———. "Conversation with Harpsichordist Denise Restout," *The Harpsichord* VII:1 (1974):6–11, 14–23.

———. "Interview with Sylvia Marlowe," *The Harpsichord* IV:3 (1971):6–11, 18–20.

———. "Interview with Fernando Valenti," *The Harpsichord* II:1 (1969):4–6.

———. "Portrait of a Builder: John Challis," *The Harpsichord* II:3 (1969):14–23.

———. "Portrait of a Builder: William Dowd," *The Harpsichord* IV:1 (1971):8–19.

———. "Portrait of a Builder: Frank Hubbard," *The Harpsichord* V:1 (1972):5–9, 14–17.

Harding, James. *Massenet*. New York: St. Martin's Press, 1970.

Harich-Schneider, Eta. *Charaktere und Katastrophen*. Berlin: Ullstein, 1978.

———. *Die Kunst des Cembalospiels*. 3d ed. Kassel: Bärenreiter, 1970.

"A Harpsichord Romance," *Musical Courier* 19:25 (18 December 1889):520.

Henahan, Donal. "Harpsichordists Turn the Tables," *New York Times*, 14 January 1972.

Hess, Albert G. "The Transition from Harpsichord to Piano," *Galpin Society Journal* VI (1953):75–94.

Heylbut, Rose. "The Harpsichord Today: An Interview with Ralph Kirkpatrick," *The Etude* 72 (August 1954):9, 51.

Hill, Edward Burlingame. "An Apostle of Old Music," *The New Music Review* 6 (1906–1907):625–629.

Hipkins, Alfred J. *A Description and History of the Pianoforte and of the Older Keyboard Stringed Instruments*. 3d ed. London, 1929. Republished with an introduction by Edwin M. Ripin, Detroit: Detroit Reprints in Music, 1975.

———. "A Lecture on Spinets, Harpsichords, and Clavichords," *Musical Times* 26 (November 1885):646–649.

Hoover, Cynthia. "Music at the Smithsonian," *The Smithsonian Journal of History* II:1 (Spring 1967):55–66.

Hubbard, Frank. "Reconstructing the Harpsichord." In *The Historical Harpsichord*, I, edited by Howard Schott. New York. Pendragon Press, 1984.

———. *Three Centuries of Harpsichord Making*. Cambridge: Harvard University Press, 1965.

Hyams, Ben. "Wanda Landowska Called Her Momo," *Honolulu Magazine*, September 1980, p.107.

International Who Is Who in Music. 5th ed. Chicago, 1951.

Johnson, William Lyman. "Musical Life in Boston," Library of the Harvard Musical Association, *Bulletin* No. 14 (April 1946), n. p.

———. "Return to the Harpsichord," *Christian Science Monitor*, 23 June 1937, p.6.

Kilvert, Rev. Francis. *Selections from the Diary*. Edited by William Plomer. London: J. Cape, 1938–1940.

Kinkle, Roger D. *The Complete Encyclopedia of Popular Music and Jazz 1900–1950*. New Rochelle, NY: Arlington House, 1974.

Kirkpatrick, Ralph. *Early Years*. New York: Peter Lang, 1985.

———. "European Journal," *Musical America*, November 1985, pp.33–37.

———. "Fifty Years of Harpsichord Playing," *Early Music*, January 1983, pp.31–41.

———. *Interpreting Bach's Well-Tempered Clavier, A Performer's Discourse of Method*. New Haven: Yale University Press, 1984.

———. "On Playing the Clavichord," *Early Music* IX:3 (July 1981):293–305.

———, ed. *Bach's Goldberg Variations*. New York: G. Schirmer, 1938.

Lincoln, Stoddard. "The Harpsichord on the Contemporary Scene: Roots for a Tradition," *Bulletin of the American Composers' Alliance* 7:2 (1958):18–22.

Lindorff, Joyce Zankel. "Contemporary Harpsichord Music: Issues for Composers and Performers." D.M.A. diss., The Juilliard School, 1982.

Loesser, Arthur. "Return of the Harpsichord," *House Beautiful*, January 1956, p.82.

Lownsberry, Eloise. "Nelly Custis' Harpsichord," *The Etude* 59 (February 1941):92.

Lyons, Sister Stephen Marie. "Reawakening Interest in the Harpsichord." M. A. thesis, St. Joseph College, 1966.

Mason, Daniel Gregory. *Music in My Time and Other Reminiscences*. 1938. Reprint, Freeport, New York: Books for Libraries Press, 1970.

Mendel, Arthur, and Hans T. David. *The Bach Reader*. Rev. ed. New York: Norton, 1966.

Michotte, Edmond. *Richard Wagner's Visit to Rossini: Paris, 1860*. Translated by Herbert Weinstock. Chicago: University of Chicago Press, 1968.

Moscheles, Charlotte. *Life of Moscheles with Selections from his Diaries and Correspondence*. Translated by A. D. Coleridge. London: Hurst and Blackett, 1873. Published as *Recent Music and Musicians*, New York: 1874.

Moses, Julian Morton. *Collectors' Guide to American Recording 1895–1925*. 1949. Reprint, New York: Dover, 1977.

Nurmi, Ruth. *A Plain and Easy Introduction to the Harpsichord.* Albuquerque: University of New Mexico Press, 1974.

O'Meara, Eva J. "Historic Instruments in the Steinert Collection," *Yale Alumni Weekly,* 29 March 1929, pp.795–796.

Orenstein, Arbie. *Ravel, Man and Musician.* New York; Columbia University Press, 1975.

Overmyer, Grace. "Harpsichord," *American Mercury* 10 (April 1927):442–445.

Palmer, Larry. "The Concertos of Falla and Poulenc," *The Diapason,* July 1979, pp. 9–11.

———. "Harpsichord Repertoire in the 20th Century: the Busoni Sonatina," *The Diapason,* September 1973, pp.10–11.

———. "In Search of Scarlatti," *The Diapason,* December 1985, p.13.

———. "Ralph Kirkpatrick and Bach's Goldberg Variations," *The Diapason,* May 1973, p.7.

———. "Some Literary References to the Harpsichord and Clavichord: 1855–1923," *The Diapason,* September 1983, pp. 18–19.

———. "Vincent Persichetti: A Love for the Harpsichord—Some Words to Mark his Seventieth Birthday," *The Diapason,* June 1985, p.8.

Philipp, Isidor. "Charles-Marie Widor: A Portrait," *Musical Quarterly* 30:2 (April 1944):125–132.

Poulenc, Francis. *Poulenc: My Friends and Myself.* Conversations assembled by Stephane Audel, translated by James Harding. London: Dennis Dobson, 1978.

"President Roosevelt Greatly Interested in Clavichord," *Music Trades,* 26 December 1908, p.9; signed "D.L.L."

Restout, Denise. "Mamusia: Vignettes of Wanda Landowska," *High Fidelity Magazine,* October 1960, pp.42–47, 136–138.

———. Program booklet to Landowska recordings of Mozart, *Piano Concertos* 13 and 22, and *Sonata* in F, K.332; and Poulenc, *Concert Champêtre.* International Piano Library Limited Editions, IPL 106 and 107, 1969.

———. "Wanda Landowska's Centenary," *The Diapason,* July 1979, pp.1, 12–15.

Restout, Denise, and Robert Hawkins, eds. *Landowska on Music.* New York: Stein and Day, 1964.

Richard, J. A. "The Pleyel Harpsichord," *The English Harpsichord Magazine* II:5 (October 1979):110–113.

Robertson, Josephine. "Harpsichord Popularity Is Seen Growing," *Cleveland Plain Dealer,* 15 December 1960.

Roche, Elizabeth, "George Moore's Evelyn Innes: a Victorian 'early music' novel," *Early Music* XI:1 (January 1983):71–73.

Rodzinski, Halina. *Our Two Lives.* New York: Scribner's, 1976.

Rorem, Ned. *The Paris Diary.* New York: George Braziller, 1966.

Rosenfeld, Paul. *Discoveries of a Music Critic.* New York: Harcourt, Brace & Co., c. 1936. Reprint 1972.

"Rossini's Harpsichord," *The Music Trade Review* 38:17 (1904):26.

Ruff, Willie. "A Musician's Legacy: Ralph Kirkpatrick Remembered," *Yale Alumni Magazine,* April 1985, pp.20–23.

Russcol, Herbert. "Boom Goes the Harpsichord," *House and Garden,* October 1968, pp.74–78.

Russell, Raymond. *The Harpsichord and Clavichord: An Introductory Study.* 2d ed., revised by Howard Schott. New York: Norton, 1973.

———. "The Harpsichord Since 1800," *Proceedings of the Royal Musical Association* 82 (1955/56):61–74. Reprints, Nendeln/Liechtenstein: Kraus Reprint Ltd, 1968.

Sabin, Robert. "Harpsichord Seen as 'Timeless' by Sylvia Marlowe," *Musical America,* 15 December 1954, p.16

———. "Poulenc: 'The Essence is Simplicity,' " *Musical America,* 15 November 1949, p. 27.

Sachs, Harvey. *Virtuoso: The Life and Art of Paganini, Liszt, Anton Rubinstein, Paderewski, Kreisler, Casals, Wanda Landowska, Horowitz, Gould*. London: Thames and Hudson, 1982.

Sanborn, Pitts. "Landowska's Contribution," *The Nation* 121 (5 August 1925):175.

———. "The 1925–26 Season," *Modern Music* III:4 (May–June 1926):3–9.

———. "Wanda Landowska," *The Nation* 118 (9 April 1924):404–405.

Schonberg, Harold C. "American in Orient," *New York Times*, 22 April 1956.

———. *The Great Pianists*. New York: Simon and Schuster, 1963.

Schott, Howard. *Playing the Harpsichord*. New York: St. Martin's Press, 1971.

———. "The Harpsichord Revival," *Early Music* II:2 (April 1974):85–96.

———, ed. *The Historical Harpsichord*, vol. I. New York: Pendragon Press, 1984.

Schulze, Richard Allen. *How to Build a Baroque Concert Harpsichord*. New York: Pageant Press, 1954.

Shattuck, Arthur. *The Memoirs of Arthur Shattuck*. Edited by S. F. Shattuck, with an account of his career by Willard Luedtke. Neenah, Wisconsin: privately printed, 1961.

Shaw, George Bernard. *The Great Composers*. Reviews and Bombardments by Bernard Shaw. Edited with an introduction by Louis Crompton. Berkeley: University of California Press, 1978.

———. *Music in London 1890–1894*. London: Constable, 1932.

Simosko, Vladimir. "Artie Shaw and his Gramercy Fives," *Journal of Jazz Studies* I:1 (1973):34.

Slom, Stanley H. "A Sort of Mild Mania for Doing it Yourself Hits the Music World," *Wall Street Journal*, 25 January 1974, pp.1, 17.

Slonimsky, Nicolas. *Baker's Biographical Dictionary of Music*. 5th ed. New York: G. Schirmer, 1958. 6th ed., New York: G. Schirmer, 1978.

———. *Perfect Pitch: A Life Story*. Oxford and New York: Oxford University Press, 1988.

Smith, Fanny Morris. "The Revival of the Harpsichord," *The Etude* 17 (August 1899):254.

Spaeth, Sigmund. "Musical Uplift for the Collegian," *Opera Magazine* I (April 1914):31–32.

Staatliches Institut für Musikforschung, Preussischer Kulturbesitz, *Das Musikinstrumenten-Museum Berlin—Eine Einführung in Wort und Bild* (Berlin, 1968).

Stanley, Albert A. *Catalogue of the Stearns Collection of Musical Instruments*. Ann Arbor: University of Michigan, 1921.

Steinert, Morris. *Reminiscences*. Compiled by Jane Marlin. New York: Putnam's, 1900.

Stevens, David, "A Harpsichordist Who Dares to Buck the Tide," *New York Times*, 6 October 1985, p.H23.

Stoddard, Hope. "The Harpsichord—Past and Present," *International Musician*, December 1951, pp.24–25.

Stone, Else, and Kurt Stone. *The Writings of Elliott Carter*. Bloomington: Indiana University Press, 1977.

Straus, Noel. "Sylvia Marlowe in Classic Works," *New York Times*, 17 January 1946, p.21.

Sween, P. "The Nineteenth-Century View of the Old Harpsichord," *The English Harpsichord Magazine* II:7 (April 1979):92–95.

Symons, Arthur. "A Reflection at a Dolmetsch Concert," in *Plays, Acting and Music*. New York: Dutton, 1909.

Taubman, Howard. "Priestess of the Harpsichord," *New York Times Magazine*, 11 Feburary 1951, p.16.

Thomson, Virgil. *The Art of Judging Music*. New York: Knopf, 1948.

———. *The Musical Scene*. New York: Knopf, 1947.

Thorp, Keith Andrew. "The 20th-Century Harpsichord: Approaches to Composition and Performance Practice as Evidenced by the Contemporary Repertoire." D.M.A. diss., University of Illinois at Urbana-Champaign, 1981.

Toth, Gwendolyn Joyce. "Twentieth-Century Solo Harpsichord Music in the Kirkpatrick

Collection of the Library of the Yale School of Music." M.M.A. thesis, Yale University, 1981.

Troxler, Ule. *Antoinette Vischer: Dokumente zu einem Leben für das Cembalo.* Edited by Markus Kutter. Basel: Birkhäuser, 1976.

Valdes, Lesley. "The Legacy of This Harpsichord Pioneer Lives On," *New York Times,* 19 June 1983, pp.H27, 30.

Valenti, Fernando. *The Harpsichord: A Dialogue for Beginners.* Hackensack: Jerona Music, 1982.

————. "Scarlatti Forever!" *High Fidelity,* November 1954, pp.37, 108, 110, 112.

Watkins, R. Bedford. "New Life for the Harpsichord," *Clavier,* February 1970, pp.39, 42–45.

Whiting, Arthur. *The Lesson of the Clavichord.* Brochure in the Library of Congress [c. 1910].

Who's Who in American Music, Classical. 1st ed. Edited by Jaques Cattell Press. New York: R. R. Bowker, 1983.

Williams, Richard. "The Syncopated Harpsichord," *House Beautiful* 95 (January 1953):10.

Williamson, Narcissa. "Musical Instruments—To Be Seen or Heard?" *Museum News,* January 1967, pp.34–36.

Winternitz, Emanuel. *Keyboard Instruments in the Metropolitan Museum of Art.* New York: Metropolitan Museum of Art, 1961.

Yale Collection of Musical Instruments: Checklist. New Haven: Yale University, 1968.

Zuckermann, Wolfgang Joachim. *The Modern Harpsichord. 20th Century Instruments and Their Makers.* New York: October House, 1969.

Index